BEST PRACTICES
for SCHOOL LIBRARY
MEDIA PROFESSIONALS

The School Library

MEDIA
FACILITIES
PLANNER

Thomas L. Hart

NEAL-SCHUMAN PUBLISHERS, INC.

NEW YORK   **LONDON**

Published by Neal-Schuman Publishers, Inc.
100 William St., Suite 2004
New York, NY 10038

Library of Congress Cataloging-in-Publication Data

Hart, Thomas L.
  The school library media facilities planner / Thomas L. Hart.
       p. cm. — (Best practices for school library media professionals)
  Includes bibliographical references and index.
    ISBN 1-55570-503-0 (alk. paper)
  1. Instructional materials centers—United States—Design and
construction. 2. Instructional materials centers—United States—
Planning. 3. School libraries—United States—Design and construction.
4. Media programs (Education)—United States—Planning. I. Title. II.
Series.
    Z675.S3H2674 2006
    027.8—dc22
                                                    2004047424

Contents

PART IV
"Facilities Speak": Resources that Better Equip You to Work with Building Professionals

List of Figures

Preface

Exceptional school library media programs impact curriculum, enhance teaching and learning, and foster a lifelong love of reading. No other aspect of the school experience affects every learner as much as a quality library media program—one that encompasses a knowledgeable specialist, helpful staff, carefully chosen collections, and a well-planned information literacy curriculum. But even with these elements, the program can fail if its facility is not in line with its purposes. If students and faculty find the library media space unappealing, confusingly organized, or otherwise difficult to use, they will not reap its benefits. If they find its entrance inviting, the reading areas comfortable, and the technology spaces conducive to learning, they will *want* to use it.

The School Library Media Facilities Planner helps you become more familiar with facility design and offers tips and techniques for designing the best center possible. The information in this practical handbook is important for school library media specialists, architects, district level media coordinators, and administrators.

In my decades as a professor and as a library consultant, I have both researched and experienced firsthand the process of designing and building school library media centers. I have learned many lessons the hard way. I studied spaces that appeared functional in the planning stages but proved problematic in their day-to-day use, and encountered low-cost solutions that turned into high-priced, long-term headaches. *The Planner* shares my experiences and offers guidance for planning, designing, and constructing facilities that work. You will find many examples—both good and bad—of projects I have worked on over the years, which illuminate key points. There are also numerous photos and plans that bring the discussion to life. I hope that by highlighting these projects, you will be inspired to seek out your own exemplary models. I cannot stress enough the importance of looking and walking through other libraries en route to designing or redesigning your own.

The School Library Media Facilities Planner may be used in two ways. First, you can read through it well ahead of constructing, designing, or even considering a new facilities project. You may even find some quick-fix ideas that will vastly change your library without significant effort. Second, I urge you to use this book as a reference tool. For example, the design specifications, sample contracts, and glossaries can all better equip you to be an active participant in the entire remodeling or building project.

Organization

Part I, "Before You Begin: Essential Background and Vision" helps set the scene, providing the initial information you need before proceeding. In these chapters, you will begin to develop the fundamental knowledge base needed to understand what separates good and bad school library media centers and how to tell the two apart. Chapter 1, "Introduction to Facility Planning Basics," provides crucial information for those who are new to the planning process. It goes over the role of collaboration and communication in design, the evaluation of needs, and the beginning steps of creating a plan to address them. These issues are then put into practical terms in Chapter 2, "Develop a Vision: Looking at Successful Library Media Center Designs." Here, we evaluate the plans for various kinds of school library media centers, evaluating the compromises made and the decisions reached over the course of the design phase. More than a simple exercise in looking at architecture, this will help you understand how to relate to architectural ideas and innovations. In the third chapter, "Take the DVD Tour," we will go over the contents of the enclosed DVD, describing its various features, discussing how the information it contains can best be put to use. Included in this chapter are additional floor plans for the school library media centers that are explored in the video tours on the disk.

Part II, "Planning the Facility," delves deeper into the specifics, describing in detail what is different about school library media centers and what those working on them need to know. As the title of Chapter 4 suggests, "How to Develop Comprehensive Planning Documents," the primary goal in this section of the book is to demonstrate how the special needs of these unique spaces can be systematically articulated. Among other things, we will consider questions of spatial flexibility, collection development and program activities, focusing on how to describe these issues in such a way that they can be understood by all. Chapter 5, "How to Allocate Space and Determine Library Media Specific Details," goes still further into the particularities of these facilities. We will discuss the different rooms that a media center should contain and reflect on the ways they can relate to one another. Further, we will indicate how the activities in such facilities inform everything from acoustical control to security. Next, Chapter 6, "How to Select Furniture and Storage Units," talks about how to ensure that the center's furnishings, whether built-in or mobile, support the institution's educational community and program goals. Included in this chapter are extensive photographs of many of the options available for circulation desks, cabinetry, table configurations, and so on.

Part III, "Building and Moving into the New or Remodeled Library Media Center," discusses the ways in which dream becomes reality. In these four chapters, we will move the library out of planning and into design and construction.

Chapter 7, "How to Select the Right Architect," discusses the ways school systems advertise for, solicit bids from, and ultimately contract those who will design the facility. It suggests questions that should be asked and warning signs that should be watched for, helping avert potential problems long before they arise. Once the selection phase has been completed, the dialogue about how the building should look begins, bringing us to Chapter 8, "How to Collaborate with Architects to Design a Facility that Works." This chapter is especially relevant to those schools building freestanding library facilities, but all should be served by the overview it provides of how to look at plans as they come into being and propose changes as the phase proceeds. When the design is complete, a construction team must be hired to interpret and implement the architectural schematics and designs. A good contractor makes all the difference when it comes to ensuring the quality of the final facility, but even the best require oversight and careful attention. Accordingly, Chapter 9, "How to Select and Work with a Contractor," provides tips and tools to ensure that the erection of the facility goes as smoothly as possible. Finally, Chapter 10, "How to Move Into and Open a New or Remodeled Library Media Center," brings the project to a close by suggesting strategies that will guarantee a successful shift from an old facility to a new one.

The final part of this book, "'Facilities Speak': Resources that Better Equip You to Work with Building Professionals" provides readers unfamiliar with the design process with a variety of tools to make facilities planning and design more comprehensible. "Resource A: Glossary of Architectural Styles and Terminology," provides alphabetical listing and definitions of architectural styles, construction terms, and more. "Resource B: Sample Planning Document" reproduces portions of a planning document for a significant project on which I worked, providing a reference point for those striving to put together such information for their own facilities. This is included so that you can pick and choose elements you can adopt and use for your own project without "reinventing the wheel." "Resource C: Sample Contract and Request for Bids" looks at model documents used in the selection process for architects and contractors.

Remember always that the first goal of facilities design is to keep in mind the interests of the students and larger educational community that the library will serve. A love and respect for the work of learning informs every aspect of this book, and I hope that *The School Library Media Facilities Planner* will be a useful and much consulted resource for you. Bringing this book into the world has been a labor of love, as there few things that excite me more than exceptional libraries. May reading this book be as useful to you as writing it has been a pleasure for me.

Acknowledgments

Thanks to everyone at Neal-Schuman Publishers. I would like to express special appreciation to these particular people.

- Ken Haycock motivated me to develop this book as a part of his *Best Practices for School Library Media Professionals* series.
- Charles Harmon, Director of Publishing, selected an excellent outside reviewer and offered constant positive reinforcement—capped off when he eagerly approved a DVD to add quality video to the project.
- Michael Kelley, my first editor, offered encouraging feedback and even sent me another book to stimulate my creative juices.
- Jacob Brogan, my final editor, made timely phone calls and shared life experiences as the son of a major public library system director.

I am grateful to Mahlum Architects of Seattle for their generous donation of four photos of two of the exceptional designs in the Pacific Northwest. Thanks are also due to Nancy Teger, Media Director for Dade (Miami, Florida) County Schools and State Director for Media Services, for sharing her enthusiasm for the need for the book and DVD.

I

Before You Begin: Essential Background and Vision

1

Introduction to Facility Planning Basics

Introducing the Planning Process

Beginning school library media facility planners usually need a little help understanding what the planning process entails. For a library media center to be successful, those responsible for bringing it into being need to develop a wide knowledge base. Before the process even begins, they will have to learn how to be a part of a planning team, complete a needs assessment, and prepare a planning document. This chapter and those that follow it will attempt to provide an introduction to each of these areas. Experienced planners, by contrast, will probably only need this chapter as a refresher, but they may still find it useful to look over the following pages.

The key element of any quality school library program is an exceptional facility. Most students and teachers respond positively to clean, colorful, up-to-date environments. While older spaces can be appealingly decorated and arranged, specialized and sometimes essential activities are often curtailed or eliminated if the facility was not designed with them in mind. For example, in elementary and middle schools, a daily TV morning news show can be a powerful learning tool for students. Inadequate space for a TV studio, however, impairs such activities, limiting the benefit that can be drawn from it. If a facility is to meet the needs and fit the tastes of the community it serves, planners must approach a new project with the utmost thoughtfulness and rigor. Architecture can be truly functional only if it works in context: No building is good in a vacuum.

The planning for a library media center must be a meticulously executed formal process that begins with the recognition and documentation of needs through information gathering and assessment. This phase, which will be described in detail shortly, provides the focus for the design and construction that follow it, informing all the decisions that will subsequently be made on the project. Needless to say, it is crucial that the reader acquire a thorough understanding of it and of all that comes after. Accordingly, a brief overview of the larger process may be in order.

Needs assessment is followed by the development of a facilities planning document, which is then presented to the school board or other governing agency for approval. This important initial work is usually the responsibility of a school planning team comprised of the school library media specialist, administrators, teachers and other members of the school community.

After acceptance of the project, the school planning team finalizes the facilities planning document that will guide the design and construction program developed by the architectural team. An architectural firm is then selected, contracted with, and brought onto the design team. Once hired, the architects use the school team's planning document to develop proposed designs. Over a series of meetings and discussions, these proposals gradually become more specific and detailed, until a set of final construction drawings is completed. As will be described in the following chapters, a continuing dialogue between the school planning team and the architects is essential for success. Together they must review the subsequent iterations of the plans to be sure that expectations have been met and that work has been satisfactorily completed. They must also be able to communicate frequently to discuss unexpected problems and delays and any resulting changes or even to explore an exciting new design idea.

Selection of contractors, a process that occurs after the formal closing of the design phase, is usually the result of a competitive bid process, based in large part on cost estimates laid out by the architects. The drawings produced by the architects also give the contractors all the necessary data for the actual construction. They should thoroughly explain the design and creation of the shell (walls, floors, ceilings, windows, doors, etc.), the internal systems (air, electrical, communications, etc.), and any built-in special design elements like cabinetry or video screens.

It is the responsibility of a school or district employee known as the project manager to monitor work on the construction site, ensuring that building codes are observed and appropriate materials and methods are used. During construction, this individual serves as the intermediary between the school system and the contractors.

The selection of new equipment, furniture, and shelving should be the school team's responsibility, though it is often accomplished in consultation with the architectural team. If the furniture and shelving are not part of the general contractor's construction contract, vendors and manufacturers are invited to bid for contracts to supply the desired items, which have been identified and described. The school planning team then analyzes the bids submitted and recommends which firm should be awarded the contract.

Once construction is concluded, facilities must be inspected by both the owners and the architects. The school team evaluates the completed facility for its success in meeting educational expectations, while the architectural team evaluates on the basis of aesthetic, engineering, and construction standards. Acceptance of the facility by the school team, the installation of furniture and shelving, the opening of the facility, and the eventual evaluation of that facility complete the process, bringing the planning cycle to a close.

Collaboration and the Design Process

Most school districts have a high-level administrator in charge of planning, renovating, and building facilities. The library media center coordinator and/or the project consultant, if one is hired, need to develop a trusting relationship with this individual. They are usually hard-nosed people who have had to deal with very difficult architects and contractors at various points in their careers. To have a successful final product, it is essential for the library media specialist, project consultant, and/or the library media coordinator to become familiar with priorities of the school district facilities planner.

How do you develop a successful collaborative project?

- Involve key members of the school district planning department at the beginning of the project.
- Use all elements of documentation required by planning department.
- Hold regular meetings of the planning committee, making sure there is adequate representation of parents, teachers, administrators, and district planning department employees.
- Make sure major elements of the planning document are supported by the school district planning department and the director.
- Provide documentation, preferably supported with significant research and analysis, concerning any unique spaces in the facility and any special unusual needs for the facility.

Important as these above guidelines are, true collaboration can begin only when all parties understand the roles and responsibilities of others as well as their own. The following sections seek to describe each of the players involved in the design process of a typical school library media center.

District Coordinator for Information Technology/Library Media

Many school districts have a coordinator for information technology and/or library media. IT/LM coordinators are usually involved in the planning process at the time bond issues are being passed and/or funds are being assembled for new facilities. They usually are on the planning team and work closely with the school district facilities director and/or superintendent.

After building funds become available, IT/LM coordinators are usually involved in writing educational specifications for the facility. They will also usually consult with library media specialists working in other new facilities to obtain their advice. As projects develop, they may relinquish some control to the specific library media center specialist, but they nevertheless remain involved throughout the various phases of the total process.

If this role is split into two positions, the IT coordinator is often more interested in working toward a space that is easy to manage. By way of example, this typically entails locating the computers and other IT resources in closed labs rather than on the floor of the reading room. Library media coordinators, on the other hand, are usually most invested in building a facility that is best for users, meaning that they may advocate diffuse, universally accessible distribution of resources. Regardless of who espouses them, it is important to find common ground between these two positions. Fortunately the costs of technology are falling rapidly, and with wireless systems, the installation costs are considerably less than in the past. Accordingly, it may be possible to satisfy both parties by having good control over the technology and also providing good access for users, since the lower cost of computers makes it possible both to include more of them in a facility and to better supervise their usage over a network. As in other cases that will be discussed throughout this book, good architecture helps make such compromises easier. This makes it all the more important that such discussions happen early in the process, so that such needs can be communicated to the architects later in the process.

The Library Consultant

Under normal circumstances the school library media specialist should coordinate the planning for the library media center, with guidance from the appropriate district coordinator(s), who is often responsible for facilities planning leadership district-wide. If the school's library media specialist has little or no experience planning for construction programs, or if the district administrator recommends outside assistance, an experienced consultant can be a useful addition to the planning team. The consultant should have expertise in developing a building program and should be able to provide assistance as each phase evolves. The ideal consultant should be supportive to the library media specialist and/or district coordinator and should help facilitate the various phases of plan development. He or she should also be involved in assessing the particular problems specific to the project, guiding the planning team through the information-gathering stage and the determination of educational specifications.

The consultant may also review the documents and drawings for each step of the architectural design phase with the school staff, assist in interpretation of the drawings, and suggest changes that reflect program and staff needs. Further, the consultant typically assists in developing the furniture and shelving layout, reviewing bid specifications for furniture and shelving, analyzing bid responses, and making recommendations for awarding the bid. Lastly, the consultant can provide additional aid in inspection of the facility, furniture, and shelving to identify problems in installation and in the quality of the workmanship. The contract with the consultant should delineate the specific services to be provided and the duration of the assistance.

Planning Team

One of the most important steps in the planning process is the initial identification of the key participants who will help shape the new facility's design and, ultimately, the program: the school building planning team. The overall planning process for a new or renovated library media center must involve those individuals who shape and direct its programming as well as those who are affected by it—the school library media specialist, the district information technology/library media coordinator, the school's administration, and representatives of the faculty, student body, and community. Together they must oversee the process as described, from the formal needs assessment through the construction documents, all the way to the ultimate completion of the facility itself. This planning team must be able to fuse their collective knowledge of the current program to create an ideal facility capable of serving tomorrow's students as well as today's. Accordingly, the planning team must have a vision for the future as well as for the present. If the project is to be successful the team members must be able to anticipate such developments as changing emphases in collection balances between print and multimedia resources and radical changes in the nature of our information technologies.

SELECTING MEMBERS OF THE PLANNING TEAM

The school district facilities planner or principal of the school under construction is usually the lead person in planning a new facility. Before this can begin, funds for preliminary scoping studies and planning must be allocated by the school board. Once this is done, the district superintendent must select an appropriate planning committee to support the local project needs. How this proceeds depends on whether the planned library media center is to be part of a new school building or whether it is a remodeling project within or in addition to an existing facility.

SELECTING MEMBERS OF THE PLANNING TEAM FOR A NEW BUILDING

With a completely new building, it is rarely the case that the principal and staff members have been selected at the time the planning process is initiated. Under these circumstances, the superintendent typically appoints the school district facilities planner to coordinate and oversee the project as it develops. It is then the responsibility of this official to select the remainder of the planning team. The group is typically composed of five to six members, including:

1. A principal of the level of school being planned
2. One or more district subject area specialists
3. One or more respected teachers
4. The district media specialist and/or IT specialist
5. One or two other special area teachers (PE, guidance, etc.)

SELECTING MEMBERS OF THE PLANNING TEAM FOR AN ADDITION OR REMODELED FACILITY

When the library media center is to be built or remodeled within an existing school, the responsibility for planning typically happens at a much more local level. The principal of the school is usually assigned the responsibility of selecting the planning team, which can include:

1. A representative from the administrative team
2. The district level library media and/or IT specialists, if those positions exist
3. One or two respected teachers
4. The library media specialist
5. One or two parents

On occasion, one or two students may also be included on the team, as they can bring to the process a different perspective on the dynamics of usage of a facility. The decision to include students should always be informed by context: for example, grade school students are less likely to provide consistently helpful input than high schoolers. Should students not be included on the planning committee, whatever the reason, it is important that they be consulted in the latter phases of the project.

The Needs Assessment

The first step in planning is the production of a needs assessment. This entails the determination of teaching and learning goals, as well as objectives for the center. A truly thorough needs assessment will set the parameters for the remainder of the project. Only after this phase is complete do the other steps of the planning process really become meaningful.

Needs assessment involves two processes: first, the gathering and synthesis of information to facilitate decision-making; and second, the evaluation of programs and collections. The school planning team must become knowledgeable about a number of variables in order to adequately assess the needs of the education program, the students and teachers, and, therefore, the library media center itself. If the proposed project involves the replacement or renovation of an existing facility, then the team will evaluate the physical condition of that facility in terms of its ability to meet the current and future demands of collections and programs, as well as its ability to accommodate newer information technologies. Here, a thorough study of the current facility's usage, success in meeting its goals, and so on should guide the team's analyses. On the other hand, if there is no original facility on site, the team will have to thoughtfully theorize and speculate about the needs of the community that will eventually occupy it.

A number of useful approaches to program evaluation and to collection analysis are mentioned in the professional literature. Most schools and media centers already have program evaluations in place and have a standard procedure for going about them. For those that do not, the following pages provide a short annotated bibliography of possible evaluation tools.

Program Evaluation

http://eduscapes.com/sms/evaluation.html

This Web site was developed by the Indiana University School of Library and Information Science to explain the elements of program evaluation. This site provides ideas and guidelines to assist the library media specialist in evaluating all aspects of the program. Evaluation involves placing a value or worth on an item or activity. Evaluation is used to determine the degree of excellence being achieved. It provides a way to determine the quality of the library media program and then compare the program against the standard. The standard may be locally established or used as a way to compare your program against others.

TERMINOLOGY OF EVALUATION

There are a number of terms used in evaluation:

- *Checklist*—a prepared list of items used for the purpose of observation or evaluation
- *Criteria*—a standard, norm, or judgment selected as a basis for comparison
- *Evaluation criteria*—the standards against which the collection or program may be checked
- *Standard*—a goal, objective, or criterion of education expressed either numerically or philosophically as an ideal of excellence

QUESTIONS USED IN EVALUATION

- Is the library media collection and program responsive to changes in the school's program?
- Does the library media collection and program support curricular and instructional needs?
- Is the library media collection and program meeting the needs of users?
- Does the library media collection and program provide access to materials from outside the school?
- Does the library media collection and program include formats preferred by users?
- Does the library media collection hinder or facilitate the library media program?

STEPS IN EVALUATION

The following steps are essential in conducting evaluation:

- Identify what information needs to be collected.
- Determine how the information will be collected.
  - What effort is needed to collect he information?
  - What instrument(s) will be used?
  - What will not be measured by the instruments?
- Determine how the information will be organized and analyzed.
- Determine how information will be used and shared.

BIBLIOGRAPHY OF SOURCES FOR PROGRAM EVALUATION

Farmer, Lesley S. J. *How to Conduct Action Research: A Guide for Library Media Specialists*. Chicago: ALA, 2003.

National Study of School Evaluation. *Program Evaluation: Library Media Services*. Schaumburg, Ill.: NSSE, 1998.

Nebraska Educational Media Association. *Guide for Developing and Evaluating School Library Media Programs*. Englewood, Colo.: Libraries Unlimited, 2000.

"School Library Media Program Assessment Rubric for the 21st Century." In *A Planning Guide for Information Power: Building Partnerships for Learning.* Chicago: AASL, 1999.

New York City schools have a Web site with a school library media program rubric available in Word format and as a PowerPoint presentation: http://emsc.nysed.gov/nyc/library.html

Collection Analysis

http://eduscapes.com/sms/mapping.html

A Web site developed by Indiana University, School of Library and Information Science to explain the elements of collection analysis. They call it collection mapping, which is the process of examining the quantity and quality of your collection and identifying its strengths and weaknesses. A number of authors have written abut the process. The outcome of the process can serve as a guide during the collection analysis and development process.

An example of the documents that are used comes from the Philadelphia public schools: http://libraries.phila.k12.pa.us/misc/docs-collecmapping.html These are PDF files of a "Total Collection Work Form" (a one-page form to summarize information on age and quality of collection, divided into the important Dewey Decimal Classifications), "Emphasis Collections Work Form" (a one-page form that categorizes the information on age and quality of collection by each emphasis area in the school), and a "Total Collection Map" (a blank document to be printed for plotting the collection map).

BIBLIOGRAPHY OF SOURCES FOR COLLECTION ANALYSIS

Johnson, D. and McCaskill, S. (Fall 2002). *Policies and Procedures Manual Web Guide*
http://ths.sad44.org/library
Useful for developing a policies and procedures manual for your library media center. It has a helpful section on collection assessment.

Collection Analysis from Baltimore County Public Schools
http://bcpl.net/~dcurtis/libraryfacts/#anchor19540677
Provides ideas for how library media specialists determine the quality of the school library media collection for Baltimore County Public Schools.

Collection Assessment from University of Wyoming Libraries
http://lib.uwyo.edu/cdo/collass.htm
Introduces methods for assessing library collections for any library.

Collection Mapping from Baltimore County Public Schools
http://bcps.org/offices/lis/office/admin/cm/mapping.html
A simple guide to the collection mapping process.

Collection Map Template from South Carolina Department of Education
http://myscschools.com/offices/tech/lms/documents/curriculumMapForm.doc
A Word document designed to record information for the collection map.

Collection Evaluation Matrix from Missouri Department of Elementary and Secondary Education
http://dese.mo.gov/dvimprove/curriculum/library/handbook/collevalmatrix.htm
An html document designed to record information for the collection map.

Collection Mapping: Videos from Missouri Department of Elementary and Secondary Education
http://dese.mo.gov/dvimprove/curriculum/library/handbook/collmapvideo.htm

Coordinated Cooperative Collection Development Plan from Franklin-Essex-Hamilton School Library System
http://fehb.org/slscccdp.htm
An excellent guide for collection mapping.

Collection Mapping: A Powerful Method of Getting Money for Your Library
http://vema.gen.va.us/handouts03/Lammay.ppt
A brief PowerPoint presentation summarizing the process of collection mapping from the Virginia Educational Media Associaton.

Felker, Janice (2000). *Internet Assist for Building a School Library Collection Plan: A Beginning Handbook* by D.V. Loertscher & B. Woolls
http://lmcsource.com/tech/felker/index.html

Loertscher, D. V. *Collection Mapping in the LMC: Building Access in a World of Technology*. Castle Rock, Colo.: Hi Willow, 1996.

Facilities Needs Assessment

The team may wish to select one of the evaluation instruments described in the sections above and modify it for the local setting, or even to create a new one. It is often useful to evaluate the existing facility and program by surveying users. Such a survey can help the team members gain better qualitative understanding about current collections, services, and staffing patterns. If the project involves creating a new facility, the team may use a survey instrument to identify its own priorities for the new facility. An example needs assessment document is provided as a part of Resource B: Sample Planning Document.

Regardless of the project's scope, the team must identify the educational goals and objectives to be achieved by the library media program within the parameters of those established by the school and district. The team must examine current and projected demographics and identify curriculum trends and changes in teaching and learning styles as well as changes in accessing and using information. It must evaluate the existing or projected initial collection and project changes in the balance between print and multimedia resources.

The group must be aware of the requirements, standards, and guidelines of the local school district, the state department of education, the regional accrediting agency for schools, and such national professional organizations as the American Association of School Librarians (AASL) and the Association for Educational Communications and Technology (AECT).

The needs assessment is the foundation for the school team's most important contribution to the planning process—the creation of a program statement, or educational specifications document, that projects the space requirements for the new or renovated facility in terms of educational goals and objectives and program needs and functions. This document will, as was mentioned earlier, be the basis for the architectural design and construction phases of the project. Along with it, the team may also submit a proposal that recommends a time frame of phases for funding, planning, and construction, and contains a rationale for the project, including a consideration of alternatives to new construction, if applicable and appropriate.

There are many ways to critically examine facility needs. Many states have guidelines for school building spaces. The American Library Association has guidelines, as do some regional accrediting agencies. Even school districts sometimes have recommendations. After the overall space requirements have been estimated, usually based on local program needs and a basic square-foot allowance for student enrollment and/or special education needs, this estimate then is usually further refined using a careful analysis of each special-use area. Details for determining actual space allocations will be explained in detail in the next chapter.

THE MAJOR AREAS

There are several critical special-use areas in a school library media center:

- space to store resources for public use (often up to 30 percent of the space)
- space for reading and computer usage
- group activity space
- instructional laboratory space
- TV production and distribution space
- computer networking and management space
- staff areas including work, production, and office areas

The size of each space will be determined by formulas or a variety of other local factors

NON ASSIGNABLE SPACE

In addition to space for operations of the library media center, facilities must have space for the facility infrastructure, including:

- entrance and display
- walls
- restrooms
- stairs, elevators, and hallways
- heating, ventilating, and air conditioning equipment
- custodial, cleaning, and maintenance equipment
- deliveries and general storage

Anticipating Change and Innovation

Part of this process should involve strategizing ways to ensure that the center will both work with current technologies and be amenable to all future developments.

Planning facilities that anticipate change must take into consideration changes resulting from technological progress as well as changes in educational programming as it shifts to conform to our constantly mutating information environment. In K-12 library media centers, the following are some important considerations:

1. Most facilities of the future will probably use wireless connections and laptop computers. In many media centers, between 20 and 80 laptops are now available for checkout and use in the center. To ensure maximum functionality, the staff will need to keep the batteries charged and replaced so teachers and students can use them seamlessly for instructional purposes. This will remain an important task, as no matter what improvements are made in technology, there will still be a need for batteries and equipment maintenance.

2. The need to build library media centers' book collections will continue in the future, regardless of ongoing information developments. Many reference books are being replaced by databases, but more conventional print resources remain crucial. Accordingly, space for book collections should be preserved and room for growth should be incorporated into the plans.

3. The school library media center will continue to be the site of school community activities, such as book fairs, PTO functions, science fairs, history fairs, ethnic fairs, creativity fairs, etc.

Starting the Planning Document

The information gathered in the needs assessment is next used to develop the planning document. This is a team effort under the leadership of the library media specialist, the appropriate district coordinator, and/or the consultant. The planning document describes the needs and expectations of the school system in clear language directed at lay people and architects, not in the language of the information professions. The audience for the document will be the school's administration and board, facilities planning personnel, and, of course, the architectural team. Since architects' awareness of library media center terminology is likely to be limited, using clear, jargon-free language is essential.

Architects often have difficulty understanding the variety of activities that occur simultaneously in the school library media center facility. Multimedia presentations, such as PowerPoint or video programs developed for community groups or student orientations, can show the multiplicity of activities of a school library media center program. Visual representations of features the team has identified as desirable are also helpful. Photos taken in other school library media centers and manufacturers' product descriptions also encourage discussion. Such images should not serve to inhibit the architects' creativity but to provide a springboard for exploring possibilities.

The format of the program planning document will often be prescribed by the state's department of education. If the construction or renovation of an entire school building facility is intended, the educational specifications for the library media center will be only one component of a broader document. The goal of the school's program document is to provide administrators, decision-makers, and architects with a sense of the scope of the facility and the needs of each individual program and curricular area. The document should also provide an understanding of the organizational and program structures the facility is intended to serve.

The program statement should be specific enough to provide guidelines for the architectural firm without fully anticipating the design itself. It should therefore be descriptive, not prescriptive; the narrative should allow plenty of opportunity for the creativity of the architects who will eventually work to interpret it. Instead of attempting to provide full solutions to all potential problems, it should point to approaches the architects should take or elements of the project they should carefully consider.

For example, marketing is an important component of a successful library media center program. Features that make a facility unique, invite entry, and generate interest, excitement, and participation play a clear part in increasing awareness of the program within the school and the community. Therefore, the program narrative should include a descriptive statement to remind the architect that such marketing is important and expected. The architect should respond with design features that call attention to the school library media center, setting it apart and making it easily identifiable.

The planning document model presented in Resource B comprises eighteen sections. This sequence of topics imposes a process by which the planning team moves from broad to specific considerations as well as from textual to graphic and numeric representations of the desired facility. These eighteen sections may be grouped into two major functions: program description and special technical considerations.

Importance of the Planning Document

The beginning of any planning for new or remodeled facilities requires input from the community. Many times the initial funding comes from successful passage of a bond issue. Without strong community support, most bond issues fail. Such support can only begin with a collective investment in what the library media center means to the greater context of the school's educational culture. Recent longitudinal research concerning school library media centers reinforces the notion that investment in the library media center program provides the best investment in education. Quicker achievement gains can be obtained by investing in a quality collection and a quality library media specialist than any other educational investment.

Elements of the Sample Planning Document

Introduction

The sample planning document included in Resource B is for a comprehensive stand-alone building for the Florida State University PreK-12 School. For a remodeling or a new facility as a part of a new building, pick and choose those elements you will need to include, such as:

- Sections I through V are the introductory aspects of the program (i.e., title sheet, table of contents, signature sheet, building committee and introduction).
- Section VI, academic plan, includes recommendations from Florida Department of Education facility needs assessments.
- Section VII, space needs assessment, fleshes out the existing problems with the facility, since it needs to be replaced.
- Section VIII, analysis of impact on master plan, is Florida State University specific.
- Section IX, site analysis, is extremely detailed and will vary from project to project.

Spatial Relationship

- Section X, program area, makes an important transition from narrative to graphic representations of program facilities, functions, and equipment. There is a brief description of the functions of the various physical spaces, which are then outlined in a facilities list. This is followed by a schematic rendering of these spaces in what is called a bubble diagram, adjacency diagram, or space chart (Figure 1-1).

Figure 1-1
Spatial Relationship Diagram for Possible Layout of a School Library Media Center

SPATIAL RELATIONSHIP DIAGRAM

LEGEND
No. None
1. Entry Vestibule
2. Reading/Stacks/Copy
3. Periodical Storage
4. Technical Processing
5. Graphics Production
6. Professional Library/TBS
7. Conference Rooms
8. Staff Offices
9. A.V./C.C. Storage
10. T.V. Studio/Control Room
11. Group Viewing/O.L.
12. Video Editing
13. T.V. Distribution
14. LAN Control Room
15. Second Skills Dev. Lab

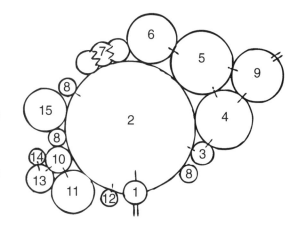

Symbols
= Facility Access
   Visual/Physical Access
– Physical Access

The bubble diagram depicts the needed spaces and shows the special relationships and traffic flow of the various areas. Transferring conceptualization of the functions and the relationships of the spaces outlined in the facilities list to the bubble diagram assures that the team will have developed its own understanding and philosophy of the functional relationships before any meeting with architects. Knowing what the program is and how it operates within the facility, then placing it in a diagram reduces the chance of confusing administrative decision-makers and the architectural team. The bubble diagram will provide the architect with a visual understanding of the program's narrative description.

Special Considerations

Chapters 4 and 5 have detailed ideas for the elements of utilities impact analysis, information/communication resource requirement, codes and standards in addition to general guidelines. These areas contain a substantial number of specific technical recommendations and standards for various design components, including:

- climate control
- acoustical control
- floor surfaces
- walls
- ceiling
- lighting
- windows
- doors
- water
- communications
- electrical control
- safety
- service drives and entrances
- built-in storage units

Addressing special considerations as part of the program statement provides the architectural team with organizational and environmental requirements that may depart from the norm. These features make the difference between a functional library media center and one that creates problems for students, staff, collection development, and program implementation. It is appropriate to repeat statements in different areas of the document; members of the architectural team may miss some considerations if they turn only to the section that affects their own work. For example, electrical requirements may be described in a section on communications and then be repeated in other sections. Repetition reinforces the need for special considerations and assures that important design components get the appropriate attention.

Later chapters go into greater detail about:

- the project schedule
- program funds
- project budget summary

These are the basic elements of the model program planning document from Florida State University (Resource B). They are all essential elements of all programs, but may only be of concern to specific members of the architectural team.

Next Steps

Completion of the program planning document is followed by school board approval of the document and identification of funding sources. An architectural firm is then selected through a process that is typically not the responsibility of school library media center professionals; instead, architect selection is a decision of the school board, other governing agency, or school administration. These processes are nevertheless described later on to help the reader understand what is at stake.

An architectural firm's familiarity with design of school library media centers may have little influence on the selection process, and a school planning team may find itself working with an inexperienced architect. The educational specifications for the library media center must, therefore, be definitive. It is critical that the program description provide an overview of the entire library media center program and various functions as well as activities of both students and staff. This written description, any additional visual representations that accompany it, and comments on special considerations are all key to the architectural firm's translation of the program into concrete concepts that are capable of meeting both present and future needs.

This model of educational specifications for a school library media center program and facility built at Florida State University (Resource B) can provide a useful springboard for schools that anticipate new or renovated facilities. The model in this section can be used as just that, a broad jumping off point for the development of programs that meet specific needs. The school media specialist who uses and adapts the model's format should find it helpful. Under no circumstances should the model given herein be seen as generic. Program needs must be confronted on a case-by-case basis, as no universal program exists. Individual school or district specifications must reflect the needs of the unique school program, curriculum, geographic and climatic factors, and, most important, the personality of the community the school serves. The sample program document in this book should provide some direction to planners and the architectural team and furnish a basis for discussion. Portions of the model may be adapted and expanded to meet the unique needs of individual schools and districts. Such adaptation should produce a program statement that meets the individual current and future needs of the school library media center.

2

Develop a Vision: Looking at Successful Library Media Center Designs

A successful library media center project is easier to accomplish if you have actual experience with the design process. If you lack experience, ask a trusted professor or friend. Equally significant is that knowing what can go wrong in the process of overseeing the design and construction of a school library media center is almost as important as knowing what to do right. Let's take a look at a few school library media centers that have met with varying degrees of success. In the following pages we will look at four media centers designed to be part of existing school buildings.

Many issues and concerns for these library media centers are the same as those for centers that are part of a new school. In this chapter, however, all of the designs were prompted by library media centers deemed inadequate to meet the needs of their communities. First will be an elementary school addition on the second floor of an old building that is being renovated. Next will be a middle school, which renovated and added onto what was the previous main office area of the school. Last will be a junior/senior high school library media center that was added onto and reconfigured to become a high school, when a new middle school was built next door.

Elementary Level Library Media Center

The floor plan shown in Figure 2-1 was the first one submitted by the architects. The library media specialist had been on the job one year, and this plan was given to her by the new principal with the mention that it would be under construction in one month. Terror struck! She immediately contacted me, since

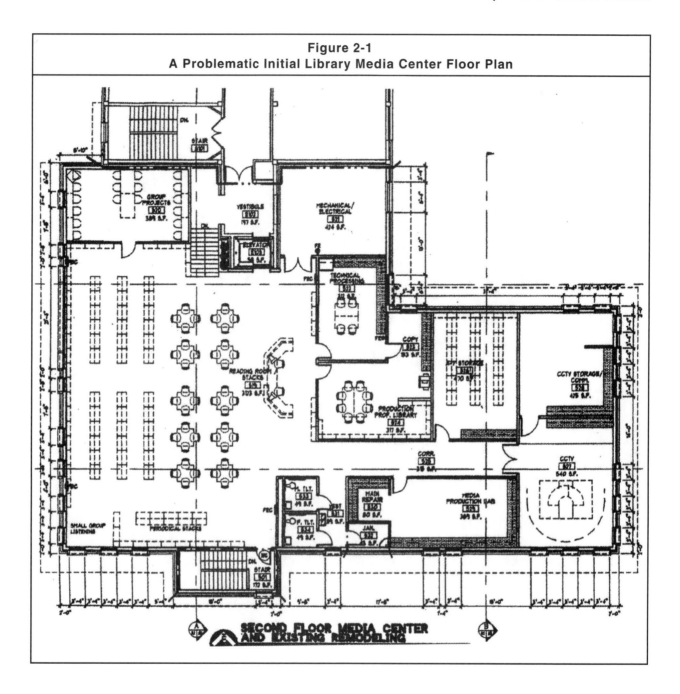

Figure 2-1
A Problematic Initial Library Media Center Floor Plan

she had been my recent student in our Master's program. Fortunately she was able to demonstrate to the principal that the plans were deeply problematic. To her considerable credit, this initial design was never built.

What is wrong with this first plan?

The following items are part of the master construction plan for this school district and also the state's master planning, but not included in this first architectural drawing:

- office for the library media specialist
- special computer area for class group use
- staff bathroom

The architects also included a large mechanicals room as part of the overall square footage for the library media center. This was not according to school district plan nor was it ever mentioned to be included in the recommended square footage for any library media center.

Additionally, a long hallway was designed to reach four very important areas of the library media center: the student media production laboratory, A-V storage, closed circuit television studio, and closed circuit television storage. All of these areas were located in such a position as to be difficult to supervise with one professional and one clerk, and there were no plans to add staff in the future.

We worked to reorganize the spaces on paper, attempting to reassemble them in a more sensible fashion. Our first priorities were ease of access and supervision. Fortunately, when the library media specialist presented our plan to the principal, it was well received. They both met with the architects, and after three revisions, the final plans were approved by all parties.

Final Plans

Immediately upon entrance into the library media center, it looks more spacious and less cluttered. The functions are grouped in logical patterns, such as:

- Small group listening area is tucked away in a corner, not evident when you first arrive, so there will be fewer distractions when other students use the library media center.
- Staff office (which didn't exist in the first plans) is located conveniently behind the circulation desk with a large window to help with observation of activity in the center.
- Student media production lab is near the entrance and can also be easily supervised.
- Professional library which will be heavily used by teachers, because multimedia production computers will be located there for teacher use.
- Group projects area (not in the first plans) with enough computer stations for a class to be instructed by the library media specialist concerning computer literacy.
- Computer lab (not in the first plans).
- Technical processing room which is enlarged and functionally arranged as compared with the first plans.
- Staff toilet which was not a part of the first plans
- A-V storage located near the back of the center. This area is primarily used for storage of classroom A-V equipment over the summer.
- Closed circuit television studio which is nearly twice the size of the original plans. This school has a daily live morning news show, a major feature of the school for years.

Comparisons of Entrance Area for the Elementary Example

The entrance area is a vital aspect of any library, since you want to make it as easy as possible for the users. In this case the library media center is an add-on

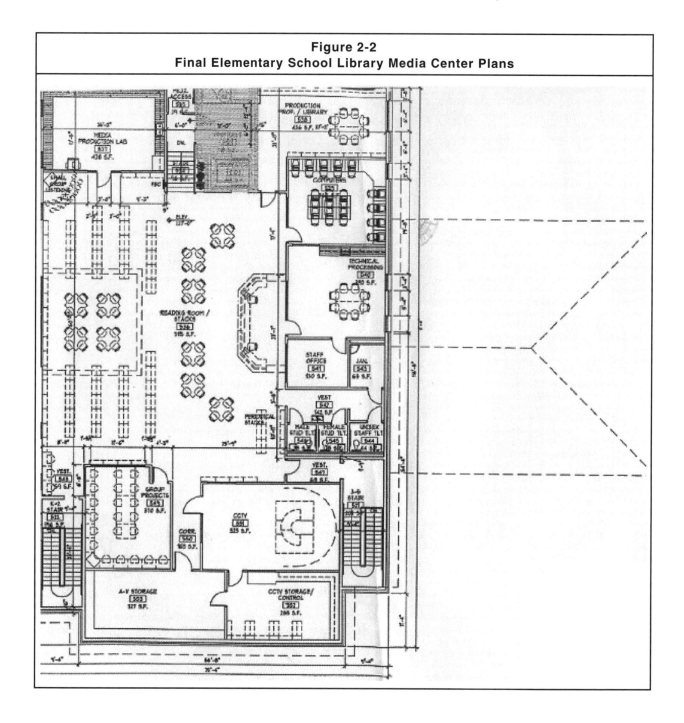

Figure 2-2
Final Elementary School Library Media Center Plans

to an existing older two-story building on a slope. It would be too expensive to build this large facility, which is over a new cafeteria, on the same level as the existing building. The present building does not have an elevator, so one is needed to meet ADA requirements for easy access by any impaired users. There were 11 regular steps in the first plans and 9 regular steps in the final plans for the rest of the users. There are minor differences from the original plans for the vestibule, such as access from the stairwell as well as the hallway.

After you enter the library media center, the view from the entrance is similar, except the special rooms are logically grouped by need for access by the users and viewing of users by the library media specialist. The first entrance (Fig. 2-3) was as follows:

Once the user has entered the large reading room, the two closest rooms were the "group projects room" and the "mechanical/electrical room." These rooms are completely changed for the final plans (Fig. 2-4).

The final entrance was as follows:

The entrance is flanked by the "media production lab" (used by groups of students and teachers, mainly to produce products for schoolwide events and various fairs) and the "production/professional library" (used by teachers). Both of these areas provide quick ingress and egress.

Comparisons of Circulation Area for the Elementary Example

The first circulation area was as shown in Figure 2-5.

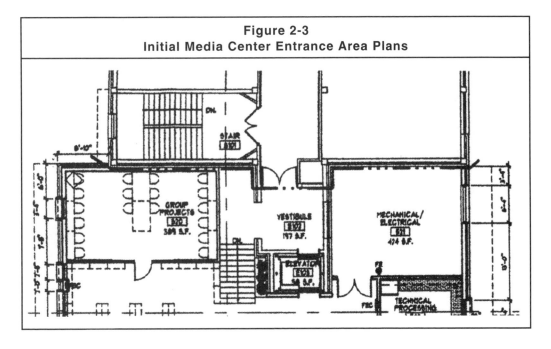

Figure 2-3
Initial Media Center Entrance Area Plans

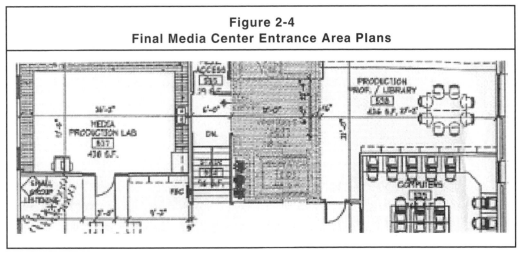

Figure 2-4
Final Media Center Entrance Area Plans

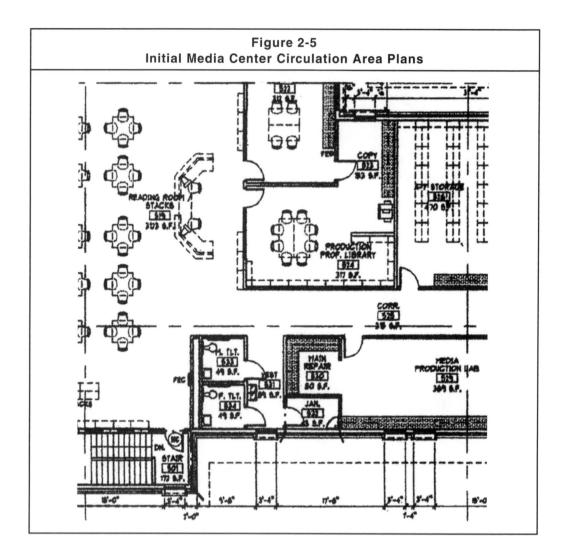

Figure 2-5
Initial Media Center Circulation Area Plans

The final circulation area was as shown in Figure 2-6.

Both the initial and final plans have an elevator and stairs at the entrance, but the two rooms on either side are completely different. The initial room was the "group projects room." This area is now in a more convenient location for the library media specialist, who will be easily able to supervise it.

As you can see, when everyone is really concerned about designing a quality library media center, it can be accomplished. If a single person in the chain of command had not been supportive, the final plan could have been very similar to the first one. It takes a lot of time and energy to plan a useful and well-organized library media center.

Middle School Library Media Center

This middle school in Florida was originally built in 1967; there have been several classroom additions since then. Recently the old library was renovated into a main office and guidance suite. The old offices were greatly expanded for the new library media center.

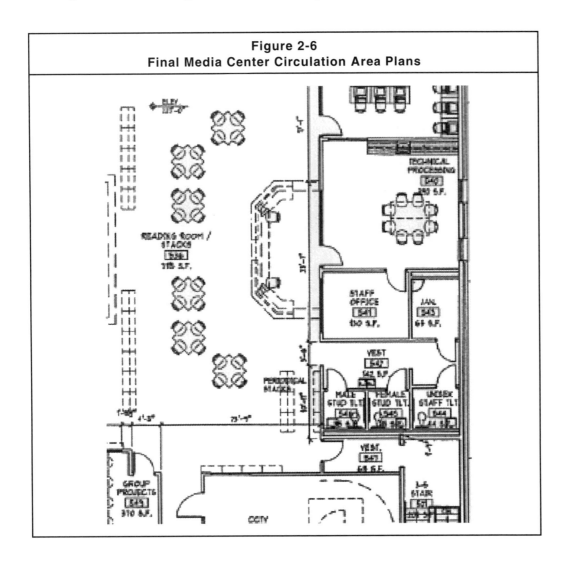

Figure 2-6
Final Media Center Circulation Area Plans

Note the typical main office floor plan (Fig. 2-7), with small waiting area and information desk, a principal's office, assistant principal's office, guidance office, bookkeeper's office, small vault, and small storage area.

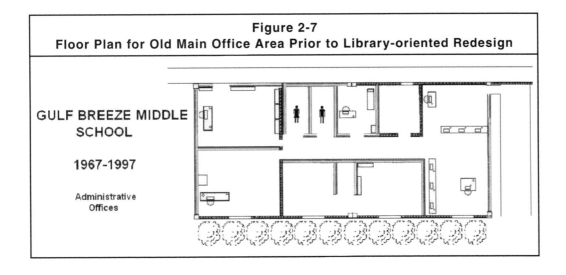

Figure 2-7
Floor Plan for Old Main Office Area Prior to Library-oriented Redesign

Library Media Center Addition

While the old library was being converted into the main office and guidance suite, the library was temporarily located for one year on the stage of the cafetorium. They moved only the heavily used resources onto the stage, and students were only allowed to come in and check out resources. The library media specialist went to the classrooms for instructional activities.

The library media specialist was actively involved in the planning and furnishing of the library media center. There were many load-bearing walls in the old main office area, so many of those original rooms were utilized for backroom functions. The ITV area would normally be located in these areas if one were being included in the plans.

Let's look at the changes made in this area (Fig. 2-8):

Where the principal and assistant principal's offices had been located, a hall was cut through to make the main entrance for the library media center. The long storeroom along the hallway into the center is used for equipment storage, TVs,

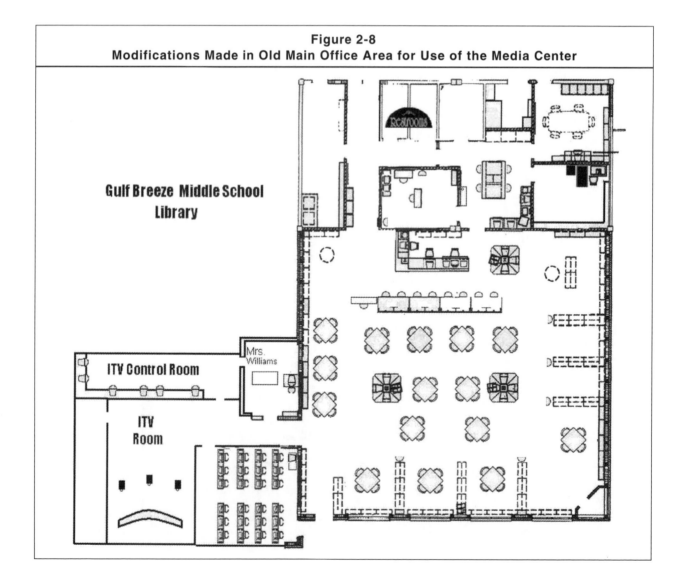

Figure 2-8
Modifications Made in Old Main Office Area for Use of the Media Center

projectors, etc. The restrooms are for teachers. To the right of the restrooms, looking toward the entrance, is a small kitchen. The library media center is the hub for all functions that require hosting. They never, ever close the library for a function. Students circulate around the area, use computers, check out books, and remember the phrase "Silence Please!" The second room is only accessible from the hallway outside the library; it is a mechanical room. A large set of cabinets to the ceiling are accessible from the processing room with the autopsy table (they use an old autopsy table as their center of processing activity) in the center. The corner room is a small conference room accessible either from the library media center or from the hall. The room below the conference room is for housing the video, CD, and DVD collections as well as the headend equipment for the computer and video networks. The office area has large windows on two sides for ease of supervision.

The large square reading room is easily supervised and can seat 60 at tables for four and 20 at computer stations. Mrs. Sharon Henderson, the library media specialist stated, "I would like to mention that the computers to the right of the circulation desk represent a creation station center where all students in the school have access to video editing software, computers with high-end Adobe design capabilities, scanners, copiers, and all sorts of neat things for them to use to communicate in a video or audio format. I have the only full theater Surround Sound system that I know of. I attended the Computers in Libraries Conference in D.C. and they were astounded. I have the same system that our bayfront auditorium has installed. It is huge. You should see the kids do their multimedia productions in here!"

Next you will notice the outside doors to the reading room and the computer room. It looks as if this could make the library media center open to the public. According to Henderson, it is used "only for emergencies, fire drills, loading and unloading book fairs, and staff entry. The administration would like the students to come through the front entrance doors down the hallway. In the early A.M., students enter with me."

The computer room was originally planned to be an instructional television classroom in the library media center. According to Henderson, "There are twenty-four total, four rows of six each. I decided to make it a search lab. Classes schedule that room to do research only. Our ITV program is a before-school program that is basically morning announcements. Two teachers volunteer to direct that. I gave that job away." The long narrow storage room adjacent to the ITV Room is used for decorations, and Mrs. Henderson *does* decorate for events and seasons.

Junior/Senior High School Library Media Center

Space Coast Junior High School was opened ten years ago (see Fig. 2-9) and started with sixth- and seventh-graders. As these students moved up they added ninth through twelfth grades. The school was originally built to accommodate 1,100 junior high students.

Through the years, as the district decided to make it a junior/senior high, more space was needed to accommodate the additional resources needed for the high school program. There was no intention to build a new library media

Figure 2-9
1995 Library Media Center Plans for Space Coast Junior High School

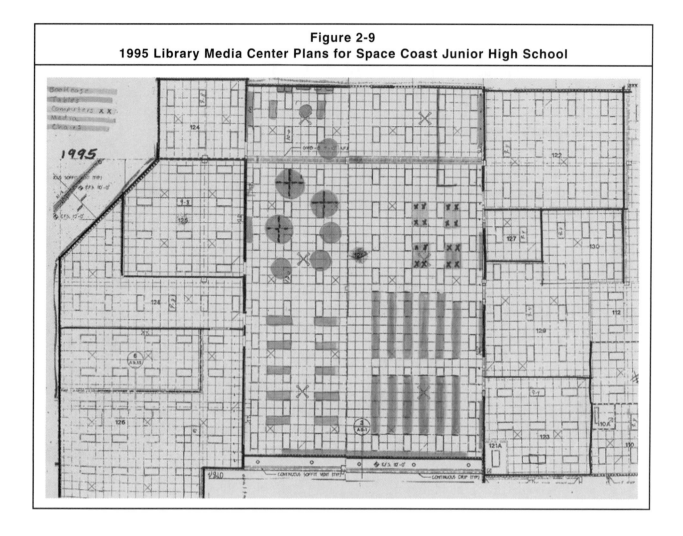

center, so changes were made to the existing area to accommodate more books to serve three additional grades. The computer lab was an enclosed room, so the wall was removed to open the space and allow for bookshelves around the lab.

The staff likes the arrangement for overall access to the facility, but the students don't "browse" the reference section because there are usually classes in the computer lab, which is not conducive to browsing behavior. They tend to forget that the reference books are available because they are located in an inconvenient area.

An additional concern shared by the staff is that they need more open-access computers than the 16 they currently have, but with the existing configuration of shelves, there is no space to add additional hard-wired computers. The best solution for this problem is to equip the library media center for wireless and add wireless laptops, which can be used easily on existing library tables.

3-D Architectural Rendering of a High School

The following school is included, not necessarily for the successful layout of its addition, but because it is the first on the Web to share a three-dimensional architectural rendering.

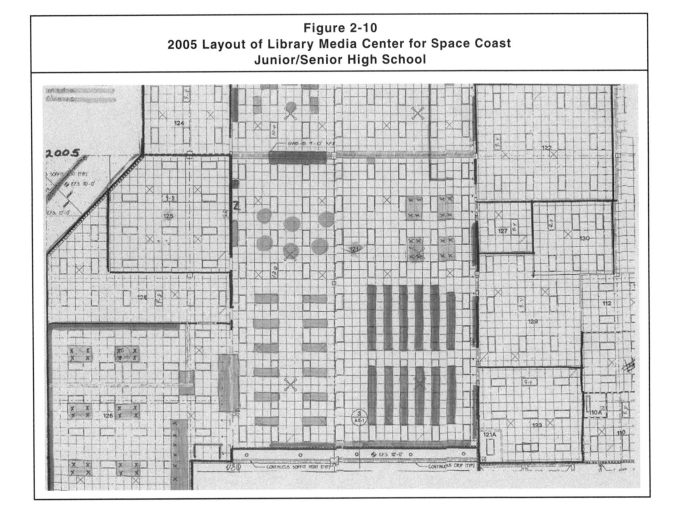

Figure 2-10
2005 Layout of Library Media Center for Space Coast
Junior/Senior High School

Maplewood Richmond Heights School District has shared their school renovation plans with the Web community, which includes a large portion of their constituents. Following is their statement about the planning:

Plans for major renovations of the Maplewood Richmond Heights High School are moving ahead with full steam. Construction managers, S. M. Wilson, and architects have spent the summer getting final drawings in place to go out for bid. It is critical to plan construction, safety measures, student traffic, and academics so that the renovations are smooth and not disruptive. Therefore all projects are being implemented in phases. Following is a list of the components of work to be done during the 2005–2006 school year:

Demolish and renovate the gymnasium; expected completion in early second semester.

Renovate remaining portion of the fourth floor into technology labs; expected completion in late fall.

Remodel existing library space into mathematics classrooms; expected completion in late fall.

While these projects are in progress, there are a few changes for students. First, all PE/Health classes will be held at the Maplewood Community Center, and a satellite library space has been created next to study hall for students to access reference materials. Once the math classes and technology rooms are complete, students will begin using those spaces to open other areas in the high school for renovations. As soon as the gym is complete, the small gym will be renovated as a new library media center. Students are also encouraged to park at the community center since there will be heavy construction traffic around the school.

Maplewood Heights High School Library Media Center

As mentioned before the remodeled library will be in the small gymnasium. The library media center (Fig. 2-11) will serve as a focal point for the high school and middle school community. It will be placed in the small gymnasium with access from the building and Lohmeyer Street. Students visiting the library will find soft seating and tables for small group study, as well as a coffee area for refreshments.

As mentioned earlier, these plans are not being included for their outstanding arrangement, but for the novelty of a new way to present plans, using a 3-D display available to the community at large as well as the planning team.

This concludes the sample design chapter. It is my hope that in reviewing these plans you will have acquired a general sense of what works and what doesn't in school library media centers. In future chapters, we will move on to look at design and construction of facilities.

Figure 2-11
Maplewood School Library Media Center Plans in 3-D

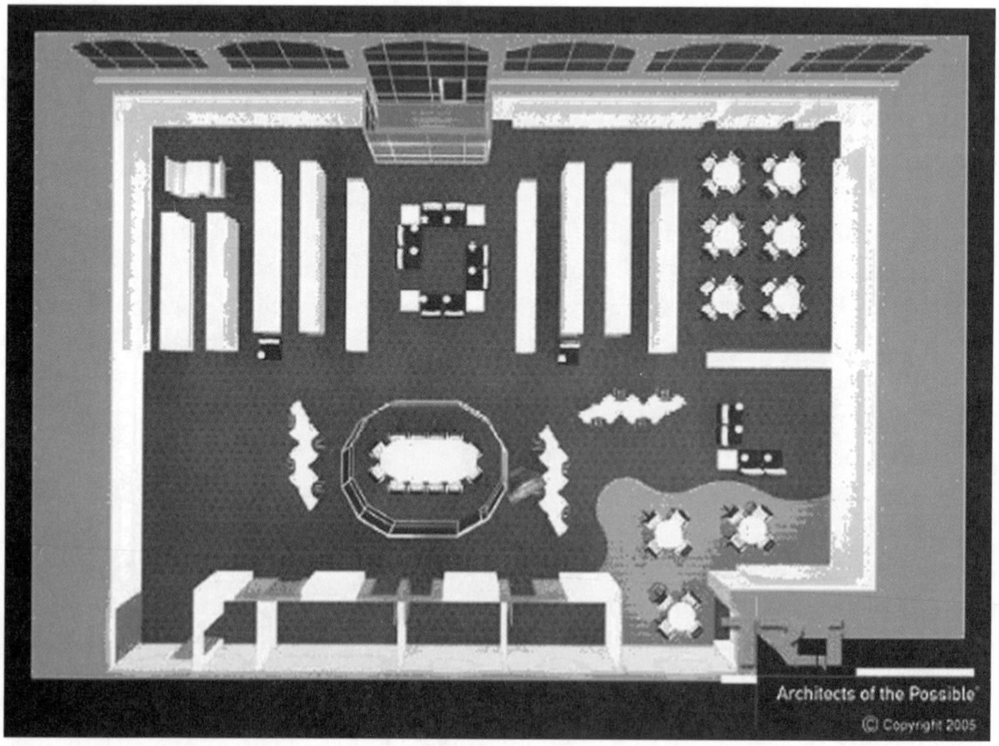

Architects of the Possible
© Copyright 2005

3

Take the DVD Tour

DVD Introduction

The introductory slide show provides a visual and oral guide to the contents of the DVD. Here the author has the ability to share color photos and video clips as well as, through his voice, his enthusiasm for this topic. There are other slide shows that provide the user with an overview of the DVD contents; introduce readers, viewers, and listeners to new technology convergences; and highlight interesting uses of special features and program as they are integrated into the facility.

Introduction to Contents (Slide Show)

The first entity listed as a part of the DVD index is the introductory slide show. Since a DVD is so powerful, it is possible to include quality video, sound, contents, and graphics. Each screen of the slide show presentation guides the user to the elements included. They are:

1. New technologies (slide show)
2. Special library media center features (slide show)
3. Tour of a knowledge center in final construction (video)
4. Tour of a new elementary school library media center (video)
5. Tour of a new middle school library media center (video)
6. Tour of a new high school library media center (video)
7. Video clips comparing important areas of the library media center (video)

New Technologies (Slide Show)

Technologies are converging. It was recently announced that Hewlett Packard is entering the video as well as the computer market. Kodak is switching from the 35mm film market to the OLED (organic light emitting diode). This provides further evidence to support this author's concept of the CommCoRe (CCR) device that will use a video-type screen and natural language communication devices, similar to video remote controls.

Samples of the new applications for CCRs are provided, ranging from flat screen applications to portable devices with rollup screens. These samples hopefully will provide a vision for planners. The slide show can be presented to decision-makers and constituents to assist them in understanding the future implications for these technology convergences and the new paradigms they will support.

Special Library Media Center Features (Slide Show)

Planners and architects generally plan and design areas as a part of the facility that can feature local areas of interest, such as waterwheels, nautical themes, trains, etc. These can be implemented as murals and 3-D displays. The slide show shares special features, which can be used in generic settings.

1. papire mâché figures—animals, objects, etc.
2. stained glass windows
3. milk jug igloo shapes

Video Tours of Library Media Centers

Tour of Library Media Center Under Final Construction (Video)

It is not often that there is an opportunity to tour a new facility in the final stages of construction. This tour provides an opportunity for the knowledge manager and specialist to describe their vision for the use of these facilities.

The Florida State University library media center for a PreK-12 school is shown in Figure 3-1.

The main entrance has a huge lighted display case on one side and a wonderful stained-glass window "tree of knowledge" created specially for the school. In addition there is an outlet for a future computer kiosk, so special features can be presented for users and potential users. Since this is a PreK-12 school the main reading room is zoned for primary students and another area for secondary students. The circulation desk is the first visible area seen as you enter. The entrance is attractively tiled from the entrance through to the fire exit at the rear of the building. The primary area is directly across from the circulation desk. The furnishings are sized for users, and there is an interesting kiosk with special seating and features for the primary level students.

To the right of the entrance is the computer lab, where students and other users have access to work-station-type computers for multimedia production. This area is adjacent to the TV studio and control area as well as TV prop storage. The large corner room is designed for special purpose projects. Sometimes

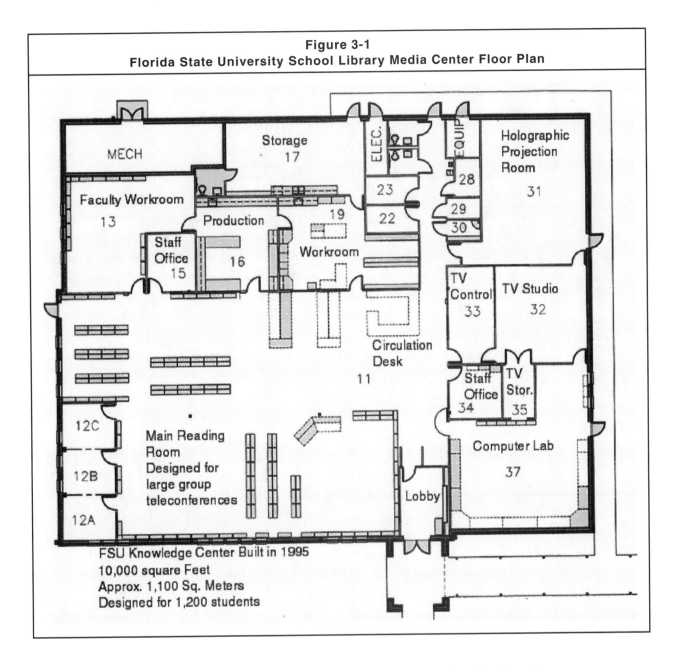

Figure 3-1
Florida State University School Library Media Center Floor Plan

it is an experimental room for science research-type projects associated with university-level research projects. Other times it serves as a seminar room or an area for science and history fair projects.

At the back of the center are the various workrooms, such as a faculty workroom with computers and other resources to prepare curriculum. It also includes a production lab encompassing a publishing center where third- and fifth-graders wrote and illustrated a book; hard laminated covers were placed on the book and it was cataloged and added to the special collection area. There is also a workroom for the staff as well as a periodicals storage area. Behind these areas is a storage area for audiovisual equipment. Since most of the equipment is permanently installed in classrooms, this area provides a convenient storage area for multimedia resources, including a large number of realia (real objects and/or models).

The main reading room includes three conference rooms with truly sound-proof folding walls. These rooms provide users with small group study areas. The microcomputers in the reading room are mainly located near the circulation area for ease of supervision. There are a few terminals located in the stack areas to be used only for searching the online card catalog.

Tour of a High School Media Center (Video)

The library media specialist at Gulf Coast High School on the edge of Naples, Florida, provides an excellent tour of their facility. For the past seven years they have served 2,000 students per year of grades 9–12. This past summer they added 1,000 new computers and a wireless network to the school. They also have a signal tower from which they provide wireless access to other schools in their area. The library media specialist and her professional colleagues serve as co-leaders for the library media programs in their school district. The floor plan in Figure 3-2 provides the DVD user with an orientation to where spaces in the tour are located.

This school building is wonderfully organized. On entry, one first passes the main office, where much of the administrative work of the facility takes place. Continuing down the hall, one comes to the guidance area, and then arrives shortly thereafter at the principal's office. His office overlooks the main court-yard of the school and across the corridor is the main entrance for the library media center. The center is entered through two sets of large glass double doors.

After entering the library media center, the visitor is greeted by a large and attractive area with informal reading furniture and quality space for displays. In fact, the school clubs (called academies) hold their major functions, including science, history, medieval, classics, humanities, and ethnic fairs, in the entry area. It has ceramic tile on the floor, so food can be served there without any difficulty.

The main reading room can seat 200 users comfortably. In addition, there are two 30-station computer labs and a set of 30 wireless laptop computers, which can be used in the main reading area. There are two electric screens, which can be lowered in the main reading room and, along with video projectors, can be used to instruct large groups simultaneously.

Another feature of the center is equipment for students and teachers to produce quality multimedia computer products. The equipment is located in the combination office and workroom for the media center staff. They have a color plotter printer, scanners, digital cameras, and the proper software to digitize many formats of multimedia.

The lighting of the center was a major problem. When the school was planned ten years ago, indirect lighting was in vogue. The large reading room with 18-foot-high ceilings was lit via sodium indirect lights. There were not enough of them to provide adequate foot candles for reading at the tables. Also, whenever the electricity is turned off and then on again, it takes time for the sodium lights to re-brighten. To solve the problem, extra fluorescent lights were added to provide adequate foot candles for reading at the tables.

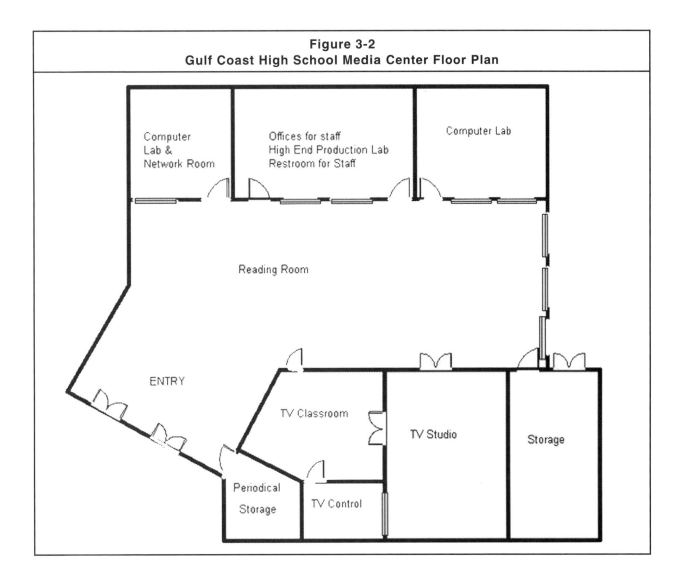

Figure 3-2
Gulf Coast High School Media Center Floor Plan

Their TV studio and classroom is well placed, staffed, and equipped. There is a full-time teacher assigned to this area who works as part of a team with the media staff, teachers, students, and parents. Collectively, they have won many local, state, and national television production awards.

The video points out the convenience of their equipment storage area, with easy access to the main parking lot and the rest of the school. The media center manager points out several flaws in the planning that were corrected when the two new high schools opened sometime later.

Tour of Golden Gate High School (Video)

This high school is also in Collier County, Naples, Florida. It is one of two new high schools opened this fall. The floor plan is shown in Figure 3-3.

The media center is on the second floor, with windows overlooking the central courtyard. The sun goes across the media center and doesn't shine through the expansive windows. The layout is an improvement over Gulf Coast High School. There are appropriate windows located throughout the facility, as was

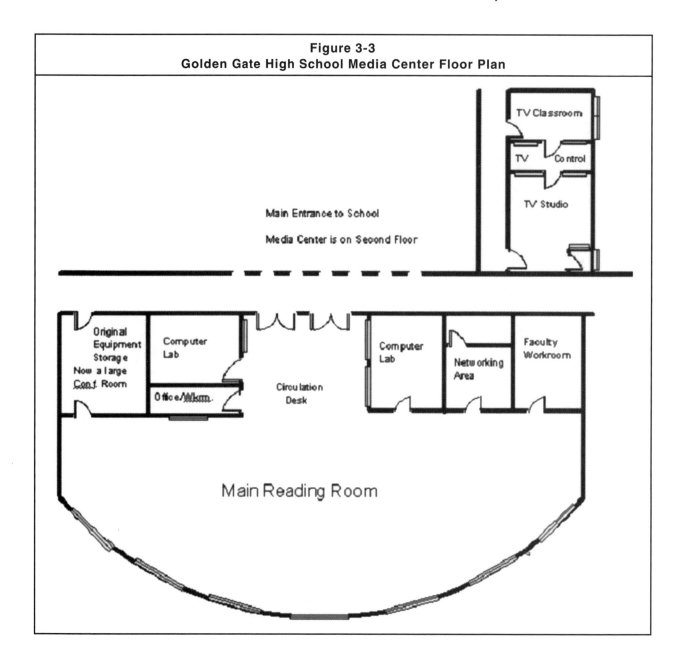

Figure 3-3
Golden Gate High School Media Center Floor Plan

TV Classroom

TV   Control

TV Studio

Main Entrance to School

Media Center is on Second Floor

Original
Equipment
Storage
Now a large
Conf. Room

Computer
Lab

Office/Wkrm.

Circulation
Desk

Computer
Lab

Networking
Area

Faculty
Workroom

Main Reading Room

recommended to the architects. The TV area, although across the hall, is wonderfully arranged for easy supervision. This school is not included in the video tour on the DVD, but portions of it are included in the video including comparison of special area solutions in library media centers.

Tour of a Middle School Library Media Center (Video)

Varsity Lakes Middle School's library media center floor plan is shown in Figure 3-4. This middle school is in the process of opening; not all areas were completed at the time of the tour. An interesting feature is the different furniture in two areas of the reading room. One area is designed with tables and roll-around chairs at the appropriate height to use wireless laptop computers for one

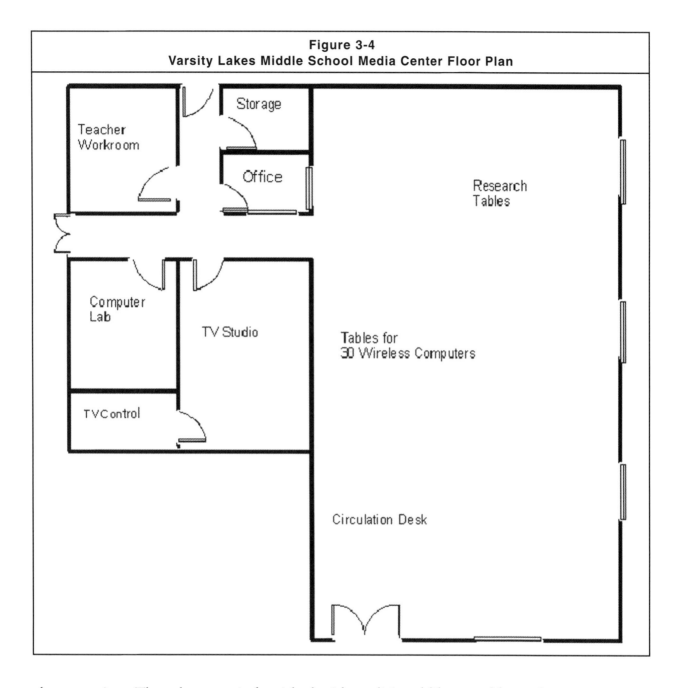

Figure 3-4
Varsity Lakes Middle School Media Center Floor Plan

class at a time. The other area is furnished with traditional library tables and chairs for one class at a time to complete traditional research activities.

The TV studio is interesting, because it is large enough to accommodate three sets of activities at one time. It is well equipped with proper cameras and lighting. One corner has an interviewing area with two overstuffed chairs, with an attractive bookshelf in the background for formal interviews. In the middle of one wall of the studio is the news anchor desk, and the last area is reserved for two chairs and a microphone on a stand for quick announcements.

The media specialist's office is located properly with windows overlooking the main reading room. She has decorated it with objects that are illustrative of her professional personality.

The rest of the library media center was not toured, because it was not furnished at this time. The equipment and furniture were still being moved in.

Tour of an Elementary School Library Media Center (Video)

Calusa Park Elementary School is arranged as shown in Figure 3-5. This elementary school represents the blend between excellent traditional program services and all the high-tech features planned for the future.

You can enter the center either from the administrative office or a major corridor of the school. Users are greeted with a wonderful lighted display case. Immediately in front of them is the circulation desk, where the clerk is always available to the user. The teacher area has been converted into a "story room," with a colorful area rug.

The shelving has been reorganized to meet the needs of the collection, rather than perfectly balanced according to the architectural plan. The computer and

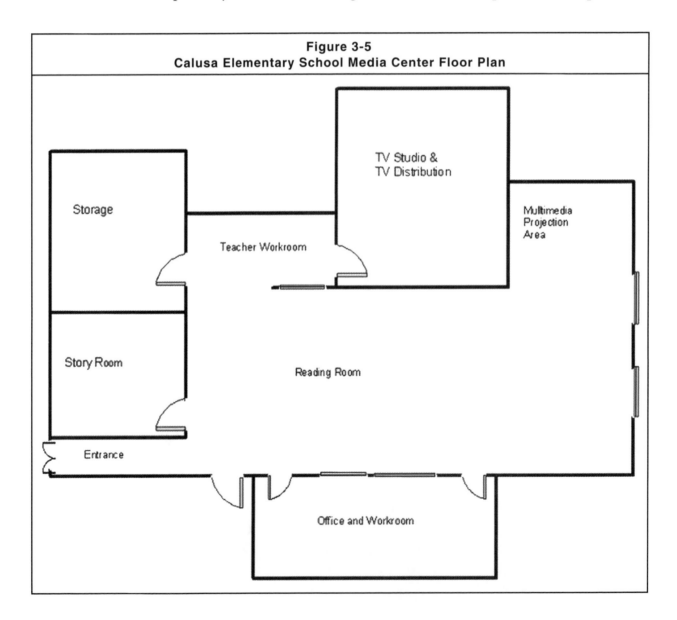

**Figure 3-5
Calusa Elementary School Media Center Floor Plan**

reading areas are conveniently located, but as with many reading rooms, the electrical outlets in the floor are not located conveniently for practical use.

A wonderful feature is the original "story area," which has been converted to a flexible space for instruction and schoolwide meetings. There are narrow tables to locate the wireless portables for use by students, faculty, and/or parents. The library media specialist has a video projector mounted in the ceiling and a screen for projections. All teachers have audio sticks (wireless microphones connected to a neck loop). There is also an additional one for each area of the school for students to use when they need to address the whole class.

An equipment storage area has been converted to be used by teachers and teacher assistants to copy, laminate, and prepare instructional resources. There is also a large area for multimedia resources to be organized for use by teachers and classes of students.

The TV studio is a combination editing and production center. It is easily supervised and well arranged for an elementary school. Also, it is well equipped to produce a quality product.

There is a combination office and workroom behind the circulation area. It is well arranged and convenient for use.

Video Clips of Special Areas

These video clips are arranged to help planners compare different solutions to problems and provide sample color schemes. A wonderful feature of a DVD is the ability to capture single frames and print them for in-depth study and analysis.

TV Studio Solutions

The two high schools featured here provide proof that planning can improve instructional options. The first school had an elaborate classroom, control room, and TV studio. There weren't any windows between the three large areas. The second video clip of the TV area in the newest high school demonstrates the improvements in planning.

The middle school sample illustrates excellent planning in set organization. This TV studio has a wonderful layout for instructional activities.

Entrance and Circulation Areas

There are many examples of solutions for circulation areas. There is no one solution for this aspect of the library media center. These come from elementary, middle, and high schools.

Multiuse Areas

These video clips provide interesting solutions to program concerns. One shows an elementary school that has reutilized a storage area for children's programming. The second examines a high school that has converted a large storage area into a space for club meetings and other school events.

Singapore Knowledge Manager Project

This document included on the DVD provides important background information for facilities planning and should be carefully examined by the readers. This project for the improvement of the schools in Singapore, completed in 2000, was established to justify the transition of their traditional school libraries into media centers. Private schools in Singapore have had library media centers just like those in the United States for years, but the 385 public schools of Singapore had libraries managed by clerks under the supervision of teachers on assignment (like lunchroom duty in the United States). It is included on the DVD to provide an electronic version of the project that could prove useful in planning for new facilities.

The media resource library (MRL) in Singapore schools is envisaged to play a very important and central role in support of education in the information age. It is a vital instrument of the education process in aspects of both teaching and learning. The MRL is the central depository of tangible information resources, supplemented by offline and online digital resources available through network connection to other parts of the school, or even to the homes of students and teachers.

This document traces the major milestones of events and activities that have impinged and impacted on the schools' MRLs to their present form today, and reviews the current status of MRLs. Challenges and opportunities for these MRLs in the advent of the information-age schools are identified and discussed, specifically the staffing and training aspects deemed necessary to implement and sustain a successful MRL. The findings and recommendations are based upon the research and proven successful MRL examples of U.S. information-age schools.

The Master of Science in Information Studies program, M.Sc. (Info Studies), at Nanyang Technological University, which introduced a full-time mode of study in July 2000, is presented. It has a special track designed specifically for the training and education of teachers to fulfill their duties and roles as MRL appointment holders and stakeholders in schools. Various modes in which the M.Sc. (Info Studies) program can be undertaken and completed and the role the Ministry of Education can play to support this aspect of training are proposed and outlined.

This document, therefore, serves as an agenda for deliberation, with the main aim of systematic training and education of teachers to equip them with specialized information skills and knowledge in the foreseeable future. This, in turn, will transform and leapfrog Singapore schools to reach the frontier of information-age schools in this region, and to fulfill the government's vision of "thinking schools, learning nation."

II

Planning the Facility

4

How to Develop Comprehensive Planning Documents

One of the most crucial steps when proposing a new school library media center is the preparation of the planning documents. Before the design specifications—the layout of rooms, selections of furniture, and so on—can be considered in detail, a number of general questions must be posed. Concerns to be answered in this preliminary phase include the demographics of the school, the library media center's programmatic philosophy, where the facility will be located, and how the collection is expected to develop and change over the coming years. A thorough investigation of these and other topics outlined in this chapter will greatly inform the specifics of the planning process, providing an anchor for the entire project as it moves through design, into construction, and toward completion, and offering reminders of what is at stake through each phase of the process.

Planning documents typically go through several versions, depending on school district procedure and the ease with which agreement can be reached by all involved parties. Final documents need to be supported by the entire planning team. The school library media coordinator and/or district coordinator will need to guide the final version of the document through the planning process. There are many important considerations for a planning document. The model in this chapter is meant only to stimulate discussion and assist in developing the final successful product.

School Demographics

The data entered into the following worksheet can provide the administrative decision-makers and the architectural team with the numerical information needed for planning total square footage and budget allocations for the new or remodeled library media center construction program. This is important whether the proposed library media center will be built in an existing school or as part of a wholly new facility. Such information will be used to determine square footage allocations, and it is therefore important that this be determined as early as possible. Without this data it may be difficult for architects and others to determine the ideal size of furniture, extent of staff work areas, and so on. The "Anticipated special uses of space" section should include information about kitchenettes, recording studios, and other spaces hoped for in the new media center. In some cases it may be impossible to predict these figures, but the better the estimate, the better the facility can be tailored to serve its community.

Worksheet

Professional staff-student ratio: _____

User capacity: _____

Total number of professional staff: _____

Total number of support staff: _____

Grade levels or age levels for which program is intended:

_____

_____

Hours per day space will be used: _____

Anticipated special uses of space: _____

_____

_____

_____

_____

_____

_____

_____

_____

_____

_____

_____

_____

Program Philosophy

In this section of the document, try to discuss the school library media center's educational and programmatic philosophy. This should be a mission statement of sorts, but it also serves to remind all parties involved in the planning, design, and construction of the media center of the ideals that will underlie the facility's day-to-day function. Be sure in this area to discuss how the school is situated within the larger educational community. In particular, be sure to articulate the reasons why the resources it provides are important, its orientation toward service, and its commitment to equal access. The following is a generic example of such a statement that can be retooled to fit specific needs:

Sample Program Philosophy Statement

The school library media center serves as the school's information hub, providing resources and activities that enable students and staff to use ideas and information effectively and stimulating personal and intellectual growth of students and other patrons. The center and its resources provide learning experiences, both active and passive, that will prepare students for success in the information age. In the process, the center will ensure that students and staff alike are thoughtful and informed users of information and technology.

The school library media center program and its environment are managed by a staff of skilled professionals who serve in different roles as information specialists, teachers, and instructional consultants to provide an effective learning environment. Professional library media center personnel encourage awareness of all the opportunities of the program. Instruction, guidance, assistance, and motivation are offered through resources and activities that promote lifelong learning. Locating, evaluating, and using information are taught as skills necessary to participate fully in a technological society. Through careful selection, planning, organization, and continuous reevaluation, library media center professionals and support staff keep the collection and services of the center responsive to the long-range goals of the educational system as well as to the immediate needs of the students and staff.

The library media center program must circulate and/or offer appropriate resources and services to meet the specific educational needs of its school, providing the maximum possible support for the institution's curriculum and other programming. Naturally, where appropriate, the library media center should be designed to support noncurricular resources as well, especially insofar as this helps to make the library media center an appealing, nonthreatening environment.

If the library media center is to play an active part in the life of the school, it must not be a mere secondary classroom space. The school library media center program must be flexible enough to accommodate groups of different sizes as well as individual instruction. Service to groups should never preclude service to individual users, meaning that the center should be designed in such a way as to allow simultaneous use of multiple types of activity. Consistent with this commitment, the center must make its resources available as freely and easily as possible to students and staff at all times during open hours.

Program Goals

In this section try to describe what the center hopes to achieve with its services. While the previous section worked through the center's approach to serving its patrons, this one should be more concerned with the anticipated payoff of those efforts. It may be appropriate here to discuss the findings of any recent studies of the role of school library media centers in the educational development of students. It is especially important to keep in mind here the specific demographics served by the school, as this will allow for a more thoroughgoing description of how the center can best serve the institution's users over time.

Sample Program Goal Statement

The school library media center facility is designed to support the teaching-learning process by providing access to resources and services to satisfy both the instructional and individual needs of students. Likewise, programming will aim to create an atmosphere that promotes inquiry, creativity, self-direction, and communication of ideas. Further, the center provides an environment in which different learning styles can be accommodated and in which individuals and groups both large and small can obtain access to information through a variety of resources. Teaching information literacy, which continues to grow in stature as an educational discipline, will also be a crucial activity of the center.

Building a Flexible Media Center

As teaching and learning change, so too must the library media center facility. In this section of the planning documents, clearly articulate what can be done to ensure that the center can change as education does. Unfortunately, schools rarely have the resources to fully remodel library facilities with regularity. Accordingly, it is crucial that the facility be designed in such a way it never need fall out of touch with the latest developments in educational culture. All too often library media centers have been designed with concrete block walls dividing areas of the facility, making later renovations expensive and difficult. Many older schools have simply converted classrooms to library facilities as needs have changed. This is problematic insofar as it breaks up the spatial continuity that is crucial to a successful library media center. Others have been built with load bearing interior walls making it difficult to create the open, squarer spaces helpful for the main reading rooms in library media centers. These and other problems can be avoided by clearing articulating the need for spaces that can change over time and by providing suggestions for how this might be done. Make it clear here that situations like those described above must be avoided in order to guarantee that the final facility can be responsive to the inevitable changes and developments that will come in time. Below is a sample statement that can probably be adapted for use on many projects.

Sample Flexibility Statement

The needs provided for by library media center facilities change with the educational climate and the larger structures of society. Flexibility in design helps to ensure that the physical space will be able to meet future program needs without necessitating expensive redesigns. While it is impossible to anticipate exactly what changes will take place in coming years, past experience suggests that spatial configurations will have to be modified frequently as school demographics and educational needs change. Most developments are likely to be internal to the facility, meaning that they will have little effect on its overall superstructure or total architectural footprint. In general, they will likely be necessitated by new developments in the educational use and availability of technologies and other resources. The total square footage of the facility is likely to change little unless the size of the school's student body fluctuates significantly, so it is essential that the interior of the facility itself be as flexible as possible. Accordingly, there should be few, if any, interior load-bearing walls, allowing internal spaces to be renegotiated as new needs emerge.

Rapid technological advances will continue to affect the procedures for locating information as well as those for circulation, inventory, and delivery of information. These advances will also affect the classroom connections to the library media center. The pace of technological change makes it difficult to predict what types of equipment and spatial accommodations will be needed in the future.

Information carriers—online public access catalogs, databases, subscription-based Web sites, and so on—will be accessible from terminals in the library media center and, where appropriate, may also be accessible via proxy connections from remote locations. Whatever the setup, learners will be able to make use of the library media center facility's resources from both inside and outside the building, and all planning should take this fact into account. The library media center of the future will likely function as an organizational hub from which users will be able to set out on their personal quests for information. Regardless of how the dynamics of usage change, however, it is crucial that the possibility of both internal and external usage of resources be maintained. However things change, the library media center must be maintained as a space in which learning happens. Under no circumstances should the library media center ever be imagined as a space through which users merely pass on their way to satisfying educational goals. It should instead be continually reaffirmed as a place where users actively engage with information through the media and means of the moment. Flexible facilities are vital facilities, riding the currents of change rather than being sucked under by them.

Facilities with built-in flexibility will allow the incorporation of new technology with a minimum of expense and disruption. Openness to current multimedia equipment and other emerging technologies throughout the library media center necessitates the inclusion of adequate electrical outlets throughout the facility, not only on perimeter walls but through grids in the floor area or ceiling. Also necessary are conduits to carry telephone, television, and/or fiberoptic cables. Space should also be alloted to subtitute other information pipes as the need arises. Lastly, workstations will have to be networked, so they can be served by common delivery systems. Whenever possible, all of the library's digital resources should be accessible from any terminal in the library media center.

Maintaining flexibility necessitates the installation of a multipurpose grid for distribution and networking of electronic equipment throughout the open floor space of the reading, listening, and viewing areas. If the school district is willing to provide for and support wireless capability, then the need for some floor grids may be reduced, though they are still necessary in the present and may well remain an important part of connectivity in the future.

Portable space dividers, freestanding shelving, and movable and flexible carrels are also essential elements of a flexible facilities plan. The more built-in furniture included in a facility, the more difficult it will be to vary spatial configurations over time. Some such units may be unavoidable, but the more they can be kept out of the facility, the easier changes will be in the long term.

Location of Facility and Patterns of Use

Properly situating a school library media center within the larger educational facility makes all the difference in shaping the way students, teachers, and support staff make use of it. In this section, describe who will be using the facility and attempt to determine how to best guarantee their access. Because this information, more than many of the other sections in this sample planning document, is highly contingent on the school's physical location and design, the language

Figure 4-1
Entrance of Chief Leschi School

(Photo by Eckert & Eckert)

that follows should be seen as highly provisional. Note that the considerations at stake for a library media center being built within a single school building are very different from those intended for freestanding buildings on an educational campus. Adapt the following statement as appropriate to your program.

Sample Facility Location Statements

The general trend in planning the location of a library media center is to place it at the heart of the academic section of the school building or complex. This ensures that those most likely to use it will have easy access to its resources, ensuring that the center will play a fundamental role in the day-to-day life of teachers and students alike. When a library media center is being designed within a larger school facility, however, the location of the center and the decisions that are made about the spaces around it will often be contingent on a variety of factors. Locating the center close to classrooms eases the distribution of equipment and resources directly to classrooms. It also lessens the amount of time needed to mobilize classes and bring them to the library, encouraging group use of the facility. In multiple-story structures, the center should be located near an elevator to accommodate the physically handicapped and to facilitate transport of heavy multimedia equipment and delivery of shipments. Provision of restrooms in or immediately adjacent to the library media center for staff and patrons is important, particularly if the library media center is used during special activity hours when other parts of the school are not accessible.

If a separate building is being built to house the library media center, the facility should still be centrally located with easy access from all instructional areas of the school as well as from exterior areas, access drives, and parking. As discussed in prior sections of this document, the key to good design is an inherent flexibility that allows a variety of activities, accommodates changes and new emphases in curriculum, and provides for changing technology. Equally important is that the center be designed in such a way as to enable a traffic flow that maximizes the number of users who can access and pass through the center at any given time while minimizing interruptions and distractions to those already present.

These ideals should be kept in mind when incorporating the center into an larger building as well, meaning that the design team should work to guarantee that students and teachers alike have the highest possible degree of access. They should be able to access the facility without significantly interrupting or otherwise impairing their curricular work. As stated earlier, it is important to locate the facility in the heart of the academic program areas. Additionally, consideration should be given for after-hours access in some schools where usage of the facility by after-school programs, community groups, and so on is desired.

In some situations patterns of library media center use may change throughout the day. Day care, early childhood programs, before- and after-school programs, and community use of facilities may require access to the library media center when school is not in session. Likewise, the concept of year-round learning, before- and after-school programming, possible open hours on Saturday mornings and/or Sunday afternoons, and the need to connect the library media center to the community may also necessitate some changes. Under such circumstances, the center should be located closer to the perimeter of school, where users have access

Figure 4-2
Exterior View of Library for Cedar Valley Community School

(Photo by Benjamin Benschneider)

to drives and parking areas; a library media center that is easy to find will be easy to use. Even so, the facility should remain as central as possible to classroom areas, encouraging interaction between the library media center program and classroom learning activities. It is not always possible to accomplish both objectives. Given that activities during school hours are essential for the success of the program, the need for central placement should take priority.

When facilities are a part of a larger building it may be more difficult to guarantee access for noncurricular activities. Ideally, the center should be located near the front, side, or rear of the building, with direct access to the outside. If this is not possible, especially if the facility is not on the ground floor, then other areas of the school should be equipped with gates or other security systems to restrict access to the rest of the building, keeping users accessing the media center at odd hours from wandering too far afield. This is possible but sometimes difficult to implement, and architects must keep it in mind from the beginning of the design process if it is desired.

Collection Size and Formats

In this section, discuss the materials currently in circulation in the library media center. Further, remember to note that collection size and formats will change dramatically in the future. Recent studies concerning the impact of library media centers on achievement foreshadow this. In this section describe how such anticipated changes should inform design choices.

Figure 4-3
Interior View of Cedar Valley Community School

(Photo by Benjamin Benschneider)

Sample Collection Size and Format Statement

Collection size and formats of the library collection must be adjusted to the impact of new technologies, delivery systems, and changes in curriculum and instruction. Available resources must also be responsive to changes in enrollment size. Recent studies concerning the significance of library media centers suggest the need for increases in collection size and scope. Placing a pedagogical emphasis on critical thinking requires a wider variety of resources and modes of delivery to meet individual learning styles and depth of inquiry. In placing an increasing emphasis on information literacy, schools no longer simply teach the basic skills of reading, writing, and arithmetic. While these skills are still fundamental, new teaching methods and learning activities create the need for more in-depth and high-quality resources than did the cursory look at information resources of the back-to-basics movement.

The center's resources must also take into account the fact that many teachers are increasingly moving away from simply lecturing; they are working to develop more fully engaged lesson plans that take the interests and abilities of individual students into account. Accordingly, resources should reflect the constantly changing interests of students as fully as funding and space allows. Tangible materials like books will remain a crucial part of satisfying such needs.

The need for some print resources is currently in decline, since databases and indexes that once occupied library shelves are now largely available in electronic format. Likewise, texts that occupied bound volumes and rolls of microfilm are being transferred to special formats to be read on computers at individual workstations, reducing the space needed to store them. Numerous other print resources remain on the shelves, however, suggesting that while reference collections may continue to shrink, they are unlikely to disappear outright. Further, this process of digitization frees up space for other print resources, allowing for the inclusion of high-quality texts dedicated to particular topics. Consider, for example that in some categories, such as multicultural materials, the print collection will increase as students and teachers use more resources in their teaching-learning activities.

Recommended Space Allocations for Various Formats

Use the following chart to calculate the approximate space needed for the various physical resources in most collections.

BOOKS AND DISKS PER SQUARE AND LINEAR FOOT OF SHELVES

Type of Item	Per Square Ft.	Items Per Linear Ft.
Young Adult Resources:		
Circulating	1 SF per 10 books	8 vols.
Reference	1 SF per 8 books	6–7 vols.
CDs/DVDs	1 SF per 20 disks	4 disks (cover facing out)
Paperbacks	1 SF per 20 books	15 vols.
Current/Display	1 SF per 5 books	5–10 vols.
Children's Resources:		
Circulating	1 SF per 18 books	10 vols.
Easy/Picture	1 SF per 26 books	14 vols.
CDs/DVDs	1 SF per 20 disks	4 disks (cover facing out)

Where possible, resources available on CD-ROMs and DVDs should be displayed with the face of the disk covers showing so the user will be aware of their contents. Also, as noted in previous sections, the ability to move and remove shelving stacks and to replace traditional shelving with storage configurations yet unknown is critical to accommodate changing collection emphases. All this must be able to be accomplished without significantly altering the facility's superstructure.

Program Activities

This section describes the different types of learning activities, both active and passive, that occur concurrently in the library media center. This diverse range of functions encompassed by the modern library media center is often difficult for those unfamiliar with them to comprehend. Accordingly, this section of the document can be highly informative for architects and others, helping anchor them in the various functions of the facility for which they will be responsible. Be sure to adapt the following statement as appropriate for your own library, adding information where necessary and removing those items that do not match your school's programmatic goals.

Sample Program Activities Statement

The library media center should be a space amenable to both planned and spontaneous activity. Further, its program is action-centered: It facilitates attainment of knowledge by both individuals and groups using different learning modes and different technologies for transmitting information. As a learning facility, the library media center must provide flexibility to permit both active and passive participation.

Activities going on in the learning center at any given time might include:

- Individual students and teachers browse through databases and the Web
- Students study individually or work in small groups at tables
- Students browse the collection and read at tables
- Teachers and professional library media center staff instruct large and small groups of students in the use of library media center resources and their accompanying technologies
- Students participate in live dramatic presentations, such as puppet shows, role-playing, and storytelling
- Students use computers to access information services beyond their own library media center
- Students work with teachers and library media center staff on television productions to be distributed throughout the school
- Students and teachers create multimedia projects in the production area
- Students are taught to use television cameras and video editors through schoolwide television programs, such as a student delivered video news show
- Teachers consult with the library media center staff to select appropriate materials for teaching curriculum units
- Community volunteers listen to students read aloud
- Staff members participate in professional growth activities and learn the use of new technologies
- Adult volunteers serve as mentors, assisting students in research
- Library media center staff members create displays and exhibits that market the center's program and resources
- Students listen to or view multimedia programs in small groups
- Media center staff circulate, retrieve, and store the multimedia and computing equipment
- Library media center staff ship and receive materials and equipment.

Program Facilities, Functions, and Equipment

In this crucial section, describe the particular needs of the facility, discussing the various programming specific rooms needed, the overall layout and so on. The general narrative statements that provide guidance for architects come before the specifics required for space allocation, types of facilities, and special conditions within the library media center.

Sample Program Facilities, Functions, and Equipment

A library media center must provide the space and resources such that a variety of dissimilar activities can occur simultaneously. The center should include features that will market both the program and the facility to the school and to the community. The library media center should be recognizable, invite entry, and have "curb appeal." It should have features that will generate interest and encourage students and teachers to participate in the activities it offers.

Be sure to provide a thorough argument for the importance of each need to the overall success of your school. The statement should be inclusive, but brief and to the point, as in the example in Resource B.

5

How to Allocate Space and Determine Library Media Specific Details

Naturally, every school library media center will be different, depending on the community it serves, the resources of the school to which it is attached, and so on. An exhaustive account of all the different styles and strategies that can be employed in the design of these facilities would take hundreds, if not thousands, of pages. Doing so would, however, be pointless, as many of the available layouts, furniture possibilities, and so on are inappropriate, nonfunctional, or unattractive. This chapter attempts to describe a wide variety of the best options currently available.

Space Allocation

The assignment of physical space—that is, the layout of rooms and resources—within the library media facility should match program functions, so that each need can be filled at specific, easily recognizable locations. This is critical to effective use of the library media center by students and teachers. Strategic location of program functions within the total allocated square footage will market the program and facilitate the effective use of staff time. The spatial relationships within the center should provide for efficient flow of traffic. Additionally, the design flexibility in the center must allow for change and easy adaptation of spaces. Lastly, the center's aesthetics need to stimulate a positive response to the work environment. All of these factors in organizing the space within the library media facility should respond to the school's total program and will serve to market the library media center program to both the school and its community.

Planning for the library media center's physical space allocations must be in accord with the total school program. It must reflect the regional accreditation and state standards for square footage, seating, and program functions and should also reflect the current national school library media guidelines.

Facilities List

The facilities list will reflect the special terms given to the different areas of the school library by the state department of education or school board. Education department guidelines usually define space terminology and present a range of square footage allocations for these spaces. It is from these that administrators and school board or governing agencies select the spaces and allocations to meet the individual school or district's program requirements. Private and independent schools have greater latitude in such choices, as they do not have to comply with the standards imposed on publicly supported institutions. See Resource B for a sample facilities list for a library media center.

Following is a list of spaces and the types of furnishings/equipment to be matched with functions/activities/special considerations. Note that many of the spaces in this list will not be ideal or accessible for all library media center types. In particular, media production rooms may not be apt for schools that lack the budget to develop or support them:

Figure 5-1 **School Library Media Spaces, Furnishings, and Functions Chart**		
Library media center spaces	*Special furnishings/equipment*	*Functions/activities/special considerations*
Entry area, circulation center, display space	Provides space for traffic control and the opportunity to market library media center program to the school and community. Provides physical access to library media center. Will provide adequate space for checking resources in and out. Should provide access for handicapped. Should also have ceramic tile for ease of maintenance and be large enough for serving as a display and eating area for special events and fairs (science, history, ethnic, cultural, humanities, etc.).	Circulation center Work chairs Computer terminals and printer Copy machine Display cases Electronic security
Reading, listening, viewing	Provides shelving to house collection of print and multimedia materials. Shelving may define areas to accommodate different sized groups and functions. Seating for individuals and for groups of different sizes should be available in areas defined by shelving. Visible control by library media center personnel is a consideration.	Workstations CD-Rom, DVD devices and printers OPAC access and printers Atlas stand Dictionary stand Tables Chairs Lounge furniture Shelving

(cont'd.)

	Figure 5-1	
School Library Media Spaces, Furnishings, and Functions Chart *(Continued)*		
Library media center spaces	*Special furnishings/equipment*	*Functions/activities/special considerations*
Project room	Provides area for production of multimedia of all types. Should be accessible by large groups without disrupting activities in reading/browsing/listening area, and visible from areas staffed by library media center personnel.	Built-in cabinets with locks Island counter with built-in light tables to view transparent multimedia Cabinets and drawers of varying sizes beneath the counter Work surface counters with recessed and dropped areas to accommo-date computers and typewriters (still a few are needed) Refrigerator Microwave Sink
Group viewing	Provides classroom-size area for different types of presentations and instruction. Should accommodate the use of all types of media and accommodate teleconferences. Should be set up in such a way as to facilitate visual control by library media center personnel.	Flexible tables Chairs Podium Screen (wall or rear view) Smart board Computers
Conference spaces	Multipurpose areas under supervision of library media center personnel. Acoustics provide for use of multimedia equipment; portable computer table. Movable walls provide for flexible use by different sized groups.	Chairs Conference tables Computer tables Counter with built-in cabinets and locks Computers
Professional collection	Provides storage area for professional books and periodicals. Conference and planning area used by small groups or individual teachers. Area for previewing, selecting, evaluating print and multimedia resources and equipment.	Shelving Comfortable chairs Tables Computers and connectors
Television studio, distribution and editing	Provides space for students and teachers engaged in production and distribution of programs to classrooms, auditorium, cafeteria, library media center carrels, and conference areas. Convenient access to media production laboratory, equipment storage, and reading/listening/ viewing areas. Should be accessible by groups without disrupting activities in reading/browsing/listening area. Includes area for production of sound recordings. Must be soundproof and provide area for editing and distribution of multimedia programs. Should be secure.	Built-in cabinets with locks Television cameras Tripods, dollies Video decks Mixers Microphones Track lighting Backdrop Audio recording equipment Editing equipment Head end equipment Amplifiers Tables Chairs Counter work surfaces

(cont'd.)

Figure 5-1 School Library Media Spaces, Furnishings, and Functions Chart *(Continued)*		
Library media center spaces	*Special furnishings/equipment*	*Functions/activities/special considerations*
Television instruction classroom (only needed if there are plans for a full-time instructor)	Provides a classroom adjacent to the TV studio and editing areas, with glass windows between the classroom, control room and studio.	White board Tables Chairs Computers
Multimedia production laboratory	Provides area for production of electronic multimedia, visuals, models, sound recordings. Locate adjacent to equipment storage area. Should be accessible by groups without disrupting activities in reading/browsing/listening area, and visible from areas staffed by library media center personnel.	Built-in cabinets with locks Flexible tables Chairs Cabinets and drawers of varying sizes beneath Work surface counters with recessed and dropped areas to accommodate computers and typewriters (a few are still needed) Scanners, multimedia computers, digital cameras, digitizing equipment
Offices	Provide areas for quiet work by professional staff. Accommodate interviews and planning with teachers.	Desk Chairs Cabinets Shelving
Multimedia equipment	Provides storage for small and large equipment on shelves or rolling projection carts, parts for repairs, consumable supplies, lamps; counter-height cabinetry and work surfaces to facilitate routine maintenance and minor repair of equipment. Location should be near corridors, loading docks, elevator. Area should be secure.	Built-in cabinets with locks Shelving Stools Tables Test equipment
Workroom	Area for technical processing and repair of materials, used by staff. Adjacent to entrance, circulation, display, media production laboratory. Includes periodical storage shelving. Physical and visual access to other support and production areas of library media center. Provides storage area for back issues of magazines. Located near areas for library media center personnel.	Built-in cabinets, drawers, desk, storage areas Shelving Desks for library media center personnel Computers Fax equipment Copy equipment Sink Chairs Tables
Large-group instruction	Provides arge area for different types of presentations and instruction for groups larger than a class. Should accommodate the use of all types of media and accommodate teleconferences. Visual control by library media center personnel.	Lecture tables Chairs Podium Screen (wall) Computers

Location of Computers

Computers are usually located in laboratories near special curriculum areas and/or as separate lab areas in library media centers. As schools implement more wireless configurations, these labs can be phased out, and laptops on carts can be distributed to classrooms when needed. When not in use, they should be located in an area within the library media center or in a special area of the library media center reading room. Keeping the possibility of such changes in mind, computers labs should be designed as, and located in, flexible spaces that can be turned to other purposes as needs change. Furniture in these areas should also be as modular as possible, allowing for adaptation to new, heretofore unanticipated devices and technologies that might come into use.

Advantages and Disadvantages of Wireless Systems

Wireless technologies are an increasingly important part of educational facilities, and nearly all new buildings are equipped for connectivity of this kind. Even so, it is important to consider the relative pluses and minuses of such systems before calling for one in the building plans.

Advantages

1. Laptops are rendered easier to use and so are used more often. To connect to the network, a student merely opens the laptop, turns on the machine, and logs on to the wireless network. That's all. The wireless connection eliminates the need to find a hub, unravel a cord, walk or reach several feet, and plug in.

2. The ease of access to the network encourages precisely what schools want to see: greater integration of information technology into the curriculum and day-to-day life of the school. Faculty members put off by the effort of getting a room of students online will be more likely to consider assignments that make use of the Web. Ease of use also encourages spontaneity. Inside or outside class, students and faculty can turn to their laptops to collaborate or answer questions as soon as the need arises.

3. The system saves time. With access easy, setup is fast. Valuable as this is for one user, it is even more so for several—notably, groups of students in classrooms. With wires, teachers report up to five minutes spent setting up and shutting down the laptops for class. A wireless network frees as many as ten minutes of extra learning time each period—potentially as much as an hour a day for students who are using laptops in several different courses.

4. Wireless connections also improve productivity outside the classroom. Students can get to work in any area without hassle. Faculty will find it easier to use small moments of free time.

5. Wireless works anywhere, so users can move around. No longer tethered to a 15-foot patch cord, students and teachers with working batteries can

move around the classroom, even rearrange desks if desired. Outside class, students and faculty can move from classroom to the library media center as they choose without logging on and off and plugging in and unplugging.

6. Media centers are safer. Without a tangle of wires on the floor, spaces are easier to navigate. Students are less likely to trip over wires and hurt themselves, hurt others, accidentally yank a machine off a desk, or pull out and break a network cord.

7. Wireless systems can be easier and less expensive to install than a wired network. While costs vary, a wireless system can be less expensive to install in an existing facility because fewer wires must be run through walls and ceilings.

DISADVANTAGES

1. Wireless systems are sometimes slower. Existing wireless technology comes close to the performance of wired systems, but can be slower. How much slower it operates depends on the task at hand. While there is little difference in simple and frequent uses, such as checking e-mail and browsing the Web, more complex tasks such as downloading large files and using multimedia software can go far more slowly. That being said, the difference between the speed of wired and wireless systems is not significant when dealing with sites on the Internet that are not located on the school server. The speed of access to the outside world largely determines the speed of the flow of information. A T-1, for example, runs at 1.536 megabytes per second. By contrast, both ISDN and ordinary phone lines run at a small fraction of that speed. Significantly, this situation may be about to change with the introduction of a new generation of wireless products.

2. Wireless systems are harder to supervise in the classroom. Some students take advantage of the ease of use of wireless to send e-mail, play games, or otherwise tune out during class. Of course, classroom distractions have always been part of school, but wireless systems do make it easier for students to avoid the task at hand. As a result, teachers are encouraged to make their students active and involved participants in class rather than passive recipients of explanations or lectures.

3. Wireless laptops are not truly wireless. While wireless technology eliminates the need for a cord connecting the user to the network, students still need to plug their laptops into an electrical outlet unless their batteries are charged. Students are not always reliable about recharging their batteries at night, charges run out, and many aging batteries hold charges poorly. Consequently, electrical wires remain unavoidable, and vigilant care of these connections is a necessity.

4. Laptops can be easily stolen, so security is essential in installations that make use of them. This is doubly the case when technology is circulated to classrooms.

5. Wireless still necessitates the widespread distribution of hubs throughout the school from which the signal is broadcast.

6. Regularly moving laptops from classroom to classroom increases wear and tear on the machines, potentially putting a strain on a school's technology budget.

Although this discussion has emphasized the use of laptops with wireless systems, desktop computers can also be used in a wireless configuration. Desktops are usually located in labs, but can also be located in the main reading room of the library media center.

Spatial Relationship Diagrams

Differences in school programs, levels, and specific communities served will affect the spatial relationships and allocations in the design of any library media center facility. These relationships are depicted on a space chart, or "bubble diagram" (see Resource B). A chart of this kind specific to your library should be developed as part of the plan. Spatial relationships and the amount of square footage allocated will also reflect criteria in state planning guidelines and the program philosophy of individual districts and schools. For example, elementary school diagrams may include a story/presentation area. Secondary school space charts may show carrel areas or computer workstations in carrel-like configurations within the large open area. Special education centers may have sections of wall space for sensory activities and manipulatives (games and other resources that involve learners actively rather than passively). Some space charts may include computer-assisted instruction laboratories, multimedia production areas, a television studio, and an instructional classroom. The space chart will depict those areas selected for inclusion in the school library media center by the school planning team.

The diagram will show spatial relationships and approximate proportional sizes of individual areas to the whole. Whether ovals, circles, or some other geometric forms are used, the message relayed by the bubble diagram needs to be comprehensible to the architectural team.

These diagrams should be drawn in light pencil for the first few drafts. We usually start with the main reading room since this is the primary area of the school library media center. It is the largest circle in the middle. Then we add areas around the central circle, based on their need to be close to the entrance, circulation desk, and/or library media specialist office and workroom. The closer they are to the main reading room, they either overlap slightly or are connected by a very short line. We also try to keep the size of the other circles in relationship to their size and the main reading room. This is not an exact science. That is also why we do the first few drafts in light pencil. It is then the responsibility of the architect to interpret this "bubble diagram" and fit it into the first set of architectural drawings.

A sample bubble diagram follows:

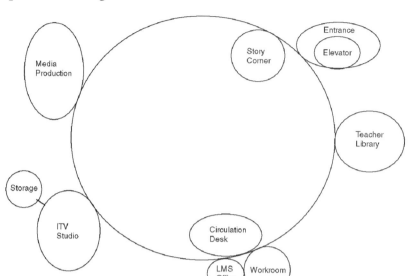

Special Facilities Considerations

This section provides a special look at the facilities requirements that depart from the norm of conventional construction projects but are critical to the successful operation of library media center programs. This section will reflect the specific needs generated by local geographic and climatic conditions.

Climate Control

While climate control can be accomplished in a variety of ways, from cross-ventilation to entire energy management systems, maintenance of humidity at 60 percent is essential to the preservation of resources and equipment in all climates. This level of moisture prevents drying out of materials in heated facilities and the growth of mold and mildew in more humid areas. Traditionally schools were heated with gas-, coal-, or oil-fired furnaces, which used steam water pipes to distribute the heat throughout the building. With the advent of air conditioning, these systems were inefficient, so many schools switched to heat pumps, which could be reversed to cool in late spring, summer, and early fall. They still used multiple energy sources to generate the "heat pump" concept. Recently there have been new breakthroughs in "geothermal" heating and cooling. Pipes are installed underground at the proper level for your location. The underground earth temperature ranges from 50 to 70 percent winter and summer. A mixture of water and glycol is circulated in a closed system, and the heat or cool is extracted; it is similar to a heat pump, but more efficient. Geothermal heating and cooling can be considered in areas where it is feasible, but such systems tend to generate more humidity, and this *must* be controlled to protect the resources.

The entire library media center should have a climate control system for air and heat. It is important that the library media center have a separate, independent heating/cooling system that can be regulated to control the temperature and humidity so critical to the handling, storage, and preservation of materials and equipment. An independent climate control system permits use of the library media center for off-calendar events, such as summer reading programs. Windows should enable exchange of fresh air and provide ventilation when the climate control system is not in use.

Humidity must be maintained at a maximum of 60 percent at all times by means of the following systems:

- The normal heating/air conditioning system for this area is to maintain temperature and humidity during periods when the area is occupied and is to be controlled by the building energy management system.
- Separate humidifying/dehumidifying equipment is to maintain a maximum of 60 percent relative humidity when the area is unoccupied and the normal air conditioning is off. This is to be controlled by the energy management system.
- Air conditioning units should have electrostatic filters.
- The temperature must be maintained at a level between 70° and 77° F., with humidity at 60 percent in the library media center.

In areas used for equipment storage and maintenance, television and audio studios, and in the telecommunications distribution area, the temperature is to be maintained at a set point of 76° F. +/- 1° F. when the areas are in use. This is accomplished by the building's air conditioning/heating and ventilation system. A control unit must be installed to limit temperature to 76° F. This temperature control is also required in the television studio when there is use of high wattage studio lighting.

Supply and return air ducts should be located high on the walls or in the ceiling, with air velocities low enough to prevent problems created by moving paper, hair, or clothing. Supply and return air vents should not create noise in production areas. Sound from any subsystem of the air conditioning should be suppressed so that it cannot be audible in sound recordings.

Restrooms should have forced ventilation to the outside and have a ventilation control.

Since wall space for shelving is a primary concern, return air vents should be positioned high on walls (at least 86 inches from floor) or installed in the ceiling.

Acoustical Control

Attention should be given to the acoustics in all areas. Acoustical drop ceilings in all areas are generally preferred.

ACOUSTICS AND SPECIAL NEEDS

Acoustical performance is an important consideration in the design of school library media centers. Research indicates that high levels of background noise, much of it from heating and cooling systems, adversely affect learning environments, particularly for young children, who require optimal conditions for hearing and comprehension. Given that many school libraries are multiuse facilities, noise control is likely to be a crucial concern. If this is amplified by excessive ambient noise generated by the facility itself, it may be difficult for many patrons to make full use of the library. It is therefore crucial during this phase of development that the architects show evidence that they are making plans to install appropriate acoustical paneling around any machinery in the facility.

Poor acoustics are a particular barrier to children with a hearing loss. At risk are children with mild to moderate hearing loss, as well as those who have cochlear implants or who use hearing aids and assistive listening devices, since these assistive technologies amplify both wanted and unwanted sound, including reverberation and background noise. Children with temporary hearing loss, who may comprise up to 15 percent of the school-age population, according to the Centers for Disease control, are also significantly affected, as are children with speech impairments or learning disabilities.

The Acoustical Society of America has several publications to assist with the specific requirements needed to provide a quality classroom acoustical environment. These guidelines are also useful for library media centers.

Conference rooms should be provided with sufficient acoustical treatment to prevent external noise sources from interfering with recordings. Walls in both the television studio area and conference rooms should have special acoustical treatment to facilitate recording. Mechanical equipment rooms and air handling equipment should be accessed from the exterior of the library media center and have sound barriers to isolate noise and vibrations. Air handling units should be removed from reading/listening/viewing areas and from entrance/circulation areas and should have provision for reduction of vibration when in operation. Air conditioning vents should be low velocity, to minimize ambient noise.

Floor Surfaces

Carpeting should be continuous where equipment is moved on rolling carts. It is required in the following areas:

- Reading, listening, viewing
- Group viewing
- Conference rooms
- Professional collection
- Large-group instruction area

Carpeting in the vicinity of the circulation area should be higher grade.

Vinyl or tile flooring is recommended for all other areas and in areas where running water is used. These often include:

- Main entrance (ceramic tile is best)
- Workroom

- Circulation area
- Project room
- Television studio area
- Telecommunications distribution areas
- Media production laboratory
- Multimedia equipment storage, distribution, and maintenance areas

The main entrance to the library media center, a high traffic area, should be of durable material, such as quarry tile or nonskid ceramic tile.

Walls

All walls should be finished with a tackable surface and provide ample area for display of student projects and artwork. Neutral colors on the wall surfaces will allow the many colors of the student projects and the library materials to brighten the rooms.

Signage and limited graphics to highlight areas can be part of the overall design. In general, they are added later, but if they are a feature of the school, then those in the library media center should be consistent with the rest of the school.

If the facility's elevation is one story and it is adjacent to classroom areas, the walls surrounding the media center and the area for equipment storage, distribution, and maintenance should be designed to extend above the drop ceiling to the roof to prevent unauthorized entry and ambient noise into these areas through the ceiling crawl space.

If the school has the resources to develop, maintain, and make use of a television or video recording studio in the library media center, one wall must be painted light blue to provide a production backdrop. A curtain, which can also function as a backdrop, should also be considered. Should conference rooms be included in the plans, they should have special acoustical treatment to facilitate recording. If the school plans to build a television studio, its walls should have a similar treatment. Naturally, many of these resources will be either inaccessible or inapt for many school systems.

The multimedia storage room should include 20 square feet of pegboard, with fasteners mounted to the wall for cables and extra extension cords.

Walls between conference rooms should include folding or movable walls to facilitate change in size of conference facilities. These walls must be as soundproof as possible.

Walls between the largest user area and support areas should include observation windows beginning at least 45 inches from the floor, leaving space for shelving and carpeting beneath. Observation windows should be in appropriate areas to provide visual control by staff from circulation and support areas. All windows must be placed to accommodate wall-mounted shelving running in 3-foot linear sections (shelving is standardized at 3-foot sections so they can handle the weight of the books and other resources).

Ceiling

The ceiling should be coated with a sound-resistant surface. If acoustical tile is used, it should be standard-type tile. The exact height of ceilings will vary according to the situation and the available space, since there is there is no basic standard for library media centers. The standard for public buildings is normally 9 feet, but this is more a generalized guide than a hard and fast rule. It is, however, important that there be room for air circulation and sprinkler systems above the stacks. New facilities often run into trouble when this is not taken into account, and it can necessitate drastic, last-minute changes, such as the lowering of bookshelves, reducing the collection size.

Ceiling tiles are used for most applications, because electrical and heating-cooling ducts are hidden above them, as well as communication and computer cables. Some main reading rooms have pitched roofs and ceilings and they may have sound retardant sprayed on, while some school libraries use natural wood for its warm look and sound control.

Lighting

Lighting is an all too often underrated element of planning, but this aspect of facility design should not be overlooked. Consider, for example, that there have

Figure 5-2
Natural and Artificial Lighting in Library of Chief Leschi School

been multiple studies indicating that natural lighting dramatically improves test scores. Studies by Kuller and Lindsten (1992), Phillips (1997), the Heschong Mahone Group (1999), Plympton, Conway, and Epstein (2000), and Benya (2001) have indicated a positive correlation between day-type lighting and academic performance. Natural lighting may not always be possible, so many school systems specify full-spectrum lighting. There have been several breakthroughs in recent years concerning lighting installation and operational costs. The price difference between cool light bulbs generally used in public places and full-spectrum lighting has historically been four to one. T12 (traditional cool light) is the type of lighting that has typically been used in public buildings in the United States, and T8 (full-spectrum light) is the newer lamp now available at nearly the same cost as the T12. There are several choices, as illustrated in the Figure 5-3. In this chart, note that ballast is the electrical device for turning on and regulating the brightness of fluorescent light bulbs.

Another solution is pendant indirect lighting, which is typically mounted 18 to 24 inches below the ceiling, requiring ceiling heights of 9 feet 6 inches or more. This type of lighting requires 80 percent reflectivity for ceilings and 65 percent reflective paint for major walls.

Light control blinds are required for observation windows and other architectural features that provide natural light.

Separate light controls should be provided for each room or area in the library media center and should be located at each door or entrance inside the room or area. The walls within the center are usually drywall, so if and when they are moved, it is also easy to change the electrical wiring. A keyed master switch controlling light for the entire library media center should be located near the staff exit to enable all areas to be darkened simultaneously. For security purposes, motion detectors should be used in rooms infrequently occupied.

Lighting fixtures should be located for uniform illumination. All too often, no one thinks to consider the placement of book stacks when lighting is being conceptualized and designed. Therefore, sections of the stacks are sometimes left unlit, or other elements of the facility are left in perpetual shadow. It is crucial also that lighting be designed so that it can reach the lowest level of the stacks. This is often more difficult to achieve than expected, so it is advised that this be taken into careful consideration when lighting decisions are being made.

Figure 5-3 Lighting Options Chart					
Lamp	Hours	Ballast (thing that turns it on and off)	Flicker	Lumens (amount of light)	Color Rendition Index (range of visible color[?])
Sun	Unlimited	None	None	Varies	100
T12	18,000	Magnetic	Yes	2800	50–70
T8	20,000 or greater	Electronic	No	3100	85–90

Security lights that operate when regular lights are turned off or when the power goes out should be strategically placed to light a clear path from all support areas. They should not, however, be placed in areas that are adjoin projection screens, as light bleed can reduce the use value of such features of the facility. Lighted exit signs for emergency evacuation and exit should be placed for maximum visibility.

Special lens systems should shield light fixtures in areas housing computers to reduce glare on the screens. Fixtures can be shielded by such systems as paracube or parabolic lenses, which reflect the light toward the ceiling and provide reflective light in computer areas. Lighting is to be zoned to permit banks to be switched off in separate areas of large, open spaces.

Lastly, in the event that a television studio is to be included in the facility, adjustable track lighting (two 16-foot tracks) is ideal for the closed-circuit television production area. Red "In-Use" lights should be located outside entrance doors to television studio.

Exterior Windows (Fenestration)

Provision must be made for fresh air exchange, and windows that open should be included where possible. Since wall-mounted shelving is of primary importance, the majority of the exterior windows should begin at least 86 inches from the floor and take up a minimum of wall space. Consideration should be given to alternative methods of providing natural light through the use of such architectural features, such as glass brick or skylights. Limited decorative windows can be placed near entrances and can provide visual access to scenic exterior areas. Decorative windows may also be located throughout the facility if placed to accommodate standard 3-foot lengths of shelving and a sufficient number of linear feet of shelving to accommodate the collection. Blinds must be provided in all areas of the library media center where natural light enters in order to keep direct light from the users.

Observation Windows

With the exception of the multimedia equipment storage, distribution, and maintenance room, all other areas of the library media center should be observable from both the center of the facility and the circulation area. Observation windows should be in all commonly shared walls. Observation windows must begin at least 45 inches from the floor to permit the installation of counter-height shelving beneath, and must not interrupt the 3-foot sections required for continuous linear footage of shelving. The minimum window width should be 72 inches. It is essential for the architect to locate and configure the space to meet this important consideration, for adequate viewing of activities in the room. Maximum window size is determined by the final library media center design and required built-ins. Only clear, tempered, or reinforced glass or Plexiglas is acceptable. Any other material could cause a danger to users.

Doors

Doors should have quiet operating mechanisms and should be light enough in weight and design to be opened easily by younger students. To assure safe transport of heavy multimedia equipment on carts, all doors should be installed without thresholds.

The work area and media production laboratory should have one door to a corridor for deliveries that leads to the delivery exit.

Special attention should be given to hardware for the doors and after-hours security considerations. The corridor should open to the outside of the library media center.

Water

No water fountains should be located in main reading, listening, viewing, or stack areas.

The workroom should be equipped with a sink having a raised gooseneck faucet, providing hot and cold water.

The media production laboratory area and project room should have a double-sized sink without a divider. The sink should be equipped with a raised gooseneck faucet, providing hot and cold water.

Sinks should be at one end of built-in counters.

All sinks should be equipped with liquid soap and paper towel dispensers.

Communications Networks

This section addresses communications networks, such as closed-circuit television systems, that are internal to the building. Although these systems may link with district systems or communitywide systems, such as cable television, the model addresses only the internal communications network of the school.

Television System: The television distribution system originates in the distribution area of the library media center and extends to all classrooms and instructional areas. It is a multichannel system capable of local origination or playback of programming on videotape decks and/or redistribution of special programs from the television connection to the outside world serving the building.

All "head-end" equipment—that is, switches and connections for the wiring for the communication distribution system—should be mounted in a television equipment rack in the telecommunications distribution area. Included in the head-end equipment will be a down converter power supply, a VHF/UHF channel converter, individual channel amplifiers, television modulators, and all necessary splitters, mixers, and filters to complete the distribution system.

The cable distribution system is to be installed with connecting outlets throughout the library media center and in all classrooms, administrative areas, the auditorium, and the cafeteria.

All television cable outlets must be installed no more than 6 inches from 110-volt electrical service outlet boxes and should be no more than 5 feet from the floor. Closed-circuit television cable and 110-volt supply must be in separate boxes. Location of these boxes should be clear of traffic patterns.

Projection Screen: One 60 × 60 inch ceiling-mounted electric projection screen with modular motor, low-voltage multiple switching, matte finish, and keystone elimination capacity should be installed in areas designated for large-group instruction and group viewing.

Telecommunications System: As part of the school's communication system, two-way communication from each classroom and instructional area of the school to the library media center can help facilitate use of the instructional television and library media center resources.

Modular telephone outlets, compatible with the school system's telecommunications equipment, should be provided in the circulation area, the offices, workroom, media production laboratory, and storage areas. The library media center staff should have access to portable phones or other wireless communications devices and/or wireless devices.

A dedicated telephone line and a portable phone is required in areas closest to the circulation area to facilitate communication. There will need to be special provisions to serve the online catalog and carrels housing computers. Provisions should be made in the grid system to link telephone lines throughout the library media center. Location must be per working drawings that locate carrels, computer stations, circulation desk, and furniture installations requiring networking.

Computers

The library media center circulation system, inventory, and public access catalog system uses computers located in the support areas, at the circulation desk, and in computers used by students and teachers. There should be provision for networked printers to serve all computers in the facility. The types and location of computers will vary according to the technology plan of individual school systems and schools. The key concern is providing the best access possible for students and teachers.

As discussed previously, many successful centers are now wireless, particularly in the library media center, so computers can be located for best use anywhere in the library media facility. There are usually 8 to 10 computers located near the entrance of the center for quick user access, primarily to the electronic card catalog. Large numbers of laptops should be available for in-house checkout at the circulation desk. Additionally, computers should be located conveniently within the reading room.

In some especially well-equipped libraries, another computer concern is access to powerful workstations where students and teachers can create quality multimedia products. Such machines should have scanners, digital cameras, CD and DVD burning capabilities, etc.

Electrical Grid and/or Wireless Systems

A system of outlets designed on a 10-foot-square grid should be installed in the floor to accommodate electrical service, television, and communications distribution throughout area, unless a wireless system is planned. This grid system should provide for linkage among the support areas, the circulation area, and workstations. The grid system should be large enough to carry electric power, networking cables, and telephone lines, all while eliminating interference or "cross talk" as thoroughly as possible. Access panels for installation of outlets will be on 10-foot centers at minimum. Location and number of floor outlets will be according to the working drawings that locate workstation computers, circulation area, and other furniture installations requiring electrical service and networking. Most school districts have developed systemwide standards for number of circuits and outlets. Double duplex electrical outlets, each with dedicated circuits, should be installed at each of the proposed workstations in the library media center, per working drawings.

Floor outlets should be of sturdy construction, flush to the floor, with hinged covers opened with a single key. Electric outlets along walls should be located at 10-foot intervals. They should also be located in all support columns and at a minimum of 5-foot intervals along all work counters.

In the circulation desk area double duplex electrical outlets, each on dedicated circuits, internet connections and telephone jacks should be installed.

All dedicated circuits should be clearly labeled with information about what is to be plugged into them.

Electrical Control

Electrical considerations addressed in the preceding section, "Communications Networks," are repeated in this section devoted entirely to the topic of electrical requirements. Inclusion under "Communications Networks" is necessary in the planning documents because despite the interrelationships of these major aspects of design, there is always the possibility that members of large architectural firms may look only at those areas of the educational specifications that relate to their own work assignments.

Since wall space for shelving is of primary concern, all electrical switches, fire alarm controls, intercom switches, thermostats, and other electrical controls should be concentrated vertically to use as little wall space as possible. No control should be located behind shelving-unit upright supports.

In all areas, 110-volt duplex wall outlets are to be installed every 10 feet on available wall space.

In addition to wall outlets, 110-volt duplex floor outlets are to be installed throughout the reading, browsing, listening, viewing, and stack areas in a grid system designed on a 10-foot-square grid. The system provides for the installation of 110-volt electrical service, television, and communication cables. Access panels for installation of outlets are to be on 10-foot centers. Duplex floor outlets are to be located to accommodate furniture placement shown on working drawings. Floor outlets should be of sturdy construction, flush to the floor, with hinged covers accessed by a single key.

The library media center circulation, inventory, and catalog system uses computers located in the support areas, at the circulation area, and at workstations in the reading, listening, and viewing area. There should be provision for printers to serve these workstations or a networked printer.

Dedicated 110-volt surge-suppressed circuit isolation transformer/voltage regulators are to be located at the circulation area and catalog areas for the computers. Dedicated outlets should be labeled according to their function—for example, "computer outlet."

Double duplex electrical outlets, each with a dedicated circuit, should be installed at each computer workstation in the library media center as per working drawings. Double duplex electrical outlets, each using dedicated circuits, and a telephone jack, should be installed at the circulation area.

Closed-circuit television outlets (six inches from 110-volt electrical service) should be located throughout the reading, listening, viewing, and stack areas to accommodate furniture placement on the working drawings.

Areas with built-in counters should have 110-volt strip outlets at 5-foot intervals: media production laboratory, workroom, periodical storage, professional collection (teacher/professional area), television and audio studios, telecommunications distribution, and so on. Outlets should be installed the full length of the counters, with no outlets placed within one foot of either side of the sinks.

The cable distribution system is to be installed with connecting outlets throughout the library media center, and in all classrooms, administrative areas, the auditorium, and the cafeteria.

All television cable outlets must be installed no more than 6 inches from 110-volt electrical service outlet boxes and should be no more than 5 feet from the floor. Closed-circuit television cable and 110-volt supply must be in separate boxes. The location of these boxes should be clear of traffic patterns.

Safety and Disability Issues

Local codes will determine the types of safety issues that should be addressed here. The type of building materials, the location of exits, and whether turnstiles can be installed are the architectural firm's responsibility to determine. Plans are to be drawn in compliance with local codes. Be sure, however, to make sure that the architects remember that libraries require special attention to detail. For example, shelving units should be far enough apart to allow a wheelchair to pass easily between them.

Some safety issues are covered elsewhere in the educational specifications. For example, when power failures occur and climate control systems shut down, it is important to have access to change of air and good ventilation. Other safety issues may be dealt with at another stage in the design process. For example, parents of handicapped students frequently oppose the placement of the library media center above the first floor. Elevators stop functioning in an emergency, making it difficult for those with mobility problems to evacuate the building rapidly.

Adequate aisle space between stacks and freestanding furniture is necessary to ease the movement of handicapped individuals and the movement of loaded book trucks and multimedia carts. A minimum of 3 feet of space should be allowed between stacks. A minimum of 4 feet should be left between tables in nontraffic areas, and 6 feet between tables in traffic areas. Legroom should be positioned away from aisle areas.

When fire extinguishers are being installed, consideration for the conservation of wall space and the 3-foot increments for shelving is important. Extinguishers should be placed at the ends of ranges of wall-mounted shelving for quick visual location and to prevent breaks in the ranges.

Service Drives and Entrances

As explained previously, in stand-alone library media centers located on campuses, service drives should supply the core area of the library, facilitating delivery of resources and equipment. Similar concerns should be kept in mind when libraries are situated within a larger building; access to delivery areas, major entrances, and so on should all be as smooth as possible. Library media centers on the second floor of buildings need to have a service elevator, which should be near a loading dock.

OTHER MISCELLANEOUS CONSIDERATIONS

Access to mechanical rooms and air conditioning equipment serving the library media center complex should be from exterior corridors.

To provide maximal visibility and flexible room arrangement, the use of pillars or support posts in the library media center should be placed around the perimeter walls.

Sinks shall be at one end of built-in counters.

Special consideration should be given to electronic security in all areas of the library media center. This typically includes motion detectors, but extra electronic security should be provided for the multimedia equipment storage area.

Walls in the television studio, television distribution area, and audio studio should have special acoustical treatment to facilitate recording.

Special attention should be given to architectural features that promote the program and the facility to the entire school and community.

This concludes the educational specifications section, which has attempted to address the special needs of the program not included elsewhere in the document. The educational specifications document drives the design process, and its importance is evident throughout each phase of involvement of the architectural team. The architectural team's perspective is creative, sometimes abstract, and, at other times, linear and exact. An understanding of the perspective from which the architectural team operates will help the school team communicate effectively. The dialogue critical to a successful building program only begins when the role of each team is understood by all involved partners.

Resources Consulted

Benya, J. R. 2001. "Lighting for schools." Washington, D.C.: National Clearinghouse for Educational Facilities. (January 2005). Available: http://edfacilities.org/pubs/lighting.html.

Heschong Mahone Group. 1999. "Daylighting in schools: An investigation into the relationship between daylighting and human performance." San Francisco: Pacific Gas and Electric Company. (January 2005). Available: http://pge.com/003_save_energy/003c_edu_train/pec/daylight/di_pubs/SchoolDetailed820App.PDF.

Kuller, R., and C. Lindsten. 1992. "Health and behavior of children in classrooms with and without windows." *Journal of Environmental Psychology* (12), pp. 305–317.

Plympton, P., S. Conway, and K. Epstein. 2000. "Daylighting in schools: improving student performance and health at a price schools can afford." Paper presented at the American Solar Energy Society Conference. Madison, Wis., June 16, 2000. (October 2004). Available: http://deptplanetearth.com/nrel_student_performance.htm.

6

How to Select Furniture and Storage Units

As with the information in the previous chapters, the material contained in the following pages is meant to be included in the planning documents. What follows are recommended design specifications for furniture and other details in school library media centers of all types. While there is tremendous range of choices, this chapter describes some of the ideal configurations and layouts for the various elements of the school library media center.

As we proceed through these recommendations, remember that many of the possibilities described here should be tailored to fit the specific demographics of the school. Tables and chairs, for example, should be sized to fit the students who will be making use of them. Wherever possible, this should be indicated in the planning documents as they are prepared. It is also important as the design process continues that architects and other responsible parties be regularly reminded not just what they are designing, but whom they are designing it for. Clear communication is one of the keys to a good building, and such communication will be all the easier later in the process if needs are clearly articulated in these documents.

Storage Units

Built-in storage units are defined as built-in cabinets or millwork and are usually custom-designed to fit the individual configuration of the library media center. These items are included in the general contractor's construction contract, as opposed to freestanding equipment and furniture that is bid and purchased by the school board or other governing agency. While built-in shelving is not always necessary, a poorly designed storage area that fails to meet specifications can lead to messy solutions once construction is complete:

Figure 6-1
Librarian's Storage Area

In Figure 6-1, note the way the lack of well-thought-out shelving has led to a cluttered space with none of the organizational clarity that befits a library. For example, finish on all built-in units should be high-pressure laminate (.050 with .050 backing, simultaneously applied) with a minimum of ¾ inch thickness. Laminate is important to provide durability, versus varnished or painted surfaces.

Built-in cabinets should consist of several basic types that should vary in combination according to the linear feet of an available wall space. Examples of types follow:

Type 1: Drawer storage unit (Figure 6-2). A 40-inch unit includes two vertical rows of drawers with varying depths, the bottom drawer being the deepest (10-inch vertical depth) and the top drawer the shallowest (4 ½ inches vertical depth). All drawers are to be mounted on metal roller guides. Minimum drawer width should be 16 inches. Drawers should have interior adjustable dividers. Counter depth is to be 30 inches.

Type 2: Drawer/closed shelving unit. Forty-inch unit includes a closed-door cabinet with one interior, adjustable shelf (see Figure 6-3). Vertical adjustment of the shelf should be in 1-inch increments. Immediately below the countertop and above the closed cabinet area are two 4½-inch vertical-depth drawers the width of each cabinet door. Drawers should be mounted on metal roller guides. Counter depth should be 30 inches.

Type 3: Wide drawer unit. Forty-inch unit should consist of a vertical arrangement of wide, shallow drawers for the storage of flat pictures, charts,

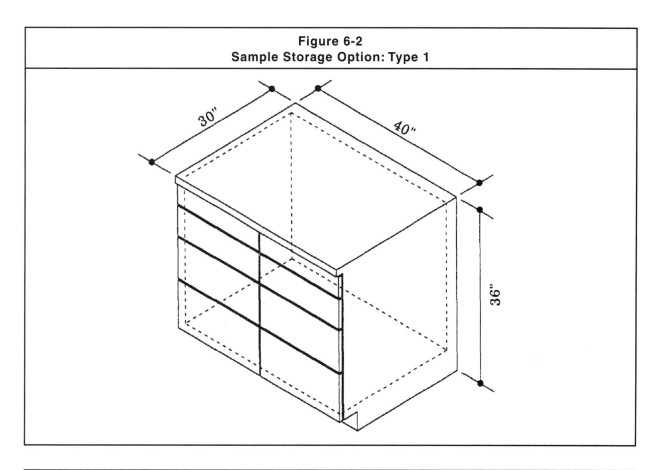

Figure 6-2
Sample Storage Option: Type 1

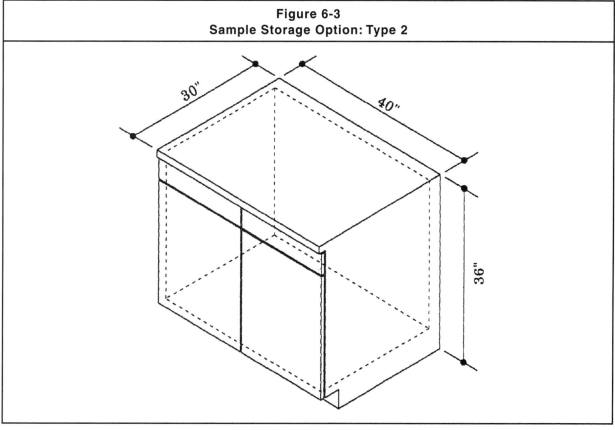

Figure 6-3
Sample Storage Option: Type 2

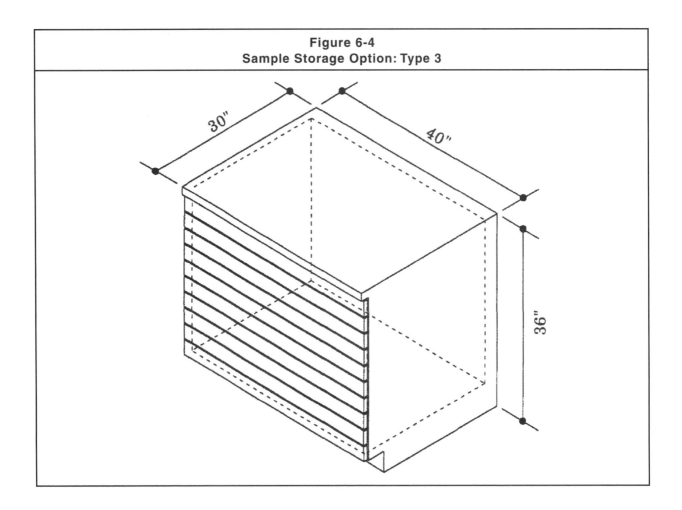

Figure 6-4
Sample Storage Option: Type 3

and other visuals (see Figure 6-4). The minimum width of drawers should be 40 inches. The maximum vertical depth of all drawers should be 3 inches. Drawers are to be mounted on metal roller guides. Counter depth should be 30 inches.

Type 4: Computer workstation. Forty-eight-inch unit should include a 26-inch-high work surface, minimum of 22 inches deep × 23 inches wide (see Figure 6-5). Kneehole width should be a minimum of 24 inches. One vertical row of drawers should be below the work surface. Drawers should be of varying vertical depth (10 inches maximum) and mounted on metal roller guides. Counter depth should be 30 inches.

Type 5: Desk unit. Forty-eight-inch unit should consist of a desk (see Figure 6-6) height (30 inches) work surface and two adjacent, shallow drawers below the work surface.

Type 6: Island counter. This unit should be accessible for work from all sides (see Fig. 6-7). Approximate overall dimensions are 12 feet long × 6 feet wide × 3 feet high. Counter should have raised area above center for double duplex outlets on each side. Each end of the unit should have one vertical row of wide drawers for the storage of posterboard and other graphic art supplies. Maximum vertical depth of all drawers should be 3 inches. Minimum width of drawers should be 44 inches. Minimum horizontal depth of drawers should be 44

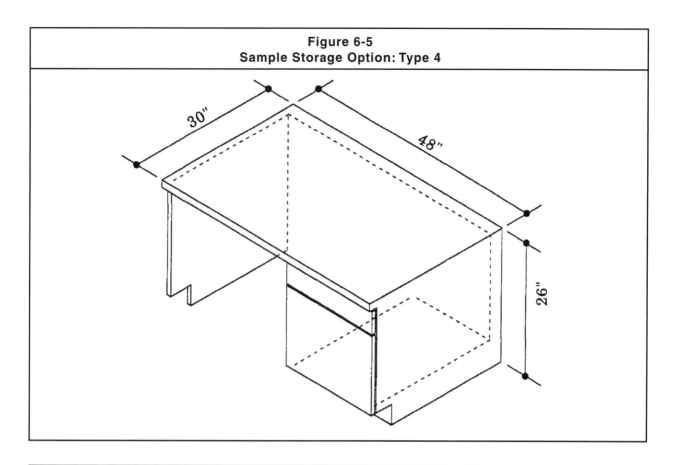

Figure 6-5
Sample Storage Option: Type 4

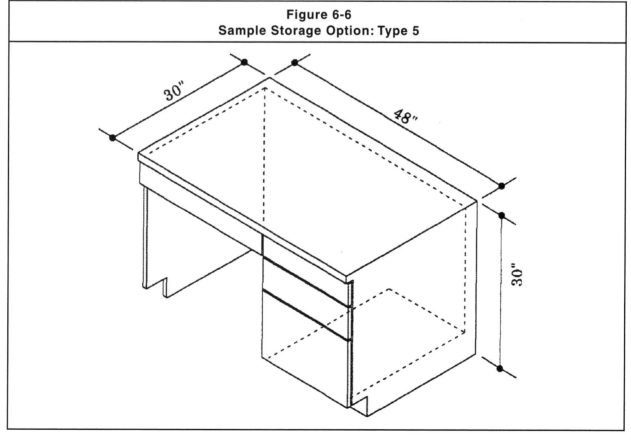

Figure 6-6
Sample Storage Option: Type 5

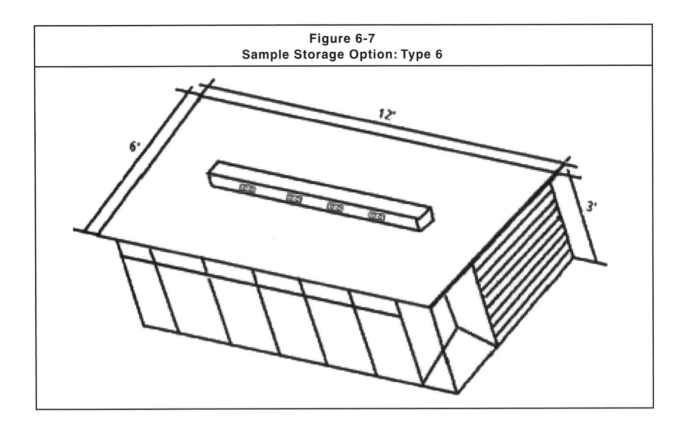

Figure 6-7
Sample Storage Option: Type 6

inches. All drawers should be installed with metal roller guides. A cabinet with one adjustable shelf should be provided for each side of center.

Type 7: Vertical map cabinet. The cabinet should be designed to hold 30 maps in the vertical position (see Fig. 6-8). Cabinet should provide enough space to accommodate rolled maps from 4 to 7 inches in diameter and 68 inches high. The storage unit should provide visual and physical accessibility to maps at rear.

Figures 6-9 through 6-14 show a series of images of built-in cabinets with various doors and drawer configurations.

Figure 6-9 is noteworthy for the range of drawer and cabinet types built into the counter. Given the variety of activities supported by library media centers, it is important that they have appropriate space to store all of the diverse materials that might be needed at any given time.

In Figure 6-10, the array of drawers, cabinets and open shelving shown in this image make for a well-organized and efficient workspace for the library media specialist. Note also the observation window at right that allows for full supervision of the facility.

Figure 6-11 shows how it is often helpful to have drawers installed with labeling systems, allowing for easy access and identification.

Figure 6-12 reveals the way space in a workroom can be leveraged to maximal effect, with further drawer space built into the island at the center of the room.

In Figure 6-13, a workroom space for both teachers and students demonstrates an ideal configuration of countertops and cabinets.

Figure 6-14 shows another possible configuration of built-in cabinetry.

Figure 6-8
Sample Storage Area: Type 7

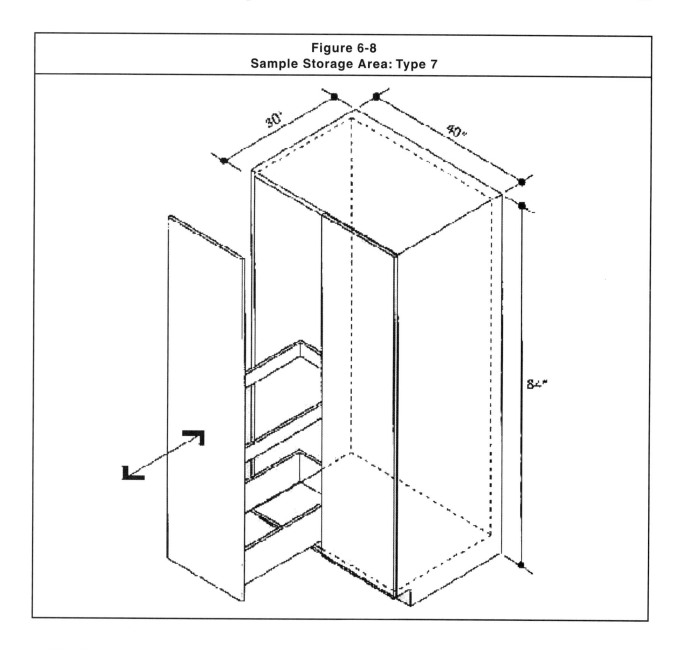

Work Counters

The workroom area (with the exception of space required for the library media center shelving units, a 4-foot open space for the catalog, and space for file cabinets) should have a work counter with a combination of closed cabinets and drawer storage units beneath (Types 1 and 2), and closed cabinets with one adjustable shelf above. This cabinetry should be placed along all available wall space. A sink should be installed at one end of the counter. Two desk units (one each of Types 4 and 5) should be located beneath the observation window.

Figures 6-15 and 6-16 suggest possible workroom configurations. This space in Figure 6-15 has been designed with a freestanding work table in the center, surrounded with cabinets and open shelves to store production resources.

**Figure 6-9
Cabinetry Configurations**

**Figure 6-10
Built-in Cabinets with Open Shelves and Sink**

Figure 6-11
Built-in Drawers with Labels to Identify Contents in Librarian's Workroom

Figure 6-12
Librarian's Workroom with Work Counter in Center Surrounded with Built-in Cabinets

Figure 6-13
Teacher and Student Production Lab Built-in Cabinets for Storing Supplies and Cardboard

Figure 6–14
Built-in Storage Multipurpose Cabinets in Teacher and Student Production Lab

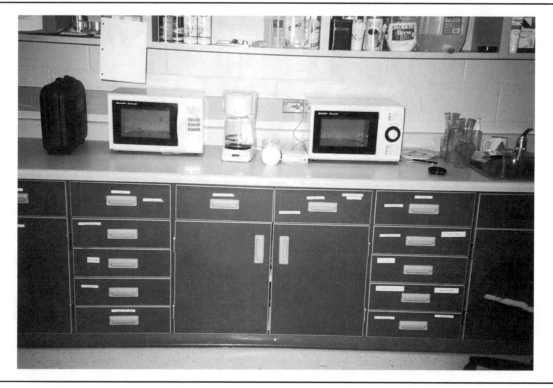

**Figure 6-15
Teacher's Workroom**

**Figure 6-16
Teacher's Workroom, Detail**

The telecommunications distribution area should include a 6-foot work counter (minimum) with a combination of closed cabinets and drawer storage units (Types 1 and 2). This unit should be located next to the closed-circuit television distribution unit. Lockable cabinets (3 feet long and 84 inches high), with 12-inch-wide adjustable shelving and accessible with one master key, should be placed along the wall and next to the work counter.

The vertical map cabinet should be designed to hold around 30 maps in the vertical position. Compartments should be wide enough to accommodate rolled maps from 4 inches to 7 inches in diameter and 68 inches high. The storage unit should provide visual and physical accessibility to maps at rear. This cabinet should be installed in the media production laboratory.

The media production laboratory, if one is to be built, should have a work counter approximately 16-plus feet in length (to provide enough open work space) installed along one wall. (Counter should consist of alternating Type 1, 2, 3, and 5 units.) A second counter, approximately 12 feet (also to provide additional open work space) with Type 2 cabinets below, should include a sink to be installed at one end of the counter. Closed cabinets with adjustable shelves should be located 24 inches above all countertops. An island counter (Type 6) should be accessible for work from all sides and should be positioned in the center of the media production laboratory and the project room. A vertical map cabinet (Type 7) for storage of rolled wall maps should be near work counters along wall. All cabinets and drawers in the 17-foot counter should have locks controlled by one master key.

Library Media Center Shelving

If the collection integrates print and multimedia in the stack area, shelving should be 15 inches actual, 16 inches nominal, depth. The height will vary according to location of the shelving. The following chart should be helpful in calculating the heights of shelving:

PRIMARY AND INTERMEDIATE LEVEL STUDENTS

- 42 inch h double-faced, aisle-type shelving
- 48 inch h single-faced, wall-type shelving
- 48 inch h double-faced, aisle-type shelving
- 60½ inch h single-faced, wall-type shelving (for intermediate only)
- 60½ inch h double-faced, aisle-type shelving (for intermediate only)

MIDDLE AND SECONDARY STUDENTS

- 48 inch h single-faced, wall-type shelving
- 48 inch h double-faced, aisle-type shelving
- 60½ inch h single-faced, wall-type shelving
- 60½ inch h double-faced, aisle-type shelving
- 82 inch h single-faced, wall-type shelving
- 82 inch h single-faced, wall-type shelving

All wall-attached and free-standing shelving in the library media center must meet requirements as per bid specifications for adjustable shelving and shall be standard 3-foot lengths. (Wall mounted shelving should be 84 inches high and counter shelving should be 46 inches high). Perimeter shelving should be used to the greatest extent possible in order to conserve floor space for furniture and program activities. Distance between free-standing shelving units and/or between shelving units and built-ins must be a minimum of 3 feet. In areas of high traffic volume, a minimum of 5 feet is required between rows of furniture and shelving. Free-standing shelving shall not exceed 15 feet in length and shall be placed as per working drawings.

Observation windows must begin a minimum of 45 inches from the floor to permit shelving beneath and should not interrupt 3-foot increments of continuous shelving of a specific height.

The reading and browsing areas should include a combination of wall-attached and free-standing shelving. The shelving will be standard adjustable library shelving to accommodate books and reference materials.

Facilities serving students who cannot be adequately provided for by more conventional means, such as those with multiple handicaps (e.g., spina bifida, cerebral palsy, and learning disabilities), will require special provisions. Distance between shelving units, built-ins, and furniture should be greater to accommodate passage by handicapped students with special mobility needs. Height and depth of shelving will change in order to store kits and manipulatives (resources with which students physically interact) and to accommodate physical access by students who have difficulty reaching and lifting.

Calculations for Books per Linear Feet of Standard Three-Foot-Long Shelving

To calculate the linear feet of shelving needed use the following estimates:

Picture/thin: 20 books per shelf foot/60 books per shelf length
Standard size: 10 books per foot/30 books per shelf length
Reference books: 6 books per foot/18 books per shelf length
Periodicals: 1 per foot for display purposes

To calculate how many linear feet of shelving are required for a collection, take the total number of volumes to be housed and divide by the number of books per foot. For example, a primary collection of 5,000 volumes consisting of picture and thin books would require a total of 250 linear feet of shelving (5,000/20). Remember, shelves should only be two-thirds full. To allow for this, multiply the number of linear feet required by 1.33. Example: $250 \times 1.33 = 332.5$, or 333 linear feet of shelving.

Specialized Shelving

The standard perimeter shelving should be single-faced and wall-attached, with 10 inches actual, 11 inches nominal depth.

Standard free-standing shelving units should be double-faced, not more than 42 inches high, with a minimum of 10 inches actual, 11 inches nominal depth. Freestanding units are not to exceed 15 feet in length. Reference shelving shall be 12 inches actual, 13 inches nominal depth. Picture-book shelving shall be 12 inches actual, 13 inches nominal depth, with upright dividers.

Periodical shelving to accommodate display of current magazines should be a minimum of 45 linear feet, and should have sloped display shelves.

The offices should have standard adjustable library-type shelving placed to accommodate books for a minimum of 45 linear feet. The shelving is to be single-faced, wall-attached, 12 inches actual, 13 inches nominal depth.

The workroom, periodical storage room, professional library, and media production laboratory should have standard adjustable library shelving, 60+ linear feet, to accommodate materials to be processed. This wall-attached shelving should be single-faced and adjustable, 15 inches actual, 16 inches nominal depth, and in 3-foot standard sections.

The standard adjustable library shelving to accommodate professional books, periodicals, and multimedia resources should allow for .25 linear feet per pupil as a rule of thumb from practical experience. This wall-attached shelving should be single-faced and adjustable, 15 inches actual, 16 inches nominal depth, and in standard 3-foot sections.

Multimedia storage requires heavy-duty, adjustable storage shelving 18 inches deep, in 3-foot lengths, to be installed around the perimeter of the room for equipment storage. Four or more additional double-sided shelving units should be installed in the center of the room to use all of the space available. Most storage rooms are long and fairly narrow. If the room is squarer, additional rows of storage units should be installed.

Display Units

Any closed glass display cases should be free-standing and located inside the library media center. No glass display cabinets should be facing exterior walls. Exhibit cases will be free-standing units that match the furniture line and will be included in the furniture and shelving bid.

All wall surfaces should be of a tackable composition, providing areas for borderless and unframed displays and assisting in sound absorption throughout the entire library media center. There should be no bordered bulletin board display areas.

One 60 × 60 inch ceiling-mounted, electric projection screen with modular motor, low-voltage multiple switching, matte finish, and keystone elimination capacity is to be installed in the multipurpose area. Location must be as per working drawings.

Circulation Desk and Area

The circulation desk should be in the middle of the reading area, convenient to entrances and exits. It should be of modular construction to meet the needs of the program. Following in Figures 6-17 through 6-22 are pictures of possible circulation desks for school library media centers, of varying degrees of success. When discussing desk possibilities with architects and vendors, remember to insist on a desk that is properly sized to serve the age of the school's students.

In Figure 6-17, note that the librarian claims the desk is too high for the school's kindergarteners.

In Figure 6-18, note the lack of built-in cabinetry, leading to messy storage solutions.

In Figure 6-19, the failure of the finished desk to meet design specifications that called for the inclusion of drawers led to the necessity of an unattractive set of plastic bins on wheels.

In Figure 6-20, note the quirky and fun circular design of the desk for the library media center of Lawton Chiles High School, Tallahassee, Florida.

Figure 6-21 shows a vast improvement on the first circulation desk. This side view of the Lawton Chiles High School desk reveals a lower area for ease of patron access.

Finally, Figure 6-22 shows the setup of its two workstations. Should more workstations be needed at any time, the desk is modular and can be enlarged. Wherever possible, such considerations should be taken into account in the

Figure 6-17
Elementary School Circulation Desk

Figure 6-18
Elementary School Circulation Desk: Rear View

Figure 6-19
Elementary School Circulation Desk: Detail

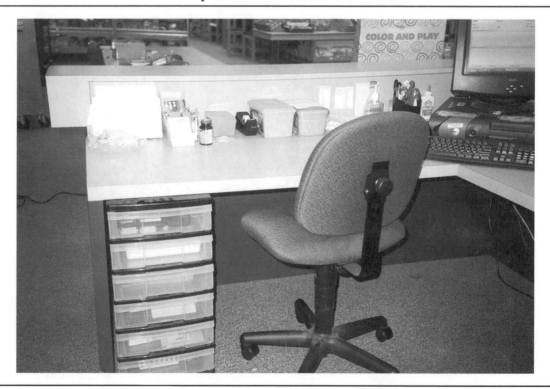

Figure 6-20
Central Round Circulation Desk

Figure 6-21
Circulation Desk: Side View

Figure 6-22
Circulation Desk from the Rear

design and selection of school library media center furnishings. Items that can be changed to fit immediate needs will lessen the need for expensive redesigns and purchases further down the road.

Moveable Furniture

Planning for moveable furnishings is as important as for fixed cabinetry. Every library media centers need tables, chairs, comfortable seating, carrels and browser bins.

Tables

Tables (see Figures 6-23 and 6-24) should be of various sizes, square and round. They should seat no more than four students per table. The height of tables and chairs will vary according to ages of students served. They should be from hardwoods and durably constructed. Usually laminates are preferred for the tops of tables.

In general, it is a good idea to select furniture on wheels (Figure 6-25), making it easier to rearrange the library at a moment's notice to best serve groups of different sizes and configurations.

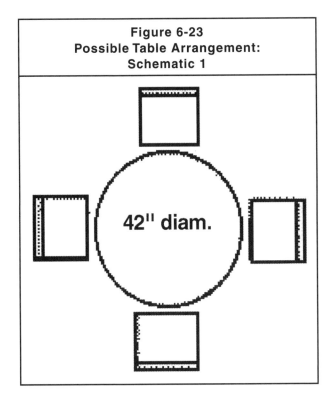

Figure 6-23
Possible Table Arrangement:
Schematic 1

42" diam.

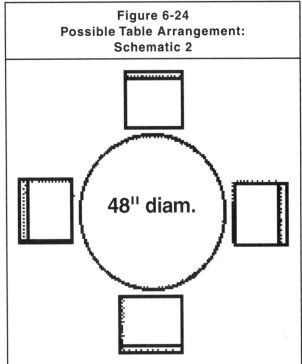

Figure 6-24
Possible Table Arrangement:
Schematic 2

48" diam.

Figure 6-25
Table and Chairs on Casters

Chairs

Should be the proper height to meet the needs of the students and teachers and built sturdily of hardwood. Examples of proper heights are:

PRIMARY LEVEL STUDENTS

- Chairs for tables and/or lounge chairs, 14 inches high
- Two-person or three-person couches, 14 inches high
- Tables, round, square and/or rectangular, 25 inches high
- Carrels 25 inches high

INTERMEDIATE LEVEL STUDENTS

- Chairs for tables and/or lounge chairs, 16 inches high
- Two-person or three-person couches, 16 inches high
- Tables, round, square, and/or rectangular, 27 inches high
- Carrels 27 inches high

MIDDLE AND/OR SECONDARY LEVEL STUDENTS

- Chairs for tables and/or lounge chairs, 18 inches high
- Two-person or three-person couches, 18 inches high
- Tables, round, square, and/or rectangular, 29 inches high
- Carrels 29 inches high

Lounge Furniture

Chairs should be appropriate height for age range of population served:

PRIMARY LEVEL STUDENTS

- Lounge chairs 14 inches high by 28 inches wide by 24½ inches deep

INTERMEDIATE LEVEL STUDENTS

- Lounge chairs 16 inches high by 28 inches wide by 26½ inches deep

MIDDLE AND/OR SECONDARY LEVEL STUDENTS

- Lounge chairs 18 inches high by 28 inches wide by 28½ inches deep

They also should have a sled base, double-doweled joints, heavy-duty floor glides, finished with a catalyzed conversion varnish (no laquer), and should be upholstered to meet fire codes. Couches should be the same height and depth of the chairs for each population group served, only 56 inches wide for two seats and 84 inches for three seats, with a sled base, double-doweled joints, heavy-duty floor glides, finished with a catalyzed conversion varnish (no lacquer), and upholstered to meet fire codes.

Browser Bins

Browser bins provide easy access to oversized picture books. Each unit should have one base and one adjustable shelf and include four wood dividers per shelf.

Select either 12-inch-deep single-faced or 24-inch-deep double-faced units in 42 and 48 inch heights.

Other Considerations

This section describes those items that do not fit in specific categories assigned by the format of the educational specifications, as well as some items that need repetition.

Individual Workstations

Individual workstations can be productively arranged around a pillar if one is needed in the facility.

Technology

This area has changed most dramatically in recent years, more than any other aspect of planning for a new facility. With the introduction of the Internet and, most recently, wireless connectivity, there are many more possibilities than in the past for more flexible access for students and teachers. In this section, your planning documents can discuss current standards that the library should aim to satisfy.

INTERNET

The facility must have a high-speed connection to the internet. This access will vary according to location of the facility; it can be fiberoptic or copper-wire-connected to a fiber cable. Usually data ports are used for Internet connections, and they need to be located wherever there is an electrical outlet in the library media

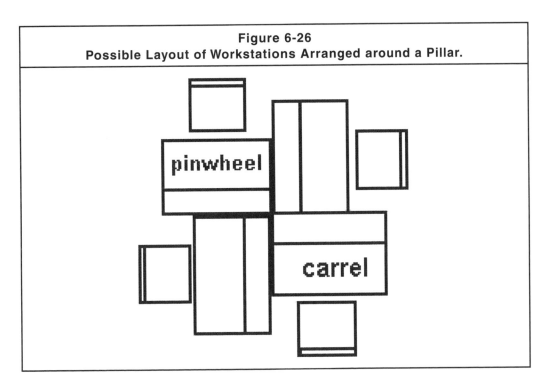

**Figure 6-26
Possible Layout of Workstations Arranged around a Pillar.**

center. Use whatever labeling identification for data ports the school system requires; there is no standard labeling at this time. If wireless connection is used, there still is a need for a grid conduit system located in the floor for electrical outlets.

MULTIMEDIA PRODUCTION AREA

If a multimedia production area is called for in the school library media center, this area will probably contain Macintosh and/or Windows computers with scanners, printers, CD-ROM burners, and graphics software for use in the production of multimedia materials (Figure 6-27).

Computers will need to be networked and equipped with software allowing the cross-platform (Macintosh and Windows computers) sharing of files over the network, if applicable.

Figure 6-28 shows an example of one part of a possible laboratory, but for computers to be an effective teaching and learning tool, there will need to be enough computers to match the average class size.

Types of equipment needed in 2006 and beyond for 30 students:

- 10 scanners
- 2 slide/negative scanners (35mm size), with stackable options
- 2 transparency scanners (originals up to 8 × 10 inches in size)
- 30 CD-ROM (CD-RW) burners (to create custom CD-ROMs)
- 30 DVD burners or equivalent when new formats are perfected

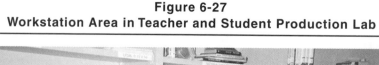

Figure 6-27
Workstation Area in Teacher and Student Production Lab

Figure 6-28
Possible Configuration for a Computer Lab

- 10 digital still cameras
- 10 digital video cameras (miniDV)
- 5 microphones and editors to digitize audio into computer files
- 5 editors to digitize video into computer files
- Printers for black-and-white images
- Printers for color
- Built-in drives on all computers

This information will have to be adjusted for the specific needs and budgetary restrictions of each individual school's curriculum. School library media specialists should consult with district IT professionals and others responsible for such long-term planning to determine what is both appropriate and reasonable.

Types of software recommended in 2006 and beyond for:

- Editing photos
- Editing digital videos
- Drawing
- Desktop publishing
- Word processing
- Preparing presentations for large groups
- Web design
- Network sharing
- Burning CDs and DVDs

Figure 6-29
Video Editing Area in Teacher and Student Production Lab

LARGE-SCREEN PROJECTION FOR CLASS GROUP VIEWING

There should be at least one large screen, which can be lowered and raised electrically. It should be strategically placed in the reading room for the best viewing by a large audience. Also, most facilities hang a video projector from the ceiling to project video and computer images.

SMART BOARD TECHNOLOGY

Smart Board technology was first introduced in 1991. Typically the size of a portable chalkboard, Smart Boards work in conjunction with a video projector and computer. Once these have been fully synched up, teachers can write on them in longhand and then save the information in text form on the computer. Users can also tap the screen and move among features of the Smart Board software.

In 2003, portable wireless Smart Boards were introduced; the size of "tablet" computers, they allow the instructor to move about the classroom. All writing on the handheld is then projected via a wireless connection on screen for the class to see. This portable unit aids the teacher in maintaining close contact with individual students while still addressing the entire class.

III

Building and Moving into the New or Remodeled Library Media Center

7

How to Select the Right Architect

Unfortunately, few architectural firms are truly dedicated to school architecture, and fewer still know anything about school library media centers. This makes it all the more important that the best possible architect be selected for the job of designing the facility. A good architect is one who is both attentive to the building plan and creative in the solutions that he or she discovers for the problems that will inevitably arise.

Architects are a unique breed of professionals, with an area of expertise unlike any other. While many are dedicated to producing innovative, attractive, and interesting buildings, others are simply looking to get the job done quickly. Be warned that even if architects have designed school library media centers in the past, they do not necessarily understand either the role or the significance of such facilities. Architectural firms that work mainly with schools have a tendency to reuse previous designs and then try to reconfigure them to meet immediate need. They refer to these recycled designs as templates. These architects may show you examples of templates in their first presentation during the selection process, which in and of itself is not necessarily a bad thing. Sometimes this helps speed up the process of design and can more than serve to meet a school's needs—but remember that good architecture rarely happens in a vacuum. Only architects able to respond to the specific site, community, and context of a school library media center facilities plan can be expected to design a truly exceptional building.

In medium and large school districts, the library media specialist is usually not involved in the architect selection process. In small districts, the specialist will be asked to be involved in many cases. Medium and large school systems usually have a director in charge of facilities. This administrator is a key member of the agency. He or she is responsible in particular for the selection of architects and facilities planning teams. The position is one of general oversight, meaning that while the administrator does not necessarily interface directly with the architects, his/her position is nevertheless a crucial one, as it is the adminis-trator's initial decisions that drive all subsequent phases of the project.

Once the architectural firm is selected, the architects will usually go through several schematic designs as related to the space relationship diagram and major elements of the building program. After the planning committee has agreed on a schematic design, then the architects develop actual exterior designs, layouts, and blueprints.

Creating Lists of Acceptable Architects

It is essential that a quality architectural firm is selected for the project. Many firms hire public relations staff to help them prepare dazzling presentations. It is the responsibility of the planning team to be discerning and to ask tough ques-tions. The team's goal should always be to find the firm best able to meet the needs of the particular project. Even the best architects in the world have their specialties. A firm that makes beautiful houses may be incapable of designing a functional school. Likewise, architecture is a discipline equally based in theory and praxis, so it is important that a firm not be chosen on the basis of good ideas alone. Precisely because the prospect of a new building can seem abstract during the lead-up to the design phase, it is essential that those responsible for the project always keep in mind that what they are shepherding into existence is a real place that will be occupied by real people.

Selecting the right architectural firm for the project is essential for a successful end product. Even though the law requires that every architectural firm that sub-mits a bid be considered, most architectural firms have an existing track record, which should be a major consideration in selection. It is the responsibility of the official in charge of planning for the agency to brief the selection committee about such histories. The planner should have records of previous projects and other information from professional colleagues to share with the selection committee.

One of the crucial points to insist on is that the architects be fiscally responsi-ble. Inquire, for example, into whether those under consideration have a history of bringing projects in on budget. Architects will sometimes claim throughout the design phase that all costs are under control, only to have contractor bids come in wildly over budget. This can lead to disastrous last-minute redesigns and may result in the removal of elements of the facility crucial to the original building plan. Obviously such situations can be avoided in part by remaining vigilant and asking the right questions during the design process, but it is also imperative that the architects' past histories be considered during the selection phase. Fiduciary oversight is primarily the responsibility of the site owners—typically the school board—but all involved in the architect selection process should work to keep such concerns on their radar.

A project manager is typically selected for each project by the facilities admin-istrator. Ideally, this individual should be brought in early as a part of the planning team, but he or she will also be involved throughout the design and construction phases, helping communicate the client's interests to the architects and contractors. The project manager sets the tone for everything related to the building project, so it is therefore crucial that he or she has some role in the determination of the architectural firm that will bring the facility to fruition. All too often, project managers only become involved when the project is under construction, meaning that they have no special insight into the project or the needs of the involved parties. They should provide their expertise in both the design and construction phases, because they have a unique perspective as the school board's on-site representative.

Advertising for an Architect

When the building program document (described in detail in Chapter 3; and a sample document appears in Resource B) is finished, it is time to advertise for an architect. This process generally follows a strict protocol. The ads are placed by the school board representative in charge of new construction in appropriate outlets that will reach the largest possible audience of architects. These ads are normally placed in newspapers, architectural trade newsletters, and so on.

Following is a sample ad:

NOTICE TO PROFESSIONAL CONSULTANTS
XXXXXX, State of XXXX, announces that Professional Services in the discipline of architecture will be required for the project listed below:
Project No. XXXX
Project and Location: XXXXXXXX
[Project location, city, state and zip code]

The project consists of a new XXXXXX facility on the [physical location] to serve [Audience]. The building site is located on [Actual description of location]. The facility is expected to be approximately XXXX gross square feet. The project will include [Any special considerations] along with the construction of other related site improvements. The selected firm will provide design, construction documents, and administration for the referenced project, which is budgeted at $[XXXX] for construction. The project delivery system will be construction management (a current term used for most construction projects).

Blanket professional liability insurance will be required for this project in the amount of $[XXXXX], and will be provided as a part of Basic Services.

INSTRUCTIONS: (specific details usually required in the application from the architectural firm)
Firms desiring to apply for consideration shall submit a letter of application.
The letter of application should have attached:
1. A completed [School System's name] "Professional Qualifications Supplement." Please use the version for this project posted on the Web site *[School system's Web site]*
2. A copy of the applicant's current Professional Registration Certificate from the appropriate governing board. An applicant must be properly registered

at the time of application to practice its profession in the State of XXXX. If the applicant is a corporation, it must be chartered by the XXXX Department to operate in [State]. Submit six (6) copies of the above requested data bound in the order listed above. Applications, which do not comply with the above instructions, may be disqualified. Application materials will not be returned.

The plans and specifications for [School system's] projects are subject to reuse in accordance with the provisions of Section XXXX, [State] Statutes. As required by Section XXXXX, [State] Statutes, an architectural firm may not submit a proposal for this project if it is on the convicted vendor list for a public entity crime committed within the past 36 months. The selected architectural firm must warrant that it will neither utilize the services of, nor contract with, any supplier, subcontractor, or consultant in excess of $XXXXX in connection with this project for a period of XX months from the date of their being placed on the convicted vendor list.

Professional Qualifications Supplement forms, descriptive project information, and selection criteria may be obtained through our Web site, *[School System's Web site]*, or by contacting: [Contact person, address, telephone and facsimile].

For further information on the project, contact: [Alternate contact person], at the address and phone listed above.

Submittals must be received in the above office, by XXXX, local time, on [day and date]. Facsimile (FAX) or electronic submittals are not acceptable and will not be considered.

Architectural Firm Selection

Upon completion of the detailed facility program, an architect can be selected. By this time in the planning process there should be a clear, consensus understanding of what the new construction or renovation project will entail. This information should have been articulated in the building program.

The first step in the architect hiring process is to establish a building committee that will see the project through all its phases. This could be the planning committee or a new committee that is similar in structure. The committee's first task is to compile a list of architects to interview for the projected new construction or renovation project. One way to begin is to determine which firms in your vicinity have designed projects that are similar in type and scale. Some of these facilities may have been visited in the earlier phases of the planning process. Other groups who are planning or who have recently completed similar work are also good sources of information, as are local chapters of the American Institute of Architects.

The selection process takes 11 steps as defined in the following, along with the critical documentation and notification requirements.

1. Narrow the list of respondents to a manageable number of firms. (Use a point system that factors in experience designing previous projects of a similar nature and the architectural firms' proximity to the construction site.)

2. Send each firm a Request for Qualifications.
3. Receive qualifications.
4. Prepare selection criteria.
5. Review submittals.
6. Reduce the list to three to five firms for more detailed consideration.
7. Check references.
8. Send each firm on the short list a request for proposal.
9. Receive proposals.
10. Interview the firms over the course of one to two days.
11. Evaluate and select.

Request for Qualifications (RFQ)

The following list describes the information that is requested from each of the architectural firms in the initial phase of information gathering (Step 2).

- Description of firm
- Résumés of key personnel
- Comparable projects within past five years
- Specific examples from one or two projects
- Drawings, photos
- NASF (net assignable square feet), GSF (gross square feet), construction cost, bid date information for the projects
- Design team members
- References

SAMPLE REQUEST FOR QUALIFICATIONS

Each respondent shall provide the following information:

A. Brief letter of introduction on Architect's letterhead transmitting all required RFQ information.
B. Experience: Provide a profile of experiences for the Architect and all members of the firm. This section shall include, but need not be limited to the following:
   1. The Architect's experience with projects for school districts.
   2. Resumes of all key members of the Architect's firm who would be working on these projects; how long the members of the firm have been working together and a list of similar projects that this "Architect" has worked on and completed.
   3. The Architect's demonstrated expertise in:
      a. School district facilities design involving the following:
         - Remodel
         - Renovation
         - Replacement of old with new
         - Upgrading existing systems
         - Interfacing new construction with existing
         - Processing plans and specs through DSA, including over-the-counter work checks

- Cost estimating
- Master planning

b. Ability to incorporate various elements into the design of a project; i.e., artistic, functionality, ease of maintenance, durability, cost savings, etc.

c. Ability to plan and execute work effectively, meet deadlines, interfaces with educators and college administrators.

d. Simplicity in the design of projects that can be constructed for available funds.

C. Identify the members of the proposed design team. Provide firm experience and individual resumes for the design consultants that will make up your team. Provide a list of consultants that you may use that are not normally needed for a typical construction project.

D. Information and references on public project work, preferably school districts, performed by the Architect. Include a minimum of five (5) projects, dates of completion, members of the Architectural firm directly involved in the design and/or engineering work, budgets, and references.

E. Provide information on the types and amounts of insurance carried by the Architect, including GLC, automobile liability, Workers Compensation, and Professional Liability Coverage.

F. Please list and submit, in a sealed envelope marked "confidential," true copies of any judgments and any other evidence of liability that has been the result of alleged negligent design by the Architect or any of its current or former members during the past five (5) years preceding response to this RFQ. This information will not be made public but will be kept confidential by the school district.

G. Proposed Fees and Costs:

1. A listing of fees for all members of the Architect's firm, the design team, and include any support personnel whose time is billed directly to its clients.

2. Proposed fees shall include fees incurred working with school district committees and making presentations to various groups. Also, please include a statement of willingness (or not) to undertake designated projects for a flat fee for the project, i.e., "all inclusive" fee for all services, except for normal and customary expenses as requested in 3. (below), within the Architect's professional discipline for a specific project, start to finish.

3. Also include a statement of all normal and customary expenses, blueprinting, and reproduction costs as typically billed directly to the Architect's clients.

4. Provide authorization of the "Architect" and all principals thereof to allow the school district to make oral and/or written inquires of all references listed, regarding your qualifications, performance, reasonableness of fees and charges, and quality of final results.

5. Submit five (5) complete copies of your proposal to:

   Contract Services
   ATTN: XXXXX
   Location
   Address
   City, State and zip

The school district will evaluate the responses based on the qualifications, background, training, experience, and apparent reasonableness of the Architect's fee structure. The school district retains the right to negotiate the final proposed fee schedule prior to recommending any Architect for a consulting contract.

1. The Architect's experience with projects for school districts.
2. Résumés of all key members of the Architect's firm who would be working on these projects; how long the members of the firm have been working together and a list of similar projects that this "Architect" has worked on and completed.
3. The Architect's demonstrated expertise in:
   a. School district facilities design involving the following:
      - Remodel
      - Renovation
      - Replacement of old with new
      - Upgrading existing systems
      - Interfacing new construction with existing
      - Processing plans and specs through DSA, including over-the-counter work checks
      - Cost estimating
      - Master planning
   b. Ability to incorporate various elements into the design of a project; i.e., artistic, functionality, ease of maintenance, durability, cost savings, etc.
   c. Ability to plan and execute work effectively, meet deadlines, interfaces with educators and administrators.
   d. Simplicity in the design of projects that can be constructed for available funds.

Selection Process

The school district's selection process is as follows:

A. The selection committee shall screen and rate all of the RFQs that are submitted. Ratings shall be based on the following criteria set forth in Section I, items A through F, above.
B. The selection committee will select the short list of "Architects" that shall be invited for interviews.
C. Questions and answers. The selection committee will invite the short-listed "Architects" for a presentation/interview. The interviews will be one hour in length; the Architects will have 30 minutes for a presentation and 30 minutes for questions and answers.
D. Based upon the interview, each Architect shall be rated in each category where professional services are desired. The highest-rated Architects shall be invited to interview with executive administration.
E. The Superintendent and the Director of Facilities will select the most qualified Architect to enter into contract negotiations with the school district.
F. When the services and fees are agreed upon, the selected Architect shall be offered a consulting contract subject to Governing Board Approval.
G. If the negotiations are not successful, the school district shall enter into negotiations with the next, highest rated Architect until an agreement for services and fees acceptable to the District and the Architect are reached.

H. This Request for Qualifications does not commit the school district to pay for any direct and/or indirect costs incurred in the preparation and presentation of a response. All finalists shall pay their own costs incurred in preparing for, traveling to, and attending the interviews. The school district reserves the right to accept or reject this proposal in part, or in its entirety.

All data, documents and other products used or developed during response to this RFQ remain the property of the Architect and not the school district. Following entry into a satisfactory contract, all data, documents, drawings, calculations, and products developed by any Architects selected by the school district, in the performance of its contract with the school district, shall be the exclusive property of the school district.

Please direct any requests for information or clarification to:

Contract Services – XXXX
Place
Address
City, State, zip
Phone: XXXX
Fax: XXXX
Email: XXXX

Request for Proposal (RFP)

Information sent by the school system to the "short list" of firms (three to five) include:

- Introduction to the project
- Description of the process
- Schedule
  - Date for tour of facility and existing space, if needed
  - Date when proposals are due
  - Date for interview and selection
- Selection criteria that will be used by the owner
- Proposal requirements
- Summary facility program
  - Background and rationale
  - Site location
  - Facility organization assumptions
  - Summary of spaces

Sample Request for Proposal (RFP) for Architectural Firm

REQUEST FOR PROPOSAL:

1. (NAME OF JURISDICTION OR ORGANIZATION) (sponsor) is soliciting competitive sealedproposals from qualified architects and architectural firms to provide architectural services outlined in the **SCOPE OF SERVICES SECTION** of this request.

2. **OBJECTIVE AND BACKGROUND:** The sponsor intends to design and construct a (BRIEF PROJECT DESCRIPTION)

3. SCOPE OF SERVICES: The sponsor is requesting full architectural services for the programming, design, cost estimating, preparation of construction documents, reproduction costs, bidding, bid evaluation, construction administration, final inspection, and project acceptance. In summary the sponsor is desirous that the successful architect/firm provide a full range of professional services, exclusive of soils test and special inspections, to assist it in the successful completion of the project. Unless noted by the architect, the sponsor will assume that all costs to accomplish these goals are included in the RFP.

4. **COMPENSATION FOR SERVICES (FEE):** The sponsor intends to enter into a professional services contract with the successful architect/firm. Compensation for the services rendered, is to be based upon a time-expended basis with an agreed maximum not to exceed value.

NOTE: The selection of the successful architect/firm will not be based solely on the fee.

5. **EVALUATION CRITERIA AND SELECTION PROCEDURES:**
   A. Evaluation Criteria: Selection of the successful architect/firm will be based upon a matrix giving a predetermined value to each of the submissions required in this section. The architect is requested to provide responses to the following:
      1) The name of the project architect/firm, and the managing principal, if applicable.
      2) The architect/firm address of principal place of business.
      3) The size of the architect's/firm's staff and current workload.
      4) A record of previous relevant experience in the design and initial development (BRIEF DESCRIPTION OF SCOPE).
      5) A list of references including names, addresses, and phone numbers of no more than 8 individuals or organizations familiar with the architect/firm performance.
      6) If an architectural firm, identification and role of key individuals in the architectural team and/or its consultants.
      7) A brief response to each of the other aspects of the project as outlined in the owner's preliminary project requirements.
      8) An approximate schedule for completion of requested services.
      9) An approximation of the number hours, the related costs to perform the services required by this RFP, and the applicable hourly rates or multiplier for the base rates of individuals employed on the project.
   B. Selection Procedures:
      1) The sponsor's selection committee will consist of the (#) member board of directors, the project manager, and legal counsel.
      2) The sponsor will review all architect/firm submissions and utilizing a matrix of pre-determined, weighted values for each of the required items, select the (3) architects/firms receiving the highest scores in the evaluation process.
      3) The (3) architects/firms receiving the highest score will be invited to participate in an interview with the selection committee. The architects/firms are requested to limit the number of participants in the interview to the project architect and/or one principal of the firm. (Date, time, and location of the interview are yet to be determined.)

4) Following the interviews, the selection committee will, again utilizing a matrix of predetermined values, designate the two architects/firms receiving the highest scores as the primary and secondary architects/firms.

5) The sponsor will then enter into negotiations with the primary architect/firm to establish the value of compensation and other relevant issues.

6) In the event the sponsor is not able to negotiate a mutually acceptable contract with the primary architect/firm, it reserves the right to terminate negotiations and then undertake negotiations with the secondary architect/firm.

6. **GENERAL CONDITIONS FOR PROPOSALS:**
   A. Failure to read the Request for Proposal and comply with its instructions will be at the architect's/firm's own risk.
   B. All prices and notations must be printed in ink or typewritten. Errors may be crossed out and corrections printed in ink or typewritten, adjacent to the corrected error. Person signing the proposal must initial all corrections in ink.
   C. Corrections or modifications received after the closing time in this RFP will not be accepted.
   D. The proposal must be signed by a designated firm representative or officer who is authorized to bind the architect/firm contractually. Submission of a signed proposal to the sponsor will be interpreted to indicate the architect's/firm's willingness to comply with all terms and conditions set forth herein.

7. **PROPOSAL SUBMISSION:**
   A. Proposals must be delivered to the office of the project manager at (NAME, ADDRESS, ZIP) on or before (TIME OF DAY) on (DAY, DATE, YEAR). **PROPOSALS RECEIVED AFTER (TIME) WILL BE PLACED IN THE FILE UNOPENED AND WILL NOT BE CONSIDERED. THERE WILL BE NO EXCEPTIONS.**
   B. Proposals must be submitted in a sealed envelope clearly bearing the name of the architect/firm, address, and title of the project.
   C. The applicant must submit (NUMBER TO CORRESPOND WITH MEMBERS SERVING ON THE SELECTION COMMITTEE) copies of the complete proposal.

8. **AWARD:** The sponsor reserves the right to reject all proposals. The sponsor also reserves the right to waive any irregularity, informality, or technicality in the proposals in its best interest, and is not obligated to award a contract based upon the lowest priced submission. If terms cannot be mutually agreed upon, the sponsor will enter into negotiations with the secondary architect/firm.

9. **WRITTEN AGREEMENT:** The successful architect/firm will be required to enter into a written agreement with the sponsor in a form acceptable to the sponsor.

10. **OMISSIONS:** Should the RFP not contain sufficient information for the applicant to obtain a clear understanding of the services required by the sponsor, or should it appear that the instructions outline in the RFP are not clear or contradictory, then the architect/firm may obtain written clarification from the

project manager at least 24 hours prior to the required time and date for proposal submission. The architect/firm shall include a copy of the written clarification with its submission

11. **EQUAL OPPORTUNITY AND AFFIRMATIVE ACTION PROGRAM:** The successful applicant must covenant and agree to abide by the federal and state regulations pertaining to Equal Employment as set forth in **EXECUTIVE ORDERS 11246, 11375, 11625, and 41 CFR Part 60-4, Section III of the Housing and Urban Development Act of 1968 (12 USC 170u), as amended and HUD Regulations at 24 CFR Part 135.** In addition, the successful architect/firm must comply with Federal Labor Standards Provisions. In summary, these regulations require project participants not to discriminate against any employee or applicant for employment because of race, color, religion, sex, age disability, or national origin and project participants will take appropriate measures to employ minority owned businesses. A copy of all noted regulations can be obtained from the sponsor. Also, the sponsor will make every effort to ensure that all offers are treated fairly and equally throughout the entire advertisement, review, and selection process. The procedures established herein are designed to provide all parties reasonable access to the same basic information. The successful architect/firm must comply with all applicable CDBG and regulatory requirements in the performance of services outlined herein.

12. **ADDITIONAL INFORMATION:** For additional information regarding the services specified in this request for proposal, contact the project manager (NAME, ADDRESS, ZIP, PHONE & FAX NUMBERS).

13. **COST OF DEVELOPING PROPOSALS:** All costs related to the preparation of the proposals and any related activities are the sole responsibility of the applicant. The sponsor assumes no liability for any costs incurred throughout the entire selection process.

14. **PROPOSAL OWNERSHIP:** All proposals, including attachments, supplementary materials, rendering, sketches addenda, etc. shall become upon submission, the property of the sponsor, and will not be returned to the applicant.

15. **NON-COLLUSION:** The architect/firm guarantees that the proposal submitted is not a product of collusion with any other offer and no effort has been made to fix the proposal price of any offer or to fix any overhead, profit, or cost estimate of any proposal or its price.

Information to be Provided by Architectural Firms in Response to RFP

- Statement of design philosophy
- Approach to the project
- Consultants
- Budget
- Schedule
- Staffing and project management
- Reimbursable costs
- Sealed fee proposal

After careful consideration, which may take several sessions, if there is no clear-cut best firm for the project, a decision may be made to re-advertise.

Reviewing the Finalists

The ideal firm should provide examples of creative solutions to designing buildings. Their presentation should include samples demonstrating ways they have responded to other school library building programs. They should also demonstrate through oral and visual representations that they understand the important aspects of your building program.

During the presentation, someone intimately familiar with the library media center proposal should ask tough questions, such as:

- Will this be an original design? (Many architectural firms have templates for school buildings. A template is sections of the building that are the same for all buildings, such as gymnasium, library, auditorium, cafeteria, etc. You have the choice of where they are located on the site, but the overall arrangement of the area is the same for all structures they design.)

   Architects have a structure for charges which is usually a percentage of the projected cost for the project. These percentages rarely vary unless they really need the work. They may say there are no negotiations, but if you have two or three similarly qualified applicants, then there is usually room for negotiation.

- Do you charge less for template designs? (Usually firms charge the same fees for all construction projects.)

   It will be hard to get a specific answer from large architectural firms; medium and small firms will usually prepare a unique design for your situation. You need to be persistent in this line of questioning, since the interviews are usually recorded or there is a secretary taking specific notes for the negotiation process.

- Will you be willing to make changes to the plans if they don't reflect the specific needs of our program? (Some firms are unwilling to make specific design changes even during the process of designing the structure.)

   This aspect should become apparent in the RFP documents, but not always. Some architectural firms charge for any changes and call them change orders even if they are mentioned during the selection process. Always be careful to ask for specific answers to your questions, since they will try to have wiggle room.

- Will you always place the educational priorities over general costs?

   This can be difficult for large firms, because their margins are so close in the bidding process. Inflation factors play a large part in this decision. Again, ask for specific answers to the question and keep asking it in a different way until you get a specific answer that satisfies you. This is the last time you will be able to negotiate with the architects.

The board or other responsible parties should also be sure to look into the relative success of the past projects of the firms under consideration. Sometimes a firm may have a history of bringing projects in on budget precisely because they use low-grade materials or otherwise cut corners. As owners of the facility, the school board should remember that a new library is an investment in a school's educational future, and it is important that investment stand the test of time. If possible, school board members and others should investigate completed projects by architectural finalists. It is important to investigate buildings at the detail level on such visits. Even a building that appears beautiful when seen as a whole may have serious problems. Members of the immediate building team should speak to the owners or managers of these other projects and inquire into how well the buildings function on a day-to-day level. Issues to consider include how easy the spaces are to clean, how well the building has stood the test of time, and how well it meets its original program. Be sure also to ask the owners what the client-designer relationship was like. Here it is particularly useful to inquire into how responsive the architects were to special needs of the site or project. Board members may not interface directly with designers after the selection phase, but by making informed decisions they can make life easier for those who will do so.

Negotiating with Finalist Architectural Firm

After a firm has been selected by the planning team, there is still considerable work to be accomplished. A contract has to be written with all the essential stipulations and requirements. The library media specialist will not be involved in this process.

Developing the Contract

After a firm has been selected, then it is time to develop a formal document, which is the contract with the firm. Here too the library media specialist will not be involved in this process. This information is provided to illustrate the complexity of the process.

Both sides have a period of time to examine the contract documents. They develop a list of issues, which may need to be negotiated. The architecture firm sends their list of issues to the owner. The owner's representatives consider these issues and then send back their response. This may go back and forth several times, until an agreement can be reached that is satisfactory for both parties.

Final Negotiations

After consideration of all the issues, there is a final meeting between the parties. Lawyers are often present to make the final negotiations. If an agreement can't be reached, negotiations may need to begin again with the firm that placed second in the selection process.

Role of the Contract Document

The document is the final authority for any lawsuits that might arise during the design of the building. Usually there are no lawsuits against architects, but it is a possibility. Lawsuits can also happen after the building is completed, if there are design flaws.

Once the contract has been ratified, work can move ahead on design. The next chapter provides special guidance for those schools hoping to build freestanding libraries. For most programs, however, the most important thing will be to keep the architects focused on the demands of the planning documents. If the right choice has been made during the architect selection phase, this should be a relatively simple matter. For a sample document, see Resource C at the back of this book.

8

How to Collaborate with Architects to Design a Facility that Works

This chapter details the design phase, the exciting moment when a new facility begins to come together on paper. Here we will focus primarily on free-standing facilities, which present special concerns and add various layers of complexity to the overall process. Those working on library media centers within existing buildings or being included in a larger design and construction project may still find this chapter helpful for reference. This segment of the project consists primarily of a series of interactions between the building team and the architects as the latter group works to clarify and perfect their ideas for the library. Over the course of these meetings, it is the responsibility of the building team to ensure that design specifications are being met. Further, it will be their task to guarantee that the facility is as attractive as possible.

The building team is typically a seven- to nine-member group constituted of representatives from a wide range of constituencies. In general, the team is led by one to two individuals—usually school library media specialists—who were involved in writing the planning document. Other members should include district administrators, teachers, parents, students, and other users of the facility. Decisions are made by consensus, which ideally leads to a balancing of the various interests each member brings to the table.

While the members of the team must bring their own expertise to bear on the conversations with the architects, the library media specialist has a special responsibility. It is this member of the team's duty to guide the others through the special needs and facets of school library facilities.

First Meeting of Architects with the Building Team

During the selection process the building team becomes acquainted with the architectural firm. The first meeting is very important, insofar as it sets the tone for future meetings. In addition to the planning team, the building principal or representative and representatives from the school system planning department attend. There is often an extensive agenda, which includes:

- Introduction of committee members
- Responsibilities of school system
- Responsibilities of facility design team
- Responsibilities of the architectural firm
- Review of the building project elements
- Architectural firm discussion of design element priorities and concerns

This meeting is usually three to four hours in length. An agreement is made at the end of the meeting for the next session, which usually consists of the first presentation of several exterior elevations and interior design solutions.

Budget Shortfalls and the Recommendation of Changes

The first meeting with the architectural firm will provide initial evidence for any needed additional design requirements and changes in the building program before seeing elevations and interior design. Many times analysis of building costs in the area and type of materials and cabinetry requested will reveal that the budget is too small to meet all of the requirements. If this is true, there will be an opportunity to include alternatives in the final program. Some elements, especially those essential to make the facility fit into its surroundings or meet building code may be non-negotiable. Others, however, can often be replaced with less expensive materials that achieve much the same effect. For example:

- If a brick exterior is called for, an alternative might be to use the brick for the entrance area, with stucco and brick combinations in other areas.
- If decorative exterior wooden columns are specified, aluminum exterior columns will be less expensive and more durable.
- If appropriate, architectural shingle may substitute for more expensive roofing materials like slate or clay tile.
- Similarly, employing ceramic tile in the floor of the lobby and major walkway areas may be less expensive than slate or marble if they were originally specified.
- Asphalt tile is a cheaper alternative for lesser-used areas. This is an alternative choice also for high-traffic areas, but not very desirable.
- High-grade carpeting is usually specified in areas where noise control is important. An alternative could be lower grade carpeting in lesser used areas or, if absolutely necessary, for the whole facility.
- The simplification or outright removal of landscaping and outdoor sprinkler systems can be listed as an alternative, if absolutely necessary.

- Wall covering can likewise be simplified. Some facility programs propose expensive wallpapers that can often be replaced with less expensive materials.
- Downgrading the quality of light fixtures is rarely an acceptable alternative.

Especially if the budget is tight, the team must be prepared to make sacrifices of this kind. A good architectural team will anticipate such concerns before they become truly urgent problems. They should also be able to come up with solutions that are both aesthetically appropriate and architecturally sound.

Reviewing First Design Solutions

Notes of the discussions and agreements should be taken at the first planning meeting with the architects, which should then be shared with all involved parties. At the second major meeting of the planning group, the architects propose a number of possible designs for the exterior appearance of the building and one or more solutions for interior arrangement. This is a crucial meeting—so much so that the building team may need to have one or two meetings beforehand to prepare for it. They may also need to meet again afterward to discuss the various design proposals. After the decision has been made regarding which design is most appropriate, a process that may require further dialogue between the building team and the architects, then more detailed exterior drawings are completed.

Conforming to Design Regulations

Once the committee and architects have come to an agreement on the overall exterior appearance, the designs are usually submitted to the person in charge of approving the general architectural look of buildings for the school or district. Good architecture works in its context, fitting in with both its immediate environment and the other buildings around it. Most architectural firms will work with this fact in mind, but institutions may also have their own approval process in place to guarantee that new buildings conform to the ethos of the old. If the architects and the building team have been conscientious and aware of any regulations that are in place, this phase is likely to be little more than a formality.

Reading Blueprints

Throughout the design process it is important that you be able to make sense of the plans shown to you by architects. The first step toward this kind of architectural literacy is to gain a knowledge of the most commonly used symbols on blueprints. The chart in Figure 8-1 provides a key to common terms. See also Figure 8-2 for a chart of common electrical symbols, a useful point of reference as the project develops.

Second Meeting with Building Team

This meeting will usually take no more than two hours, because the focus will typically be on demonstrating concrete elements that follow earlier suggestions. The architectural team will present several solutions to the building program.

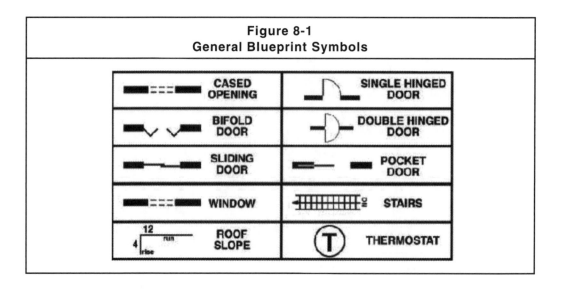

Figure 8-1
General Blueprint Symbols

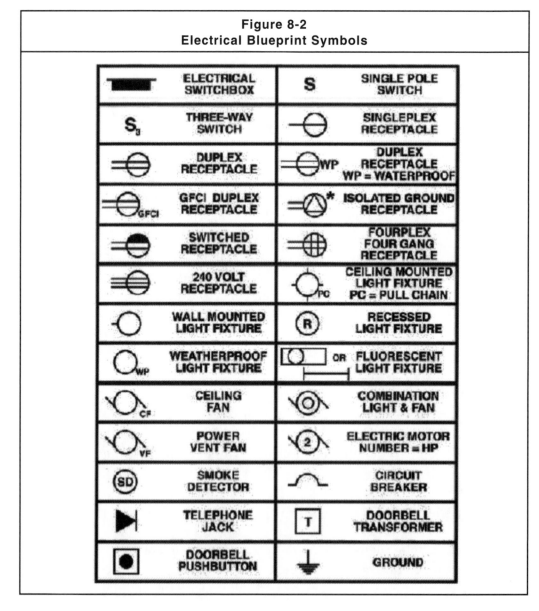

Figure 8-2
Electrical Blueprint Symbols

Usually there will be several exterior proposals and interior solutions in a bound document for every member of the team. As stated earlier, there may be four to five exterior ideas presented and one or two interior arrangements of rooms.

To provide a concrete example, the original site selection map and elevations for the Florida State University School Knowledge Center follow this discussion. (See Figure 8-3; site B was selected.)

Sample Architectural Solutions Drawings

Figures 8-4 to 8-10 offer seven possible architectural facility design solutions.

Architectural Team Makes Recommendations

During this phase of the design process the architects should thoroughly explain all aspects of their proposals for the building or facility. Particular issues to consider include:

- Reasons for the placement of the school library media center within the larger building, if this is of concern. As addressed in other chapters, the school library media center still should be located in the heart of the building, as close to the academic classroom areas of the school as possible.

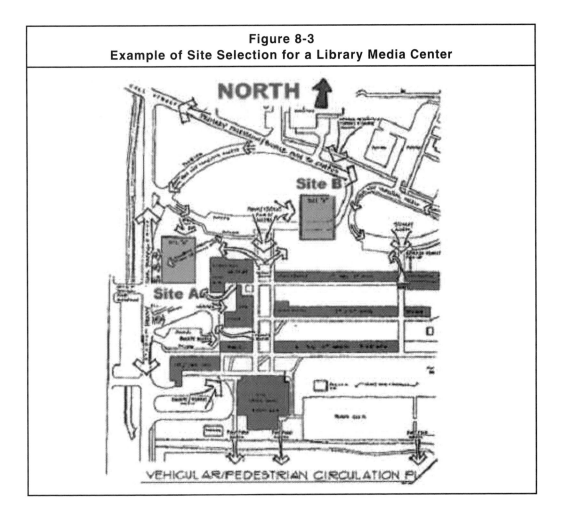

Figure 8-3
Example of Site Selection for a Library Media Center

Figure 8-4
Sample Architectural Facility Design: Solution 1

ELEVATION STUDY (A)

Figure 8-5
Sample Architectural Facility Design: Solution 2

ELEVATION STUDY (B)

Figure 8-6
Sample Architectural Facility Design: Solution 3

ELEVATION STUDY (C)

Figure 8-7
Sample Architectural Facility Design: Solution 4

Figure 8-8
Sample Architectural Facility Design: Solution 5

Figure 8-9
Sample Architectural Facility Design: Solution 6

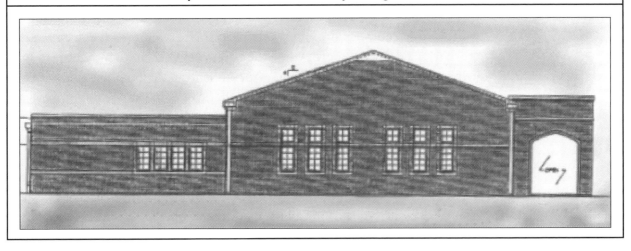

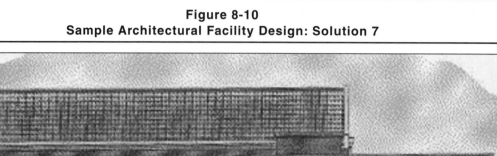

Figure 8-10
Sample Architectural Facility Design: Solution 7

- Reasons for various solutions for the exterior look of the building: height of walls; pitch of roof; and types of exterior treatments for walls, windows, and roof.
- Reasons for placement of spaces and dimensions of spaces for the interior. Of course they should, if possible, be following the spatial relationship diagram included in the building plan. If there are digressions from the spatial relationship diagram, then there should be explanations for these recommended changes.
- Evidence that ADA Standards have been followed. These are available on the Web at a variety of locations.
- Any other anomalies from the building program specifications.
- Solutions for any special needs of the facility outlined in the building plan.

Planning Team Makes Recommendations

- After the detailed presentations of the architects, the planning team asks searching questions. They then arrive through consensus at either rejection or contingent acceptance of the project. The former requires the architects to return to the drawing board, while the latter allows them to move ahead with the present plans. In either case, it is incumbent on the building committee to make clear suggestions to the architects that can help shape and improve the movement toward the final design. During this phase, clear agreements should be made with the architects regarding what will happen next.
- Interior arrangements and space solutions are generally discussed first. If the architects have been contracted for exterior elements, and if these elements are the responsibility of the library building committee, these designs should be discussed second, and one design proposal should be chosen for further elaboration.

- Sometimes agreement cannot be reached at this session, so another brief meeting is scheduled to arrive at consensus, after a cooling-off period.

Third Discussions with Building Team

These discussions, which may require only a meeting or two for simpler projects, are crucial for arriving at final plans. Every detail needs to be examined that has not already been resolved, such as:

- Traffic patterns
- Possibilities for cabinetry and furniture to fit into the allocated space configuration.
- Overall appearance of exterior (curb appeal).
- Details, finishes and special materials to get needed effects.
- Any other concerns for your building

This version of planning becomes more detailed. There should be several views of the exterior and roof layouts. A fairly detailed version of the floor plans should also be submitted. After a careful analysis of the exterior and roof layouts, the building planning team should make recommendations to the architects. If consensus cannot be reached, then the chair(s) of the planning team should meet with the head of the architectural team to negotiate differences. Those involved in these talks should submit any conclusions that arise to both the building committee and the architectural team.

Sample Interior Elevations

Figures 8-11 and 8-12 provide two examples of how interior elevation drawings look. In this case, they are emphasizing acoustical panels and their design. Figure 8-12, which displays the final version of the plans more actively meets the special acoustical needs of library media centers.

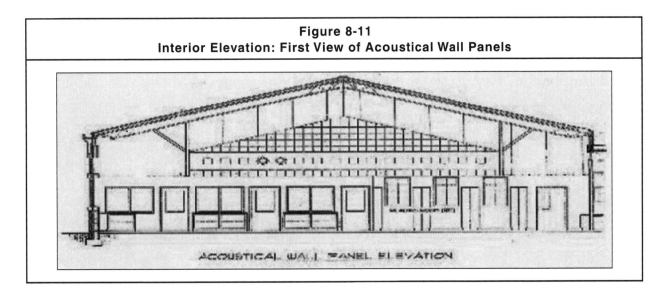

Figure 8-11
Interior Elevation: First View of Acoustical Wall Panels

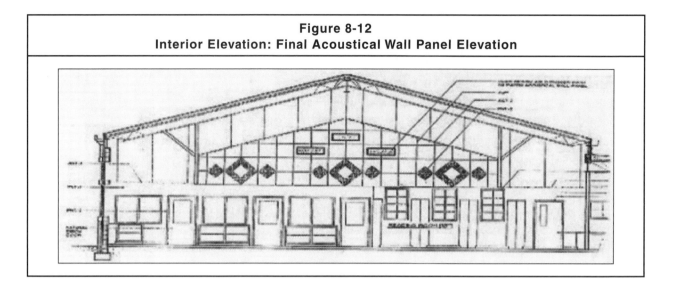

Figure 8-12
Interior Elevation: Final Acoustical Wall Panel Elevation

Fourth Discussions with Architects

If all goes smoothly in the third period of discussions, design can then move into the fourth and final phase. Now nearly final documents will be presented, and a color drawing or detailed model of the exterior will usually be displayed and turned over to the owners. There will be detailed exterior plans and interior blueprints. A full presentation will be made, rigorously presenting and analyzing every detail of the blueprints

After the presentation, the building team will approve the documents. Even after the approval, the chair(s) of the planning committee and the head architect will carefully go over every detail of the plans, room by room. Things to consider include the location of windows, window hardware, location of doors, direction of opening and closing of doors, door hardware, location of electrical outlets, location of lights, location of light switches, and placement of cabinetry, etc. It is important to check in this phase that all detail finishes are appropriate to the facility and in line with both institutional and legal code.

Once the last examination of the documents has been completed and recommendations have been offered, final changes should be made to the blueprints. If this iteration of the design meets with the planning committee's consensus approval, the design phase is all but done.

Preparation of Final Elevations and Plans

After final changes are made the blueprints and other elevations are copied. These plans are presented to the coordinators of the projects for use while the actual construction is underway. The last and final step in the design phase is the preparation by the architects of documents for the bidding process. These will break down the various elements and materials used in the facility to ensure that contractors can produce the most accurate possible estimates of building costs before they make their bids. The architects should also give a figure estimating the approximate cost per square foot of the facility. This serves in part to ensure that the project is on budget before the architects step out of the process, lessening the chance that cost-control redesigns will be required once construction has begun. As will be shown in the next chapter, this also acts as a guide to contractors, showing the budgetary range into which their proposals are expected to fall.

Resources Consulted

ARCHISEEK (online architectural resources). Architectural terms. Dublin, Ireland. (January 2005). Available: http://archiseek.com/guides/glossary/a.html.

California Energy Commission. Types of roofing. Sacramento, Calif. (January 2005). Available: http://consumerenergycenter.org/homeandwork/homes/construction/roofing.html.

Skyscrapers.com. Architectural styles. New York (January 2005). Available: http://emporis.com/en/ab/ds/sg/ra/bu/ca/ap/sy/hi/.

University of Wisconsin Milwaukee Facilities Planning Department. Building planning terms. Milwaukee, Wis. (January 2005). Available: http://uwm.edu/Dept/CFP/glossary.html.

Virginia Commonwealth University. Building façade materials. Richmond, Va. (January 2005). Available: http://vcu.edu/maps/historic/glossary/h_gloss.htm.

9

How to Select and Work with a Contractor

Once the facility is designed and there is agreement among all concerned parties, it is time to select a contractor. This process will vary according to the policies of the school authority, but there are still some common concerns, which will be discussed in this chapter. More often than not, school library media center coordinators will have little to do with this selection process, but understanding how it works can be an important part of a successful facility. Finding the right contractor for the project will help ensure that everything proceeds in a timely and satisfactory manner. Also important is that those involved understand what the construction process entails. Accordingly, this chapter provides an overview of the relevant elements of the process with an eye toward things that school library media specialists need to know at each stage.

The process for selecting, hiring, and supervising a contractor is the same for any building project. A description of the project is sent out to the sources where contractors will become aware of the project. (A sample announcement is included in the planning tools at the end of this book.) Following is the process for selecting, hiring, and managing contractors typically employed by public agencies:

- The contractors submit bids
- The representatives of the owner select a contractor
- The contractor accepts the contract to build the facility
- A project manager is selected by the contractor to represent them
- The site is cleared
- Foundations installed
- Building constructed
- Interior finishes installed
- Building accepted for occupancy

Bidding Process

Most public agencies have a bidding process to select the best and most economical builder. In general, only reputable firms are usually allowed to bid. This is most often determined through a request for qualifications. A time frame of one to two months for the preparation of bids is typically given in the initial advertisement, allowing interested contractors to carefully evaluate the plans.

As noted at the end of the previous chapter, the architects provide an estimate of the cost per square foot of the facility. Ideally, this estimate guides the bids of the competing contractors. Especially in more complicated projects, contractors typically have subcontractors for foundations, framing, roofing, plumbing, electrical, heating and cooling, exterior, and interior finishing, etc. It is the primary contractor's responsibility to anticipate the costs of this work as accurately as possible. Budgeting projections can therefore be quite complex, as the analysis of the different costs for different elements may involve communication with various other parties. In this context, the cost-per-square-foot figures are merely a limiting factor, and different elements of the building may vary wildly in cost. Experienced contractors will, of course, be aware of these disparities and will negotiate with their subcontractors accordingly.

Once the details of the bids have been finalized and selected, a committee of experts will examine them to make sure they meet all expectations. Unless none of bids meet the project specifications or all bids are higher than the funds available for construction, and assuming that all bids are of relatively equal quality, the lowest bidder is usually selected. If the bids come in too high, the architect and planning group must readjust the plans. Normally the first cost-cutting choice is a change in landscaping and sprinkler systems. Next, cheaper wall finishes and other finishes are sought and the grade of carpet and tile is reduced. Naturally, this sequence will not necessarily be appropriate in every circumstance or for every facility, but during the difficult process of deciding what must be sacrificed, many planning committees prefer to cut these more minor features. In general, it is of primary importance that they do all that they can to maintain the space and resources required to accomplish and encourage all of the facility's programmatic goals. As was noted in the previous chapters, eleventh-hour redesigns can often be prevented if the planning committee remains vigilant during the design phase, forcing the architects to provide evidence at every stage that their plan can be brought in at or under budget. Sometimes, however, unanticipated conditions can arise later in the project and all involved parties should be prepared to meet them.

Understanding Contractors

Once a contractor is approved, the real involvement with the construction project begins almost immediately. If a project manager was hired by the site owner, the head of the facility, or some other authorized official, will work with this person to begin the initial dialogue about how construction will proceed. If there is not a specific project manager, school district representative will have to spend more time on the project. Insofar as project managers have oversight of the project as their primary responsibility, they are far more able to look after the progress and satisfactoriness of the contractor's work. Their professional knowledge of the building process also makes them more comfortable than most at communicating with the contractors. In theory, they will act as intermediaries between those involved in erecting the facility and those who will ultimately occupy it. By keeping one foot in both worlds they can help protect the interests of the project owner. The cost of a project manager is small compared to that of the construction problems it can help avert.

Contractors on smaller projects are often citizens from the local area, but contracts are sometimes let with large regional contracting agencies. A local contractor has a reputation to uphold and will be confronted daily with evidence of shoddy work. Larger regional contractors, by contrast, may be concerned primarily with the bottom line. It is important that clients work to understand the overall attitude of those who will be building their facility. While a larger contractor may still do good work, a consciousness of how they approach construction will help to determine how vigilant the project manager and/or library representative should be throughout the construction period.

To ensure smooth operations during construction, contractors will usually have a building construction manager who oversees the site on a day-to-day basis. If both this individual and the client's project manager are experienced, there usually will be fewer problems. If either is new, however, more careful contact should be maintained by involved.

To save time and costs most contractors will use subcontractors for foundation work, frame construction, plumbing, electrical installation, exterior coverings, roofing, and so on. As the name suggests, these groups or individuals are under contract not with the site owner, but with the primary contractor. Nevertheless, someone from the school district must constantly supervise all installations, no matter who is doing them. This is especially important for features of the building that may be difficult to change after construction is complete. It is essential that all errors be caught as early as possible, a thing that requires full engagement from the representatives of the client. No matter how reliable contractors seem, they can never be guaranteed to catch or correct all of their mistakes. Plumbing installation should be overseen with particular care, as errors discovered after construction has been completed are often irreparable.

Need for Project Manager

Experienced project managers will have a clear sense of what to watch for. New project managers and institutional representatives (when no project manager is available) may not be as certain of their responsibilities. While no list can provide an exhaustive account of all the problems that might arise, the following concerns should be kept in mind:

- *Foundation construction.* Project managers should check on the depth of foundations and the quality of cement used. Both of these items should be specified in the original architectural plans.
- *Framework.* The project manager should examine the quality of structural steel girders, if they are used for framing.
- *Plumbing.* The installation of plumbing must be carefully observed to ensure that specifications are being followed and everything is properly connected. Few things are worse than a "finished" building in which the sinks lack drains and the toilets do not flush.
- *Electrical.* Someone must check to ensure that electricians are following specifications for installing the electrical systems.
- *Exterior.* Contractors often try to install exterior finishes of poor quality, so the project manager should check to see that they are being installed as called for in the plans.
- *Interior materials.* The project manager must guarantee that interior finish materials adhere to specifications.

Preparing for Construction

At the beginning of the actual construction phase, the contractor usually moves a trailer or trailers to the construction site to serve as their base of operations. They also install temporary water, sewer and electrical connections. A construction fence is usually specified and installed. Many recent projects have had green cloth added to the fences to conceal the major construction activity.

The site usually has to be cleared before construction begins. Sometimes it even has to be leveled, excavated and/or filled in depending on the plans for the site and the extent of construction. Trees and other greenery have to be carefully removed and/or protected during the construction phase.

After the site has been freed of obstructions, areas may need to have drainage tiles installed. Drainage tile is pipe laid in gravel that drains subsurface water away from construction areas. Many locales require holding ponds to control excess water, because of the square footage occupied by the building and parking areas. Considerable dirt is moved and relocated during this process. Runoff must be protected with bales of hay or low cloth fences.

Soil and Foundations

A building's foundation is the structure on which it rests and by which it is supported. Almost without exception, foundation systems are constructed of concrete, but beyond this fact there is tremendous potential for variety. The forms and materials of building foundations vary according to ground conditions, structural material, structural type, and other factors. Engineers design the proper foundation for the weight and height of the building. Questions of soil settlement, soil modification, braced excavations, and slope stabilization also inform the particulars of foundation selection and design.

In most buildings, the foundation (or basement) wall does not have a significant role in carrying the structural loads from the structure above, but does resist the lateral load of the soil (and any water) that the basement is constructed in. In some building systems, the floor slab is designed to assist in carrying some of the lateral loads of the building, and the floor slab thereby becomes an integral part of the framing system.

Many building projects are delayed and face change orders because of poor soil. Most projects require soil samples at the time of design, but these problems can still arise when foundations are dug. Preventing settlement problems begins with the recognition that the soil a foundation rests on is part of the foundation system; it is an element of the building, just like the joists that hold up the structure. There are significant differences among soil types, and the contractor must understand the way soils respond to building loads and be able to identify potential problems.

Naturally, total settlement must be minimized, as it can lead, among other things, to problems with entrances and utility connections. That being said, a few things should be understood about settlement. First, all buildings settle. The amount may be so small as to be undetectable or may be so uniform as to leave no signs, but that it happens is unquestionable. Second, because of both natural and construction-related variations in soil properties, not every point on a foundation settles to the same extent.

To avoid door frames that are crooked, cracking walls, and other such problems, the uneven sinking of a building's foundations, must be prevented. The distinction between total and differential settlement is important. The Palace of Fine Arts in Mexico City, for instance, has settled several meters without significant distress to the structure and remains in service because the settlement has been uniform. The Leaning Tower of Pisa, on the other hand, is useless for anything but Kodak moments for tourists.

Construction Issues

After the foundations have been completed, the real construction begins and issues of direct concern to the library media specialist at last begin to arise. The following areas provide guidance for what should be happening during the next phases of the construction process.

Pipes, Drains and Under Floor Conduits

After the foundation is finished, then it is time to locate pipes, drains and conduits in the soil which will be under the floor. Usually contractors use high grade sand and pea gravel for fill under the floor. It is easier to lay all the pipes in new clean material than in whatever soil structure exists under the building. Many communities require this for all new structures.

PIPES

The underground water pipes and/or gas pipes are installed under the concrete slab. They need to be located in a stable soil environment for corrosion and other underground issues. The library media specialist's major concern is for the placement of access points, the plans will show where they are to be located to come to the top where sinks and toilets are to be located in the library media center. It is nearly impossible to relocate these pipes after the concrete is poured.

DRAINS

The drains are also installed under the concrete slab. They need to be located in a stable soil environment to help prevent deterioration. The library media specialist's major concern is for the placement of access points; the plans will show where they are to be located, to come to the tops of sinks and toilets in the library media center. It is nearly impossible to relocate drains after the concrete is poured.

UNDER FLOOR CONDUITS

Underground conduits are another component that must be installed under the concrete slab. The library media specialist's major concern is for the placement of access points; the plans will show where they are to be located to come to the top where the outlets are in the library media center. It is impossible to relocate these conduits after the concrete is poured.

Floor

After the foundations are completed and the underground water pipes, gas pipes, drains, and conduits are properly placed, then wire mesh is placed over them to provide reinforcement. This is inspected by the architect representative, contractor, school district representative, and local building inspector. At this point, the library media specialist is not really involved in the construction phase.

Building Structure

School buildings and library media centers are usually constructed using steel beams and girders for the framework, and cement blocks for the exterior and some interior walls. It is important to note here that the steel beams are inspected before they are shipped and inspected again after they have arrived at the building site. They must meet specifications or the local building inspector will not approve their use. The exterior walls are covered with brick and/or stucco. Sometimes metal is used for the exterior, but very infrequently in school buildings. There are few problems which have to be corrected during this phase of the construction, unless there is a change order.

Roof

Pitched roofs are currently in vogue in some areas. Many structures are finished with metal roofs underlayed with foam for sound and insulation control.

Some structures will require tile, slate or other types of shingles to go along with the final architectural effect. The library media specialist needs to be more heavily involved in the design of the roof at the time the building is being designed. It is important to eliminate as many valleys and hips as possible. Some may be necessary for the integrity of the architecture to fit in with the overall plan. Try to avoid flat roofs. They seem to develop leaks from unknown sources over the years.

Change Orders

Change orders (any change from the approved blueprints after construction has begun) are budget-breaking for projects and nerve-wracking for many school districts and their facility managers during construction. While they can happen at any time they most often arise after the roof is in place. They create headaches for every one involved in the construction process—officials, architects, and contractors. Design or construction alterations will cost both the school district (which pays for additional materials and labor) and general contractor (who loses money on the administrative costs required for every change).

In addition, changes can cause the general contractor to lose momentum in the project and delay on-time delivery of the job. What seems like a simple construction modification can become a very time- and cost-consuming event. Not only must new materials be acquired, but the construction flow must be disrupted to accommodate the developments.

For example, if the request for another window is made after drywalling has been completed, the entire scheduling of contractors goes awry. First, a carpenter must cut a hole into the drywall for the window. If conduit is in the way, an electrician must be called to move the conduit. The carpenter then reframes the window and a drywall contractor repatches and tapes the wall. This one window, in effect, becomes a separate, significant job within the job.

Rescheduling each subcontractor can also become a logistics nightmare. If each sub's timetable permits, the change can be made in about two days. But if the carpenter or drywaller is booked for a few days, this one change may delay the project for a week or more until work can be assigned.

It is important to keep change orders to a minimum. One of the sources consulted in the development of this chapter stated that it is important to ask for elevations—three-dimensional-type drawings of rooms, sometimes with a view of each of the walls in a room—as the project is developed. Blueprints and elevation drawings show each wall with windows, doors, and other architectural features, as well as shelving and other built-ins. Therefore there is an opportunity to visualize the resources and users in the various areas of the library media center. Close investigation of such plans as they are produced in the design phase can prevent costly and difficult modifications after construction has begun.

Even the most vigilant clients may, however, discover problems in the building once the roof is on and rooms begin to be finished. As the building takes form, it is possible to physically walk through the various areas, often bringing to light many theretofore unnoticed concerns.

Besides the obvious design problems such as a lack of windows, structural issues may include:

- An absence of electrical outlets and secure telecommunications outlets in the lobby or foyer area
- A lack of drains for workrooms and bathrooms
- An insufficient number of secure electrical outlets and telecommunications for the checkout desk
- Electrical outlets and secure telecommunications behind permanently installed shelving
- Misaligned doors or hinges that swing in the wrong direction

As wall and floor finishes are installed, be sure that someone looks them over carefully. It is important to ensure that the proper materials are being installed in the proper place. On this account, be sure to consult both the architectural plans and the appropriate sections of this book. Also carefully monitor color schemes and patterns of tile, marble and acoustical materials. Careful attention to aesthetic detail can create a wonderful and appealing finished product. Be sure that everything works in practice as well as in theory and be willing to talk to both the contractors and the architects about the possibility of change if something seems amiss.

Keeping in mind that change in this phase can be expensive and difficult, remember that making modifications while construction is still ongoing are more likely feasible than those made after the facility has opened. Any concerns that can be solved now will not have to be confronted further down the line.

Installation of Fixed Items

After the painting is finished and the tile and/or marble is installed, then it is time to install fixed items.

They are for example:

- Display cases
- Fixed shelving
- Cabinetry
- Murals
- Stained glass panels
- Clocks
- Security systems
- TV studio

The construction manager should be helpful in supervising these installations. The facility manager will also need to be heavily involved in the process. To finish all of the installations may take several weeks.

It is important to be aware of the types of cabinetry to be installed and the timetable for installation. Many times school library media centers are finished much later than the rest of the school, because these built-ins have not been ordered in a timely manner. Usually for a new school building the principal and library media specialist are hired a year or at least a semester before the opening of the school. If this is the case then the library media specialist can be involved in the building finishing process.

Entrance

Install tile and/or marble, then wall covering and ceiling fixtures and tiles. Complete installation of electrical and telecommunications outlets. Install display cases and kiosks, if they are planned for the entrance. The exterior and interior doors may be temporary until the final items are installed.

Bathrooms

Install tile, fixtures, mirrors, outlets, light fixtures, and ceiling tile. Paint the walls and install the doors.

Cabinetry

There is usually fixed cabinetry in the workroom, production laboratory, TV studio, storage areas, etc.

Fixed Shelving

Around the perimeter area of the main reading area, in the faculty planning area, workroom, and possibly in the staff offices; fixed shelving will need to be installed. Make sure that all electrical telecommunications outlets on the walls will need to be opened and available in the shelving area.

Sample Additional Areas of the Facility

These areas will probably have the most difficult installation problems, with several vendors involved.

TV Studio

The control room will need switchers, monitors, editors, etc. installed. The studio itself will need special grid lighting and connectors for cameras and sound, as well as special acoustical treatment on the walls and floor for sound control.

Multimedia Laboratories

Many library media centers will have a lab where a teacher will instruct classes in multimedia production. As schools recognize new curricular areas and, in particular, information literacy, there will be a need for differentiated teaching roles. There will be times when teachers will be able to teach 40 to 50 students, while other teachers will have 12 to 15 students. Many students will be able to work for long periods of time on their own. Generally they will have their own computers, which meet their eventual goals and needs. There will still be a need for sophisticated multimedia production laboratories. These students will want to work with "primary sources." Many times these primary sources will still be in print format, so they will need to be converted to 3D and digital-type presentation formats (or whatever replaces these formats).

To use our present concepts, to envision what will be needed in the future, we will describe what is needed currently to allow students to develop quality multimedia formats. Today we use PowerPoint as a vehicle for presenting research and other products to be shared with others. PowerPoint allows several modes of multimedia presentation.

EQUIPMENT NEEDED FOR MULTIMEDIA LABORATORY

Essential elements of multimedia laboratories are the specialized equipment and configurations of equipment and software for successful laboratory activities. Too often spaces are built, but little attention is paid to moveable and fixed furniture. The details for this issue were discussed in detail in previous chapters. Additionally, little attention is paid to selecting equipment that will meet the needs of users. It important to not order the equipment until the last minute before it can be supplied for installation. Refer to the appropriate sections in the planning documents to determine what technologies, software programs and so on should be acquired and how they should be obtained.

Punch List Procedures

After the construction is completed and the facility is ready for occupancy, it is time to complete the punch list. The list is designed to identify flaws in the final finishes, e.g. carpet installation, painting flaws, drywall finishing flaws, leaks, etc.

The building should not be occupied until the punch list items are corrected to the owner's satisfaction. The project manager takes the lead in preparing the punch list along with the planning team.

Each room and space should be carefully looked over. Walls, floors ceilings, doors, and windows should be surveyed for flaws; sinks and other plumbing aspects should be carefully examined and used; all lighting fixtures should be turned on; and electrical outlets should be tested. Other elements should be thoroughly examined on a case-by-case basis. This may be the final opportunity for immediate fixes to problems, so it is crucial that they all be discovered now.

10

How to Move Into and Open a New or Remodeled Library Media Center

When all of the building codes and any other procedures required by the proper authorities, punch list items have been corrected, and the fire marshal has approved occupancy, it is time to move in. All fixed furniture and cabinets should have already been installed, but any remaining elements may need to be put in place by the appropriate contractors. If the building itself is new, moveable furniture and resources will probably need to be transported to the facility, unboxed, and put in place. In many cases volunteers can be organized and coordinated to facilitate this process. Transportation of materials needs to be organized and implemented. Library media center managers need to develop plans and contingencies for the move. They also need to coordinate the volunteers and/or paid staff to implement the plan. Part of this will involve determining at which stage each element should be brought into the facility. Books, for example, should not arrive until shelving has been installed. Computer equipment in particular may need to be temporarily warehoused if it arrives earlier, and some technical items may need to installed by vendors. Resources will come from multiple sources and will need to be cross-checked to see if what has been ordered has been supplied.

Basic Steps of the Move

The following lists provide suggestions for how to move materials from an old facility to a new one. Obviously, the details of different projects will create different needs, so these guidelines should only be seen as general recommendations. They can be easily tailored or reformatted to fit your own project.

Significant Dates to be Considered

1. Date the books will be due from students
2. Date the books will be due from faculty and staff
3. Date to close to study hall students
4. Date to close to classes (latest possible date)
5. Teachers adjust the dates of term papers and projects
6. Date to move books
7. Date to move backroom materials (e.g., magazines, videos)
8. Date to move equipment
9. Date when students can again sign out materials
10. Date when staff can again sign out materials
11. Date when study hall can come to the new library
12. Date when classes can come to the new library
13. When to do fine and overdue lists so that all books can be retrieved before packing
14. When other librarians can select your unneeded furniture

Resources Needed

1. Boxes for moving books
2. Pallets for shipping and storage
3. Tape dispensers to seal boxes
4. People to assist in packing
5. An approximate sense of the staff time needed for moving activities
6. A list of which, if any, of the existing furniture is to be kept

Decisions to be Made for Equipment

1. Decide the storage area for TVs and other large equipment
2. Location, and frequency, of outlets, phone lines, power poles
3. Where will deliveries be sent (e.g., books, videos)
4. Do not place computers in any areas that adjoin large pieces of machinery (or large magnetic fields). Problem spots include boiler rooms, sump pumps, copy machines, and heating and air conditioning systems. As a rule of thumb, it is a good idea to keep sensitive equipment 10 feet from such machinery.
5. Books to pack last (to place on the top of the pile) for teachers to use when they return
6. Select colors for the different areas of the room

Resources Needed

- Band-aids
- Blueprints—construction
- Blueprints—electrical
- Boxes
- Cable numbers
- Cable ties
- Chart for shelving
- Computer paper

- Graph paper
- Hard hat
- Index cards
- Inventory lists
- Labeling tape
- Laptop computer
- Maps of new layout
- Maps of old layout
- Markers—permanent
- Outlet tester
- Paper, pens
- Poster paints
- Post-it notes
- Safety glasses
- Scissors
- Screwdrivers
- Small boxes
- Storage bags
- Tape dispenser
- Tape measure

Sample Notice to Teachers About the Move

Teachers wishing to sign out materials for the summer months or for classroom use in May and June need to sign out materials by Friday, May 10th. In order to prepare, pack and move the library materials for the summer the following schedule will be followed:

Monday, May 6th—All two-week books are due.

Friday, May 10th—Last day for classes and/or student use of the Media Center.

Monday, May 13th—All overnight books are due. NO books will circulate after this date to teachers, staff or students, as we will be boxing materials.

We have alerted the (Local) Public Library staff (both Young Adult and Adult) that we will be closing down and that students' usage of their resources may increase.

THANK YOU to all teachers who were so cooperative in planning and rescheduling research papers and assignments so that they could be completed before the move takes place.

Rental Options

- Pallets (skids)—wooden racks used to hold, stack, transport boxes
- Pallet jacks—manual-powered device to move pallets
- Forklift—machine-driven device used to load and stack boxes
- Shrinkwrap—used to keep boxes from shifting on pallets

Hints

- Prepare for the unexpected.
- Do not keep anything that is obsolete.
- Pack the bottom shelves first so that the top shelves can be unpacked first.
- Install computers before reshelving books.
- Have the boxes built the night before.
- Have a fine-free period the first two weeks that school reopens.
- Don't sign out large numbers of books.
- Read shelves prior to packing any books.
- Don't mix computer parts in the same box.
- Be careful when moving heavy boxes.
- Wear clothes that can get dirty during the move.

- Only stack boxes 4 or 5 high.
- Plan on at least two boxes per shelf.
- Host the grand opening reception.

What Should be Moved and Who Should do It?

If there is an existing collection of resources and equipment, a move can be a useful time to evaluate the relevance and usefulness of the library. The staff will need to plan several months in advance to weed (deselect or remove and discard) the collection of whatever is no longer worth keeping. It is important that the time need for such an evaluative proves be taken into account when scheduling the move.

After the layout of the collection has been determined, the next question is who will move the materials? There two obvious options: a moving company or the local staff and district employees. There are a number of moving companies that specialize in moving library media collections, and other moving companies that can be considered. Library media center staff, assisted by people hired for the move or by volunteers, may help with the move. No matter which option the school system selects, there a few general questions to be considered:

- Who will be included in the planning and execution of the move and what will be the role of each individual?
- How much time can be allowed for the move? What is the window of time to plan and execute the plan? How long will the move take, given the number of hours of labor required and physical issues? Can the length of the time for the move be shortened with the addition of hours of man labor or the foreremoval of specific physical issues? Could the move be lengthened? What are the advantages and disadvantages of each option in terms of cost, access, staff time commitments, and available resources, including labor?
- Will the library media center maintain user access to the collection during the move, and, if so, how?
- How will the staff present the move to the users and what opportunities does the move provide for public relations?
- How will issues concerning the handling of materials be addressed?

If a professional moving company is being used they may be able to answer some of these questions. It may also be helpful to speak with the managers of other libraries in your area that have recently gone through like moves.

Suggestions for Moving into a New Facility

Usually the shelving and furniture will be assembled by the contractor or subcontractor before the move into the facility. As always, there should be dialogue between these individuals and the person coordinating the final move of the resources. There are many possible snags in the final preparation for a move. The following questions should probably be considered:

- Who is really in charge of decision making for the move?
  Usually the principal and library media center manager coordinate the move. The principal usually assigns the final responsibility to the knowledge manager. In larger school districts, district level personnel are generally involved.
- What if the building is not finished on time?
  Many times school buildings, especially library media centers, are not completed in a timely manner. Able managers will make alternative plans. It might be possible, for example, with the principal and other officials in arranging for a school bus to transport students and teachers in a timely manner to the nearest public library branch and/or nearest school.
- What if the furniture and shelving is not installed in a timely manner?
  Resources can be displayed on tables (even folding tables if necessary). It probably won't be possible to display the whole collection, but a highly selected and relevant group of resources would help during the interim time. Computers and peripherals can also be arranged on folding table and folding chairs, until final furnishings are available.
- How will the materials and equipment be moved?
  For a new facility, the resources will usually be shipped by the suppliers to a warehouse in the school district. Many school districts request that the resources be fully processed, ready for the shelves. The electronic card catalog information is usually supplied on a disk. Computers and peripherals are also shipped to a school district warehouse.
  The resources are then shipped from the warehouse to the school. Shipping is usually by school district transportation, if there is a special unit for transporting goods.
- Who will shelve the resources?
  The local building staff members assisted by volunteers are most often used for this purpose.
- Who will assemble and connect the technology?
  The staff at the local building assisted by school district technology staff is typically sufficient. Unusually complex technology may have to be installed by the vendors or by qualified experts.

Planning for Moving Large Collections

The suggestions for this section are based on a large existing collection. The steps can be adjusted for smaller collections.

1. Gain an overview of the current and proposed configurations, and of the Library Administration's goals/plans for the shift. Information that should be determined:

- The Library Administration's goals for this move (timelines, whether you're hiring a moving company or professional library collection movers to move books, or using internal staff).
- Whether you are going to have volunteers working on the move.
- Whether the library will be open to the public during the move.
- Who in the library has final say on plans.
- Whether you are responsible for planning the moves of offices, public study areas, etc., or just the collections.
- If non-collection areas are being moved by a separate agency, who is responsible and how the two groups relate.
- Who is responsible for publicity about the move.
- When new shelving is supposed to arrive, at what phase in construction it should be assembled (will carpet be put in and ready for shelving?, etc.), and who is in charge of this process.
- When shelving goes into new space, or gets reorganized in old space, are there ceiling height limitations? Lighting or sprinkler-head concerns? (Your architects should have this under control, but you should be aware of soffits, fire marshal regulations, etc., especially for areas in a facility that may not have been significantly remodeled but which may be used in a different way than it was previously.)
- What ADA rules you need to know and abide by.
- Who in your organization knows about safety and body mechanics, etc. and can do training.
- Who in your organization knows about preservation and can give input on care of materials during shifting, whether collection needs to be cleaned or dusted, and so on.
- Whether materials are coming out of storage and going into the library stacks, or vice versa.
- The cost of supplies.

2. Set up the planning team, begin the To Do list (the master plan).
3. Measure current collection and count current shelves.
4. Count the number of new shelves being added to the collection.
5. Decide if growth space is to be distributed evenly throughout collection.
6. Calculate fill rate of shelves.
7. Do a paper shift.
8. Determine the maximum number of simultaneous moves you want (based on number of movers, number of book trucks, amount of time to complete shift).
9. Give Library Administration an overview of the phases of the move, etc., being sure to aim in the direction they want.
10. Explain the process to the library staff.
11. If library will be open during move, set plans and publicity.
12. Make maps of move areas and paths between them, if you find it necessary.
13. Prepare moving supplies.

14. Make a timeline.
15. Test-run a move: calculate travel time/move time (sections/hour).
16. Train movers if necessary.
17. Monitor moving/make end cards for ranges.
18. Fix the mistakes.
19. Move stacks, if necessary.
20. About halfway through, *remeasure remaining collection,* recount remaining shelves, and redo a paper shift based on new information.
21. Remedy fill rates.
22. As each mini-move gets close to being done, remeasure remaining collection/recount remaining shelves and adjust your fill rate. It's okay to leave some empty sections at the end of a mini-shift: it's not okay to have some left-over books. Start reducing (drastically, if necessary) your growth rate per shelf.
23. Finish moving.
24. Revise public information: maps, information screens, pamphlets, range markers, etc.
25. Provide closure for the moving participants.

Resources Consulted

Habich, Elizabeth Chamberlain. *Moving Library Collections: A Management Handbook.* Greenwood Press, 1998, 344 pages.

> The author planned and moved an academic library collection merging several branches into the new main library in the early 1990s. The book is arranged in logical sequences. Starting with planning the space for the collection, including charts and tables of specific details. The next section is planning the collection move, with detailed questions and answers. Followed by doing the move yourself, with specific logistics and how to do ideas. The book closes with special topics: pest management control issues, cleaning collections, and moving from disorganized conditions.
>
> The author and contributors are experts and the book is readable and factual. Even though the book is designed for large library settings, it is very useful for smaller libraries and knowledge centers. This is the most current resource and is a very useful book.

Chepesiuk, Ronald. "An anatomy of a move: the Clemson University Library special collections." *Wilson Library Bulletin,* Volume 65 (June 1991, pp. 32–35).

> The move of special collections from the main university library to the Strom Thurmond Institute on Government and Public Affairs was very unique. They faced acid being sprayed on the outside of the building when the move was supposed to begin. The schedule was tight and the vice president of the United States was to give the dedication address. The planning and final move is documented and will be useful for others.

Turnstall, Patricia. "Let's move: How to move your collections without hiring movers (and without spending a fortune!)." *The Unabashed Librarian.* no. 120 (2001) pp. 8–13.

An article describing a move where library staff members were used rather than movers. The author presents a plausible argument for this choice. Next the author describes the specific details of measuring shelves, tagging books, and planning for the move. This article provides a different perspective from the other sources and will help in broadening the users perspective.

IV

"Facilities Speak": Resources that Better Equip You to Work with Building Professionals

Resource A: Glossary of Architectural Styles and Terminology

NOTE: All this information was gleaned from various Web sites and online dictionaries. It was reworded where appropriate to make it more understandable for those unfamiliar with construction and design. If you need more details, just enter the terms in your favorite Web search engine.

Architectural Styles

It is important to be able to discuss with the architect the preferred style of architecture for your building. Following are descriptions of the major styles that might be used for your project.

Historical Building Styles

BEAUX-ARTS

Named after the École des Beaux-Arts in Paris, this style is a part of neoclassicism with several refinements: paired columns, nested forms (large motifs enclosing smaller ones), tall parapets or balustrades, and strong central features, including domes, projecting facades, and pavilions. The rich decoration may include cartouches, garlands, human statuary, and wreaths.

JACOBEAN

Architecture and decoration used during the time of James the First, of England; it includes the styles used in England during this period, a combination of late Gothic and Palladian types.

NEOCLASSICAL

Neoclassical, or "new" classical, architecture describes buildings inspired by the classical architecture of ancient Greece and Rome. A Neoclassical building is likely to have some or all of the following features:

- Symmetrical shape

- Tall columns that rise the full height of the building
- Triangular pediment
- Domed roof

The most common features of the style are colonnades and arches. The facades are nearly always brick or stone. The overall building design usually follows the pattern of the classical column: a pronounced base with a ceremonial entrance, a uniform shaft with little decoration, and a distinctive or pronounced top.

NEOGOTHIC

Neogothic architecture is an American branch of the Gothic Revival style that was imported from England in the 1830s. It is a broad term and includes both the Victorian Gothic and late Gothic styles. In theory, the style lasted until the Art Deco movement of the 1930s, but in practice architectural design based on classical forms continues to the present day.

RENAISSANCE REVIVAL

Renaissance Revival is a branch of neoclassicism influenced by the palaces, fortresses, and public buildings of the Italian Renaissance, such as the Palazzo Vecchio in Florence and various Venetian landmarks.

Most buildings in this style have brick facades. Common features include towers or turrets, pyramidal roofs, castellations, large indented cornices, and rows of arched windows.

ROMANESQUE

The late nineteenth- and early twentieth-century style of Romanesque is a revival of an early medieval style, which was in turn a revival of Roman architecture. This was one of the most popular forms of architecture in the United States during the 1880s, and, along with the Chicago School, it was the first style applied to tall buildings. Many courthouses and public buildings were built in Romanesque style, even in small rural towns.

Distinguishing features include turrets, rounded arches, hipped or pointed roofs, and very heavy rusticated stonework. Proportions in this style tend to run large, both in the overall building form and in the size of the details.

SPANISH REVIVAL

A revival of Spanish and Moorish architecture from the Renaissance and Baroque periods, this style was especially popular for resort hotels in places like Florida, California, and Hawaii. Northern variants on Spanish Revival featured more elaborate detail and colorful facades without the castlelike shapes of the resort complexes. The style was also extremely popular for movie houses.

Typical features of Spanish Revival are cupolas, turrets, rounded arcades, twisted columns, red clay barrel tile roofs, iron railings, curved balconies, twisted columns, colorful tilework, small obelisks and finials, and grand bursts of white baroque ornament—all intended for exotic effect.

Transitional Building Styles

ART DECO/ART MODERNE

Art Deco and Art Moderne are two ends of a continuum, forming a style with roots in the verticality of Gothic architecture but leaning toward the simplicity of Modernism. As its name implies, Art Deco uses more decoration while Art Moderne buildings tend to have smoother, streamlined shapes.

Both Deco and Moderne use setbacks to reduce building mass and to emphasize verticality. Unlike "Wedding Cake" buildings, their shapes recede from the street gracefully, not in tiers but in gentler, more carefully positioned steps. Limestone is the most common cladding material, with brick facades common in Art Deco.

ART NOUVEAU

Art Nouveau is a style with roots in the Arts & Crafts Movement of the late nineteenth century. It replaces traditional forms and lines with naturalistic ones, generally based on organic structures such as plants, bones, or crystal formations. Designs in this style are highly original and often unique, but a few common elements can be listed, including curving lines, elegant symmetries, and complex shapes.

The main centers for Art Nouveau's development were Paris, Brussels, and the Netherlands, with related branches of the style in Barcelona, Vienna (the Secessionist movement), and Berlin (German Expressionism). The style also took hold in various other locations, including Turkey and South America.

CHICAGO SCHOOL

The "Chicago School of Architecture" was a proto-Modernist style, which arose during the building boom after the Chicago Fire. The style is a major step in the direction of simplified Modern architecture, and although it incorporates many features of historical styles, ornament is subordinated to the overall structural scheme. The style encompasses the first skyscrapers, and in many Chicago School buildings, the facade depicts nothing more than the rectangular steel grid underneath.

Buildings in this style were built in various cities, mostly in the Midwest but even in New York. Its influence was very strong in industrial architecture, and many early factories and warehouses fall into this category of design.

WEDDING CAKE

"Wedding Cake" style refers to buildings with many distinct tiers, each set back from the one below, resulting in a shape like a wedding cake. The style is almost exclusive to New York City, thanks to a zoning code that forced buildings to reduce their shadows at street level, but occasional examples are found in other cities with dense business districts.

Wedding Cake buildings range across a spectrum of early-to-mid-twenthieth-century stylistic treatments, some with eclectic or Art Moderne facades and some Modern or International. The buildings can be grouped into one style because their setbacks are usually their most distinguishing feature.

Modern Styles

BRUTALISM

Although the word Brutalism comes from the French for rough concrete *(beton brut)*, a sense of brutality is also suggested by this style. Brutalist structures are heavy and unrefined, with coarsely molded surfaces, usually exposed concrete. Their highly sculptural shapes tend to be crude and blocky, often colliding with one another.

The line between Brutalism and ordinary Modernism is not always clear, since concrete buildings are so common and run the entire spectrum of modern styles. Designs that embrace the roughness of concrete or the heavy simplicity of its natural forms are considered Brutalist. Other materials, including brick and glass, can be used in Brutalism if they contribute to a blocklike effect similar to the strongly articulated concrete forms of early brutalism.

EARLY MODERNISM

This style represents the early stages of the Modern style, in which buildings often retain traces of the Art Moderne or Neoclassical styles. Buildings in this genre frequently have streamlined shapes or facades and are very often broken into distinct masses or wings, with courtyards or open corners.

Common features include limestone or brick facades, stone framing around entrances, smooth stone columns, and rounded building or window edges. Windows are frequently arranged in strong horizontal bands, or are punched into the facade at regular intervals.

FUTURISM

Futurism is a broad trend in Modern design which aspires to create architecture of an imagined future, normally thought to be at least ten years into the future. The beginnings of Futurism go back to the visionary drawings of Italian architect Antonio Sant'Elia, as well as the "Googie" architecture of 1950s California and subsequent Space Age trends.

Early features of Futurism included fins and ledges, bubble shapes and sweeping curves. The style has been reinterpreted by different generations of architects across several decades, but is usually marked by striking shapes, clean lines, and advanced materials.

INTERNATIONAL STYLE

International Style is the purest and most minimal form of Modernism. It originated in a number of movements from Germany and the Netherlands in the 1920s, especially the Bauhaus, but was also influenced by de Stijl and the German Werkbund. Its designs are generally simple prismatic shapes, with flat roofs and uniform arrangements of windows in bands or grids.

The most common materials in International Style buildings are glass, steel, aluminum, concrete, and sometimes brick infill. Plaster, travertine marble, and polished stone are common on the interiors.

MODERNISM

The most common building style worldwide, standard Modernism has evolved from utilitarian forms introduced in the nineteenth century. Modernist buildings are generally simple in design and lack any applied ornament. Their architecture is basically a modification of the International Style but is less strict in its geometry.

After about 1960, Modernism began to play more freely with shapes and structures, producing a wider variety of designs, including cylindrical buildings, sloping roofs, and unusual shapes. This trend runs parallel to Postmodernism, which rebelled against the strictness of Modernism by reviving historical tropes. However, during this period the aesthetic and economic advantages of simplicity kept Modernism alive in all parts of the world.

POSTMODERNISM

Postmodern architecture is a counter-reaction to the strict and almost universal Modernism of the mid-twenthieth century. It reintroduces elements from historical building styles, although usually without their high level of detail. Common features include columns, pyramids, arches, obelisks, unusual or attention-getting shapes and rooflines, and combinations of stone and glass on the facade.

Postmodernism styles range from conservative imitations of classical architecture to flamboyant and playfully outrageous designs. As the style became mainstream, many buildings with a Modern form assimilated Postmodern devices into small parts of their designs.

Architectural Terms

Architects have a language of their own, so the following list is provided to help with your understanding.

Acanthus Stylized leaf motif, one of the primary decorative elements of classical architecture. It began in Greece and was adopted by Romans and transmitted into the general Classical tradition.

A-Frame Roof shape with a very steep pitch, forming a gable or "A" shape.

Air space The space provided in exterior wall construction to prevent passage of moisture and allow the wall to dry out.

Align The faces of objects that are in line with each other, or when their centerlines lie on the same axis.

Aluminum siding Lightweight material that is often painted rather than left in its natural color.

Anchor bolt Bolt or threaded rod used to secure the sill to the foundation wall.

Angle iron Provides supporting lintels for openings in masonry wall construction.

Apron The horizontal member directly beneath the stool or inside sill of a window.

Arcade Series of arches supported by piers or columns.

Arcading Uninterrupted series of arcades.

Arch Curved structure used as a support over an open space, as in a doorway. It is a semicircular opening in a wall, or a freestanding structure and depends for its structural stability on the horizontal load that is threatening to push it apart. Also it is usually made from cut stone blocks forming interlocking wedges.

Area wall The retaining wall surrounding a basement window, which is below ground level.

Areaway The excavated area between the area wall and the basement window.

Ashlar masonry Masonry construction using a square stone.

Asphalt shingle Roofing material made of a brown or black tar like substance mixed with sand or gravel.

Awning window Window hinged along the top edge.

Axis (*pl.* axes) The centerline of openings or objects that align in a row along an imaginary line. A primary element in architectural composition, which helps to create a sense of symmetry both in plan and in the elevation of a building.

Axonometric Drawing technique devised to represent three dimensional objects on flat paper. Verticals are drawn to scale, but diagonal dimensions are distorted.

Balcony Platform projecting from an upper story and enclosed by a railing.

Baluster Any of the small posts that make up a railing as in a staircase; may be plain, turned, or pierced.

Balustrade The combination of railing held up by balusters.

Base molding The decorative wooden strip along the top edge of the baseboard.

Base shoe The wooden strip (usually quarter round) along the bottom face of the baseboard at the floor level.

Baseboard Finish trim where the floor and walls meet.

Batt Precut section of insulation designed to fit between studs.

Bay window Set of two or more windows that protrude out from the wall. The window is moved away from the wall to provide more light and wider views.

Beam Horizontal load-bearing element that forms a principal part of a structure, usually using timber, steel, or concrete.

Bearing partition Interior wall supporting weight from above.

Berm Level area separating ditch from bank.

Beveled Stone cut at angles for a more decorative display.

Black asphaltum Bituminous substance applied to the outside of foundation walls beneath the ground level to waterproof walls.

Board feet Unit of measurement based on volume: 144 cubic inches of wood equals one board foot.

Bottom rail The lower rail of the bottom sash of a double-hung window.

Box sill Type of sill employing a continuous header with the appearance being responsible for the name.

Bracket Small supporting piece of wood or stone, often formed of scrolls or other decorative shapes, designed to bear a projected weight, such as a window.

Breezeway Roofed area usually found between a portion of a building and the main building designed to provide shelter and outdoor summertime comfort.

Brick sill Common type of exterior window sill in brick walls with the bricks protruding past the wall line to allow water to fall directly to the ground.

Brick veneer Type of wall constructed with facing brick covering a backing wall of frame or masonry.

Bricks One of the oldest building materials, brick is based on a mix of clay with silt and sand pressed in molds and then burned in a kiln, which gives the characteristic slightly glazed finish.

Brief The formal written instructions prepared by a client for an architect, setting out the necessary requirements for a building in functional terms. They usually include the required accommodation, size of rooms, and relationship of one space to another.

Building code Set of laws drafted by the governing body of a borough, town, or city to control building construction "to promote the public health, safety and general welfare" of the people in that locality.

Building paper Black building paper used to cover roof boards and sheathing to help control moisture and wind infiltration.

Canopy Projection or hood over a door, window, niche, etc.

Cantilever Projecting elements, such as a beam or porch, supported at a single point or along a single line by a wall or column, stabilized by s counterbalancing downward force around the point of fulcrum.

Capital The elaboration at the top of a column, pillar, pier, or pilaster.

Casement window Window that opens by swinging inward or outward much like a door. Casement windows are usually vertical in shape but are often grouped in bands.

Casing The trim bordering the inside or outside of a window or door, commonly referred to as "inside" or "outside" casing.

Caulking Puttylike substance used to seal joints against the weather.

Cement blocks Mass-produced building blocks made from pouring concrete into a mold.

Cement plaster Mixture of sand and cement that is applied to the exterior foundation wall beneath ground level to aid in watering proofing.

Ceramic tile Any of a wide range of sturdy floor and wall tiles made from fired clay and set with grout. May be glazed or unglazed. Colors and finishes vary. May be used in doors or out.

Chair-rail molding Wooden molding placed along the lower part of the wall to prevent chairs, when pushed back, from damaging the wall. Also used as decoration.

Cladding The lightweight outer skin of a building that does not carry any weight or support the building, but does keep wind and rain out. A term used to describe the siding or materials covering the exterior of a building.

Clapboard Tapered horizontal boards used as siding, thickest on their bottom edge; each overlaps the one below. Also know as weatherboard or siding.

Clerestory The fenestrated part of a building that rises above the roofs of the other parts. Upper elements of a Romanesque or Gothic style, bringing light into the center of the building from side windows pierced through stone.

Clerestory window Window (usually narrow) placed in the upper walls of a room, usually at an angle, to provide extra light.

Colonnade Row of columns forming an element of an architectural composition, carrying either a flat-topped entablature or a row of arches.

Column Slender, upright structure, usually a supporting member in a building. Freestanding or self-supporting structural element carrying forces mainly in compression; either stone, steel, or brick, or more recently, concrete.

Common brick Brick used where strength in construction is required rather than a pleasing appearance.

Concrete Mixture of sand, cement and aggregate (stone or gravel) that may be reinforced with ferrous metals.

Concrete blocks Masonry blocks commonly used for foundation and backing walls.

Contractor The responsibility for actually building an architect's design rests with the contractor, who commits to a particular price for the work, usually in competition, employs the workforce, and contracts out such specialist work as may be necessary.

Coping Flat cover of stone or brick that protects the top of a wall.

Corner post Three 2 × 4s nailed together and erected at all exterior corners of a house providing adequate nailing space for plaster lath.

Course Continuous row of building materials, such as shingle brick or stone.

Crawl space The open space beneath the first floor in a basement-less building.

Crown molding Molding where the wall and ceiling meet; uppermost molding along furniture or cabinetry.

Cupola Small, dome-like structure, on top of a building to provide ventilation and decoration.

Cut stone Large stones cut individually, used for a foundation or wall of a house.

Eave The projecting lower edge of a roof.

Elevation An orthographic view of some vertical feature of a house (front, rear, side, interior elevation).

Excavate To dig out a volume of earth for a basement, footings or foundation.

Exterior wall An outside wall.

Facade One of the exterior faces (walls) of a building.

Face brick Finished, nondefective brick yielding good appearance and construction quality.

Fascia Horizontal band or board, often used to conceal the ends of rafters; the front of an object. Same as a face board.

Fenestration The stylistic arrangement of windows in a building.

Fieldstone A stone used in its natural shape.

Finish floor Finished walking surface.

Flashing Sheet metal fitted around chimneys, valleys, drip caps, etc., to seal out moisture.

Flat roof Pitchless roof type most favorable in dry climates.

Floor plan Orthographic section of an intended floor layout with the cutting plane passing through windows and doors.

Footer The concrete slab that supports all foundation walls.

Footing Type of stone edging on a masonry wall.

Foundation The base of a house providing stability and rigidness.

Foundation wall The masonry wall that rests on the footer.

Four-way switch Electrical switches connected between three-way switches in order to control a light from three or more stations.

Foyer Area just inside the main exterior door for the removal of wraps, overshoes, etc.

Frame Wood construction members of a building.

Framing plan Top view plan of the roof of floor level showing the layout of rafters, ridge, joist headers, trimmers, etc.

French drain Basement floor drain designed to allow water to seep into the ground rather than be carried away through pipes.

Frost line The under ground level that frost will reach during the coldest days in a given locality.

Gable Triangular area of an exterior wall formed by two sloping roofs.

Girder Strong, wooden member spanning foundation walls designed to support joist ends.

Glass block Window type formed by a compilation of small translucent cubes of glass.

Gutter Metal or plastic trough along the edge of a roof that collects water off the eave and carries it to the down spout.

Hanger Formed sheet steel device that anchor together floor framing members that meet at right angles.

Head Term applied to the construction that comprises the entire lintel of a door or window.

Header This term applies to several construction features; the top horizontal support of a rough opening; the support for joist-ends on the foundation walls sill; and the support for joist-ends in a floor or roof opening.

Heat loss The heat that is lost (in BTUs) through ceilings, roof, floors, and exterior walls of a house.

Heating systems Different heating methods for heating buildings: hot water, warm air, steam, electric, heat pump, geothermal, etc.

Hip rafter The rafter at the corner of a hip roof.

Hipped roof Roof with slopes on all four sides. The "hips" are the lines formed when the slopes meet at the corners.

I-beam Steel beam often used for floor support. Cross-section of beam resembles a capital I.

Insulation Material designed to control the passing of heat and/or sound.

Interior elevation Orthographic view of an inside wall.

Jack stud Stud adding to the support of roof rafters.

Jamb The vertical members of a window or door frame.

Joist Wood framing members, usually set 16'' apart on center, carefully chosen to support all "live" and "dead" loads.

Keystone The central, topmost stone of an arch.

Lath Mesh metal, plasterboard, or thin wooden strips used as a foundation for plaster or stucco.

Lattice Grille created by criscrossing or decoratively interlacing strips of material.

Leaded window Window decorated by artistic inserts of lead.

Leader Down spout.

Light Window glass.

Lintel Horizontal supporting crosspiece over an opening.

Live load The weight of people, things and materials that are not always present at the same place in a building.

Load-bearing partition Interior wall supporting weight from above.

Louver vent Opening fitted with a series of sloping slats arranged to admit light and air but shed rain.

Mansard Roof type with two slopes on each of the four sides, the lower slope being steeper than the other; capped off with a cupola, typically Victorian.

Masonry Stonework or brickwork.

Millwork Finished woodwork, cabinetry, carving, etc.

Modular planning Planning a home in multiples of four feet in order to reduce material waste and cut labor cost.

Molding Shaped decorative outlines on projecting cornices and members in wood and stone.

Mullion The vertical member separating adjacent windows.

Newel The terminating baluster at the lower end of a handrail.

Niche Recess in a wall to place various decorations.

Nosing The rounded fore-edge of a stair tread.

Outlet Passage connecting the gutter to the down spout.

Palladian Motif having three openings, the center one being arched and larger than the other two.

Palladian window Three part window featuring a large ached center and flanking rectangular sidelights.

Paneling The lining of a wall with a wainscot.

Parquet floor Wood flooring laid to form geometric patterns.

Partition The name given to an interior wall.

Pediment Low triangular gable above a cornice, topped by raking cornices and ornamented. Used over doors, windows, or porches. A Classical style.

Pendant Bulbous, knoblike ornament which hangs downward.

Picture window One single, large windowpane that does not open from either side.

Pier Vertical, noncircular masonry support, more massive than a column.

Pilaster Rectangular vertical member projecting only slightly from a wall, with a base and capital as will a column.

Pillar Similar to but more slender than a pier, also noncircular.

Pitch The rate at which a roof or other surface slopes.

Plaster Surface covering for walls and ceilings applied wet; dries to smooth, hard protective surface.

Plaster board Name applied to many commercial products on the market used as a backing for plaster.

Plate The 2 × 4 nailed along the top edge of all stud walls. A plate also is secured to the top of all solid brick or masonry walls.

Plot plan Top view of your finished house and landscape orientation.

Pocket door Door that slides open into cavities within walls, seeming to disappear when open.

Porch Open or enclosed gallery or room on the outside of a building.

Portico Large porch usually with a pediment roof supported by classical columns or pillars.

Prefabricated Structure whose substantial parts are made entirely or in sections away from the building site.

Public utilities Those utilities, including water supply, sewage, electricity, disposal, gas, telephone, cable, etc., that are available to the public.

Quoin Stone or block reinforcing or accenting the corners of a building.

Rafter Roof beam sloping from the ridge to the wall. In most buildings, rafters are visible from the attic.

Return Wooden member nailed between the rafter-end and the stringer for bed board support.

Rib band Board set into the inside face of the stud to support a second-floor joist.

Ridge The topmost portion of a roof from which roof sides fall away.

Ridge board Decorative board standing on edge, along the ridge of a roof.

Ridge rafter The wooden member supporting rafter-ends at the ridge of a roof.

Ridgepole The horizontal beam at the ridge of a roof, to which rafters are attached.

Rise The vertical distance from one stair tread to the next.

Riser The vertical portion of a step. The board covering the open space between stair treads.

Roof pitch Degree of roof slant stated in inches rise per foot.

Roof run The horizontal distance from the outside of a bearing wall plate to the center of the ridge rafter.

Roof span Equal to twice the roof run, or the horizontal distance between the outside faces of bearing wall plates.

Roof types Style and shape of roofs: gable, gambrel, hip, mansard, shed, flat, butterfly, saltbox.

Rough opening The frame wall opening to receive a door or window unit.

Rough sill The bottom rail of a window rough opening.

Rubble Masonry construction using stones of irregular shape and size.

Saddle Small ridged roof designed to carry water away from the back side of a chimney.

Sash Individual window unit (comprised of rails, stiles, lites, muntins) that fits inside the window frame.

Schematic Diagram of electrical symbols.

Scuttle Opening in the ceiling leading to an unfinished half-story.

Shaft Long, slender part of a pillar that adds support to an overhanging structure.

Sheathing Covering over the structural frame of a building, onto which the cladding is attached.

Shed Roof type with one high pitched plane covering the entire structure.

Shingles Wood, asphalt, or other material that is applied in small sections as an outside covering on roofs of exterior walls to convey the run off of water.

Shutter Movable cover for a window used for protection from weather and intruders.

Shutter dogs Small metal structures used to hold the shutters against the wall.

Sidelights Windows on either side of a door.

Siding The finished covering on the outside of nonmasonry walls of buildings: shingles, wood siding, aluminum siding, vinyl siding, stucco, etc.

Sill Horizontal piece forming the bottom frame of a window or door opening.

Site The section of town or general location in which your building lot is located.

Skylight Window in a roof to give light to a loft or room without other lighting.

Slate Roof material made from a hard, fine-grained rock that cleaves into thin, smooth layers.

Sleepers Joist set in concrete to provide nailing strips for flooring.

Sliding window Window that opens by sliding large panes from one side to the other.

Soffit The underside of a member such as a beam or arch, or of an eave, overhang, dropped ceiling, etc. (same as bed board).

Solar orientation The relationship of a room to the sun's light.

Spandrel The part of a porch facade that reflects the balustrade.

Spanish clay tile Roofing material made from clay soil into red brick; common to Mediterranean Revival buildings.

Specifications Document that takes up where drawn plans leave off. This includes quantity and quality of material and a general description of how the work should be done and what will be included.

Square Unit of measure equal to 100 square feet. Three square of shingles, for example, will cover 300 square feet of wall or roof area.

Stairwell The enclosure of a stairway.

Steel siding Heavy siding material which remains very durable and weather resistant.

Stile The vertical sides of a window sash.

Stool The inside windowsill.

Story Horizontal division of a building, from the floor to the ceiling above it.

String-course Similar to a belt-course but thinner; a horizontal band or molding marking architectural subdivisions, such as stories.

Stringer The board nailed to the exterior wall sheathing to support returns. The diagonal supporting members for treads and riser, also called horses.

Striking joints The act of forming the mortar at the joints of brick, stone, or tile construction for the purpose of decoration.

Stucco Mixture of cement, sand, lime, and water spread over metal screening or chicken wire or wooden lath on wooden walls to form the exterior covering of an exterior wall.

Stud Vertical wood support in a frame wall.

Sub-floor Floor beneath the finish floor designed to strengthen the bearing surface and prevent dust from passing through floors.

Symmetrical When two halves of an object are mirror images of each other.

Tail beam Joist supported by header at both ends, from a header in a floor opening to the sill header.

Terra cotta Mixture of sand and baked clay commonly used to make pipe for sewage disposal systems. A mixture of sand and baked clay used to form shingles used on certain styles of architecture.

Terrazzo A colorful flooring material made of cement and marble chips or certain stones. After the floor has hardened it is ground and polished to a smooth and durable finish.

Thermopane Two or more sheets of glass set apart from one another with a vacuumed space between to prevent condensation and reduce heat loss.

Thermostat Automatic device to control heating or cooling.

Three-way switch Electrical switches installed in pairs to allow a light or appliance to be controlled from two locations.

Threshold The wooden or metal strip directly beneath an exterior door. Some have an added rubber or plastic strip feature for better weatherstripping.

Throat cut The notch cut into rafters to allow proper seating on the plate.

Timber Large wooden boards used in creating the structure of a wall.

Tongue and groove Type of wooden siding with the edge of one board fitting into the groove of the next.

Top rail The upper rail of the top sash of a double hung window.

Traffic plan or **pattern** Plan of room and door placement designed for convenience of movement in normal everyday activities.

Transom Small window just above a door.

Trap Plumbing device preventing sewage odors from entering the building.

Tread The horizontal portion of a step, usually with a rounded edge, or "nosing" which overhangs the riser.

Trimmer Two joists or rafters spiked together and run parallel to joists or roof rafters to supply needed support to a floor, ceiling or roof opening.

Truss Framework for supporting a roof.

Valley Low region on a roof between gables.

Valley jacks Rafters that run from the ridge rafter to the valley rafter.

Valley rafter The rafter under the valley proper.

Veneer wall The covering of one wall construction by a second material to enhance wall beauty, such as brick or stone over frame or brick or stone over concrete block.

Vent stack Metal, plastic, or composite pipe (usually 4 inches in diameter) leading from the sewage network out through the roof to prevent pressures during sewage flow.

Vinyl Synthetic type of siding used for its economic value and durability.

V-type ridge cover Series of clay shingles used to cover the ridge pole on tile and slate roofs.

Wainscot Paneling applied to the lower portion of a wall.

Wall tie Galvanized iron strip used to tie a veneer wall to its backing wall.

Waste pipe The name generally applied to all household drainage pipes.

Water closet Commode or toilet.

Weatherstripping Strip of fabric, plastic, rubber, or metal found around exterior wall openings to reduce infiltration.

Well-opening Stair enclosure.

Window frame The window unit less sash.

Window types

- Double-hung—two sash, vertical sliding
- Casement—side-hinged
- Awning—top-hinged
- Hopper—bottom-hinged
- Oriel—windows that generally project from an upper story, supported by a bracket
- Picture window—fixed sash
- Horizontal sliding—two or more sashes designed to slide over one another
- Bay—extends beyond the exterior face of the wall
- Bow—projected window with a curved surface often in the glass itself
- Combination—the integration of two or more of the above into one unit

Yoke The top horizontal board of a window frame

Roofing

Roofing Terms

Base flashing Flashing that is attached to or on top of the decking to direct the water flow onto the roof base cover, usually roll-type.

Built-up roof Multilayers of asphalt and plywood sheets, usually on a flat roof surface.

Chalk line Using a string or cord coated with chalk to snap a straight line. Used for making sure all elements are straight and aligned.

Closed-cut valley Describes when shingles are laid over the valley to provide a continuous shingling. For most traditional valleys there is a continuous shingle-type material laid down the valley and the regular shingles are overlapped and cut to follow the valley.

Coating A layer of molasses-type of asphalt added to the top of the base felt (material that looks like paper impregnated with asphalt) into which heavy grains or other material that reflects light and provides protection from weathering is embedded.

Condensation When water adheres to materials, usually under shingles; it can cause problems, like early deterioration of roofing.

Counter flashing The flashing that is attached to wall surfaces and sealed to attach regular flashing to them.

Cricket Generally roofs slope toward a chimney and cause leaking. A sloping pitched roof is built behind the chimney to help the water run off more quickly.

Deck or Decking The generally plywood applied over the timbers supporting the roof.

Dormer The window with a roof over the framing that projects from the roof to provide lighting for the roof area of a story and a half type of structure.

Downspout Gutters provide collection of water from the roof before it falls to the ground. Gutters have to have an outlet to remove the water from the roof to the ground.

Drip edge Usually galvanized metal or aluminum that resists corrosion laid under the shingles along the edge of the roof.

Eaves The edge of a pitched roof that is horizontal to the ground.

Eaves flashing A layer of shingles laid around the edge of the roof to protect from water damage.

Ell Extension of a building at a right angle to the rest of the building.

Exposed nail method When roll roofing is used and nailed to the surface with special nails that have special weather-resistant material that seals the nail hole, but the nails themselves remain exposed.

Flashing Long pieces of metal or roll roofing used in the valleys to provide protection from moisture. Copper is the best and most long-lasting material. If galvanized is used, it must be 26 gauge.

Gable The sloping end of a roof when the roof does not have a hip. The end of the gable is usually covered with brick, wood, or vinyl, depending on the finished look is planned.

Gable roof A roof style with sloping planes of the same pitch on each side of the ridge. Has a gable at each end.

Gambrel roof A roof style with two sloping planes of different pitch on each side of the ridge. The lower plane has a steeper slope than the upper. Has a gable at each end.

Granules Colored crushed rock that is ceramic coated and applied to the exterior surface of asphalt roofing products.

Gutter A U-shaped continuous piece of aluminum, galvanized metal, or vinyl that runs along the eaves of a roof into a downspout.

Hip Instead of a gable at the end of the roof, there are two angles that run to each corner.

Hip roof A roof style with sloping planes of the same pitch on each side of the ridge and at either end of the roof. Does not have a gable at each end.

Low slope application A special way to install regular shingles on a low two- to four-foot slope.

Mansard roof A style of roof with two slopes at a normal angle and two slopes vertical or nearly vertical. The vertical or nearly vertical slopes are shingled. Contains no gables.

Normal slope application The most common way to install asphalt shingles on roof slopes between 4 inches and 21 inches per foot.

Open valley Flashing is installed first and then shingles are overlapped and a chalk line is drawn; the shingles are cut in a straight line.

Overhang The part of the roof that hangs over the wall. Usually two to three feet of covering to protect the walls from weather.

Pitch The degree of roof incline expressed as the ratio of the rise, in feet, to the span, in feet.

Rafter The support member, usually of wood or metal that supports the roof.

Rake The area from the eave to the edge of a roof that is sloped.

Ridge The top of the roof planes where they join.

Rise From the eaves line to the ridge, this is the vertical distance.

Run One half of the span that is the horizontal distance from the eaves to a place right under the ridge.

Shed roof A roof without hips or gables. It is one slope of 4 to 21 inches per foot.

Slope The incline of the roof reflected as the number of inches per feet as it rises.

Soffit The underside of the eaves that have been covered with wood or vinyl.

Span From eaves to eaves this is the horizontal space between them.

Square Determines the area of a roof that contains 100 square feet.

Step flashing A way to apply flashing where a sloping roof portion meets a vertical portion of the roof.

UL Underwriters Laboratories, Inc.

UL label A special label indicating the level of fire and/or wind protection of asphalt roofing.

Underlayment A tarpaper-like layer which is attached to a bare decking before shingles are installed to provide protection for the decking during the construction process.

Valley When two slopes of the roof meet at an internal angle to provide a way for water to run off.

Vent A way to provide an outlet for air, called ventilation. Usually it protrudes through the roof decking, as a stack or pipe. Sometimes it can be installed on the gable of the roof as a soffit.

Woven valley A way to lay the shingles over the valley area, where they are woven together. The shingles overlap alternate courses as they are laid.. They do not expose the valley flashing.

Types of Roofing

Materials designed for roofs face very difficult environments; they are exposed on a daily basis to wide ranges of temperatures. For instance, even in temperate climates roof temperatures can range from 120 degrees in summer to below freezing in the winter. There are several destructive elements at work: rain, ice, snow and harmful ultraviolet radiation.

Asphalt Shingles

These are the most widely used type of asphalt roofing, constructed by pressing mineral granules into one of two choices: an asphalt-saturated cellulose-fiber or a fiberglass mat. There are four basic types: (1) strip shingles, (2) laminated shingles, (3) interlocking shingles, and (4) oversize shingles.

Strip shingles are usually designed with three or four tabs on the lower half of the part of the shingle that is exposed to the weather and simulates slate or wood shingles. Some strip shingles do not have tabs. They are called no-cut-out shingles and don't look like wood or slate. Their advantage is complete double-layer coverage of the roof. High-quality strip shingles are typically rated to last for 15 years and are certified to stay in place when winds are up to 60 mph. The best strip shingles have 30-year warranties and wind resistance to 80 mph. Those made with a fiberglass mat are generally more fire-retardant than those made with cellulose-fiber mats.

Even top-of-the-line strip shingles do not simulate real wood or slate shingles, so manufacturers have designed an upgrade in recent years. They are called architectural or laminate shingles, and they are the current favorite among architects and builders. Laminated shingles use more than one layer of asphalt matting, with the top layer cut in various ways to achieve a three-dimensional appearance. Shading and multicolored granules add to the shingle-, slate- or shake-like effect. The extra thickness of laminated shingles also adds to their longevity. Warranties range from 30 years to lifetime and include wind protection up to as much as 110 mph with the top product lines.

Interlocking shingles are a good solution in high wind areas because they mechanically fasten to each other for greater wind resistance and are a good choice in hurricane-prone areas. Oversize shingles are generally rectangular or hexagonal in shape; they reduce installation costs because fewer are needed to cover a given area.

Shingles are rated or certified for fire, impact, and wind resistance. Class A shingles have the highest fire-resistance rating. Class C has the lowest. Class 4 shingles have the best impact resistance, a consideration if hail is a problem in your area. Ratings are printed on shingle packaging or you can visit manufacturers' Web sites. Shingles that have been certified as wind-resistant typically employ extra strips of self-sealing adhesive under the tabs and integral locking tabs to resist high winds. In addition, they often require six nails versus the usual four when fastening them to the roof deck, so installation of this type of shingle takes longer and costs more.

In a warm climate and high-humidity area, shingles that prohibit algae growth will be required, as this can cause discoloration and may damage your roof. These shingles are covered with zinc- or copper-coated ceramic granules.

WOOD SHINGLES

Wood and shake shingles come in a variety of sizes and styles. These require specific installation methods, such as skip sheathing (long boards, spaced several inches apart, that the shingles are nailed to), and are more difficult to install than asphalt shingles. Generally made from cedar, they look great—so much so that many other roofing products try to imitate them. The shingles have smooth surfaces and square edges, while the shakes are split instead of cut. This yields a rough surface and irregular edges. Wood roofs breathe (release water vapor), so attic ventilation is not quite the critical concern it is with nonbreathing asphalt materials. Wood shingles are long-lasting—up to 40 years—and are made from a renewable resource.

Unfortunately, wood roofing is expensive, typically three times the cost of a premium asphalt roof. It also requires periodic treatment with preservatives to keep the wood from drying out, warping, and cracking. Wood is more suscepti-ble to discoloration, mildew, fungus, rot, and wind-driven fire. Furthermore, the Clean Water Act prohibits the use of preservatives that were once used on wood roofs to prevent the growth of fungus, mold, and mildew. While there are new water-based products that show promise, typically sold in gray and cedar colors, their track record is too short to make a recommendation. Recently introduced pressure-treated cedar roofing may eventually be the answer to fungal decay problems.

FIBER-CEMENT SHINGLES

Fiber-cement roofing slates are made from Portland cement and aggregate. Fibers, once asbestos but now cellulose, are added for strength. Fiber-cement shingles look good—at first, anyway. While fiber-cement siding performs well, consumers have complained that fiber-cement roof slates deteriorate prema-turely, according to nationally recognized authoritative organizations making recommendations for building products. Also, they aren't cheap. A fiber-cement slate roof can easily cost three times that of a premium asphalt roof.

METAL ROOFING

Metal roofing, usually of steel or copper, is available in several forms. Verti-cally installed steel panels, joined together edge-to-edge onsite are called stand-ing-seam roofing. Also available are ribbed panels (about 3 feet wide and from 10 to 20 feet long) that have lapped joints on the ends. These products look good on some high-end contemporary buildings and are becoming popular on the steep roofs of areas prone to large snowfalls. Snow will slide off them easily, eliminating the task of shoveling snow from the roof. Steel roofing is prefinished in a variety of colors.

Metal roofs are low-maintenance, impact- and wind-resistant, and durable—with a life expectancy of 20 to 50 years, depending on the product. And, you won't have to tear off the old roof before installing it. The big negatives for a steel roof, especially a standing-seam metal roof, are its high cost and commercial or institutional look when installed on a traditional-style building. Depending upon the complexity of the roof, a standing-seam metal roof is between two and four times the cost of a premium asphalt roof.

Other metal roofing includes horizontally installed steel panels that are formed to look like shingles, shakes, or Mission-style tiles. They are prefinished with textured protective coatings. Shingles made from copper are nice for roofs that are prominently seen, such as those over bay windows, entryways, dormers, and gazebos. Copper shingles are not prefinished, and they weather naturally from new-penny-bright to a soft green patina.

Tile

Tile roofs should be considered if they fit into the architectural style of the area. Tile is a beautiful material that has proved itself over hundreds of years and is the preferred roofing product in many European countries.

Mission-style clay tiles have a half-round shape that is slightly tapered so that one course neatly fits under the next. Ceramic roof tiles are available in many colors and shapes, including slate- and shake-like products. Tiles cast from integrally colored concrete are a lower-cost alternative to clay and ceramic tiles.

Advantages of tile includes durability—expect 50 years or more of service—superior resistance to ultraviolet rays, wind, and fire; low maintenance; and easy repair, assuming some spare tiles have been stored. Disadvantages include breakage from impact (for example, from a fallen tree branch), heavy weight, and high initial price. A tile roof will cost between two and three times more than a premium asphalt roof—more if the tile is not available locally and must be shipped.

Slate

Slate is another good-looking roofing product, popular in regions where it's quarried, but less so otherwise due to shipping costs. Like tile, it is extremely durable and resistant to fire and wind damage, but it's even more expensive than tile.

Building Facade Materials

There are many alternatives for building facade materials. It is important to be aware of their advantages and disadvantages.

Metal

ALUMINUM

Aluminum is a lightweight silvery metal which is very common, constituting 7.3 percent of the earth's mass. Unlike many other metals, it requires advanced technology to extract in pure form, and was not even discovered as a distinct element until 1808 (by British scientist Humphrey Davy). In 1889, Karl Josef Bayer in Austria invented the Bayer Process to smelt aluminum from bauxite, which is today the most efficient means of producing the metal.

As a building material, aluminum offers several advantages. The metal does not corrode and therefore requires almost no maintenance. It is extremely light, and its reflective and insulating properties work together to conserve energy.

When the element was discovered, Davy proposed the name "alumium," but the longer "aluminium" was soon adopted as the standard. In 1925, the American Chemical Society dropped the last "i" from the word, and "aluminum" has since become the standard spelling.

BRONZE

Bronze has been used for centuries. Recently buildings have begun to use extruded bronze mullions (slender vertical members that form a division between units of a window, door, or screen, or are used decoratively) and bronze spandrels (the sometimes ornamented spaces between the right or left exterior curve of an arch and an enclosing right angle) as well as other bronze features.

COPPER

Exterior architectural copper panel systems are composed of dual-laminated copper panels with a polyethylene core. Copper is shiny when installed, but it soon weathers.

COR-TEN STEEL

Cor-Ten Steel is a type of steel which oxidizes naturally over time, giving it an orange-brown color and a rough texture. It has a very high tensile strength, and in spite of its rusted appearance it is actually more resistant to damaging corrosion than standard forms of carbon steel.

STAINLESS STEEL

One of the most durable materials used in architecture. However, stainless steel is not one material; there are many different types with different properties and, most important, different levels of corrosion resistance. If an appropriate stainless steel grade is selected and if it is properly maintained, its appearance will remain unchanged over its lifetime.

Glass

Glass is a transparent or translucent material made by melting sand into a homogeneous, moldable form. Almost all buildings use glass for windows, so a facade is only labeled as "glass" if the opaque parts of the surface (i.e., areas that are NOT windows) are also clad in glass.

Stone

NATURAL STONE

Ultra-Lite Stone Panels have proven performance in bond strength and flexural strength following acid freeze/thaw and UV radiation exposure, according to the experts who have studied them over the years. They have been successful on the exterior of buildings throughout the world. Ultra-Lite Stone is impervious to water penetration, even with open structured stones such as travertine. The fiber-reinforced epoxy skin, directly behind the stone, provides a waterproof barrier, eliminating the need for a secondary layer of protection. Ultra-Lite Stone Panels can be economically fabricated to form natural stone column covers, cornices, and other massive shapes. They offer the advantages of construction speed, durability, and cost-effectiveness for buildings.

GRANITE

Granite is an igneous type of rock formed when magma is cooled deep within the earth. It is extremely hard, and can be recognized by its speckled, grainy composition. The material comes in a wide variety of colors, and can be either rough or polished. This type of stone is extremely durable and highly resistant to stains, weathering, and corrosion. Granite is not as porous as other cladding stones, and thus is not affected by repeated cycles of freezing and thawing.

LIMESTONE

Limestone is a sedimentary rock derived from the fossil deposits of marine animals. Its mineral content includes calcites and dolomites. The material has a uniform consistency and texture, and it cannot be polished. Limestone is usually a buff yellow or off-white color, but it can also be gray or very light in appearance.

Limestone is generally less expensive than other cladding stones and gives a special appearance to a building. It is the most common material used in the Art Deco and Neogothic styles of architecture.

MARBLE

Marble is a metamorphic rock formed when limestone is transformed under extreme pressure. Pure marble is a white calcite crystal, but most marbles are enriched by impurities, which give it special colors and patterns. It is softer and more brittle than granite, but as a cladding stone it is considered a luxury material prized for its distinctive mottled look. It is usually polished but can also be used in rough form.

Other polished stones, including onyx, travertine and serpentine, are sometimes referred to as marble. Although scientifically incorrect, this classification is accepted for some commercial uses.

Quartz

Quartz-based stones vary widely in color because of different materials and clays contained within the stone. These stones can be found in varying hues of light gray, yellow, green, and red. (The dark, reddish-brown "brownstone" was widely used in building construction in the northeastern United States and Canada in the early 1900s.) They may be either sedimentary in formation (such as bluestones, brownstones, and sandstones) or metamorphic (as in quartzite that is formed in exceedingly hard layers). Most common uses: interior and exterior wall covering, interior and exterior paving.

Sandstone

Sandstone is a sedimentary rock typically formed at the sites of ancient beaches or sand deposits. The rock is composed of individual grains of sand (usually quartz) cemented together. Formation occurs under pressure when the grains dissolve partially and become cemented together by the liquid silica. Under higher heat or pressure the same minerals will eventually become quartzite.

Sandstone is softer than many other rocks, and easily carved. As a building facade it is valued for its textural properties and attractive natural colors. Common impurities such as iron, feldspar, hematite, and mica give it a variety of different colors, including, brown, red, and yellow.

Travertine

Travertine marble is a variety of limestone formed in pools by the slow precipitation of hot, mineral-rich spring water. The "holes" characteristic of travertine were created when carbon dioxide bubbles were trapped as the stone was being formed. [Although the classic travertines are recognizable by their homogenous light to dark color: dark reds to reddish with dark brown veining.]

Industrial Materials

Aggregate

Aggregate stone facades use manufactured sheets of joined rocks or pebbles. The composition of these panels can include any variety of stone types, or may be composed of a single stone type.

Brick

Bricks are small masonry units made of clay or shale, mixed with water and fired in a kiln. They are often coated with sand or lime, and are available in a wide range of colors.

Advantages of bricks include architectural flexibility, low maintenance, energy efficiency and durability. Individual bricks can be shaped according to specification and arranged in decorative patterns. In many buildings they provide the primary structural means of support, but bricks can also be applied as a curtain wall or supplementary finish to other materials.

CINDER BLOCK

Cinder blocks are masonry units made of concrete, often mixed with coal cinders. They are usually hollow with holes on two sides. Sometimes the holes are configured to form geometric patterns (e.g., pinwheels), and stacked with the holes facing outward. Cinder blocks are very often painted, unless used as a back or side facade material.

CONCRETE

Concrete is a manufactured substance with properties very similar to stone. Its ingredients include cement, gravel, lime, and water. As a facade material, it comes in two main forms: poured-in-place and precast. Frequently the structural concrete (which is reinforced with steel) is left exposed on the building's surface, though it is usually painted. Precast concrete panels are hung as a curtain wall over the structural frame.

STUCCO

Stucco is a thick plaster used for its insulating and textural properties. The material can be made in almost any color and can be applied as a smooth surface or in geometric or random patterns.

TERRA-COTTA

A kiln-dried clay product popular in the late nineteenth and early twentieth centuries, often employed as decorating details and features on historic buildings and structures. Careful assessment and handling of this material during preservation work is important, as it is difficult to replace.

Types of Foundations

There are many types of foundations, each with their specific advantages and some with advantages and disadvantages. Following is a discussion of the choices to help make a decision for a specific location.

Spread Foundations

Spread foundation systems are just as the words mean: The structural load is spread out over a broad area under the structure. They utilize one or more horizontal mats, or pads, to anchor the structure as a whole or to anchor individual columns or sections separately. Spread foundations are also known as "footing foundations" and are a type of foundation often utilized in low-rise structures.

Pile Foundations

Foundations consisting of vertical structural columns that are forced into the ground by impact, from a machine called a pile driver. Some early tall buildings utilized wood piles, but steel and concrete became more practical at the beginning of the twentieth century. Piles can be driven to bedrock or, more commonly, "to refusal"—that is, until underlying soil resists the pile being driven significantly further into the soil. These types of foundations are required in sandy areas.

Caisson Foundations

Caisson foundations are similar in form to pile foundations, but are installed using a different method. Caissons, also sometimes called "piers," are created by auguring a deep hole into the ground and then filling it with concrete. Steel reinforcement is sometimes utilized for a portion of the length of the caisson. Caissons are drilled either to bedrock (called "rock caissons") or deep into the underlying soil strata if a geotechnical engineer discovers the soil suitable to carry the load. When caissons rest on soil, they are generally "belled" at the bottom to spread the load over a wider area. Special drilling bits are used to remove the soil for this type of foundation.

Mat Foundations

Mat foundations, also known as "raft foundations," are a foundation system in which essentially the entire building is placed on a large continuous footing. Mat foundations found some use as early as the nineteenth century and have continued to be utilized to resolve special soil or design conditions. In locations where the soil is weak and the bedrock is extremely deep, "floating or compensated mat foundations" are sometimes utilized. For this type of foundation, the amount of soil removed and the resulting uplift (on the foundation) caused by groundwater, is equalized by the downward forces of the building and foundation. Yet another variation of the mat foundation is to use it in combination with caissons or piles to give it more stability.

Load-bearing Wall Foundations

Many building foundations, including most buildings that have basement levels, use slurry walls at the edges to keep out the surrounding earth. In very few cases, this slurry wall or another underground wall element becomes a major load-bearing part of a high-rise building's foundation. This foundation type is usually found in combination with one of the previously mentioned types.

Types of Framing Systems

Once the foundation is determined, then there are several choices to frame the building. Following are some of the most common.

Rigid Frame

Rigid framing is a structural framework in which all elements and the joints between can resist bending moments without deflection; examples are arched bridges and buildings with arches. Today they are usually poured concrete columns and cement floors.

Trussed Frame

Framing made of wood or metal, supported at two points with the least possible strain across the length of any part of the frame, called trusses. Those which are designed to be visible, as in open timber roofs, often contain framing not needed for construction, or are built with greater size than is required or are composed in unorthodox ways to emphasize style.

Shear Wall

Shear is a force of the wind that acts in the plane of a framing part and, ultimately, causes adjacent fibers to slip by each other. It is also one of the hardest forces to demonstrate. A number of materials can be used to resist shear wind forces. Their rated capacities to resist shear wind forces without failure are related to their general strength characteristics—in particular their ability to resist loads and return to their previous shape once those loads are removed. Following are examples of shear wall applications:

STUCCO

The stucco (cement plaster) wall is listed as a shear-resisting system. If properly installed over building paper and with embedded wire mesh, the allowable shear on these walls is 180 pounds per foot. Stucco has a dual purpose: It functions as a decorative finish (depending on texture) and it resists lateral loads.

LATH AND PLASTER

In many building codes there is a reference to a $\frac{3}{8}''$ lath nailed with plasterboard blued nails. In this system, a thinner, perforated gypboard is nailed to the walls; then the plaster finish is troweled over the board to create the finish. An older type of construction that used horizontal wood lath with a top coat of plaster should not be considered a shear wind-resisting system.

PLYWOOD

Before the acceptance of performance-rated panels, this was the sheet product of choice for constructing wood shear walls. The panel thickness, panel grade, nail type, and nail spacing could be combined in different ways to achieve a wall with the right design strength. With the advent of performance-rated products (like Oriented Strand Board), another variable was added: the strength of the panel. Manufacturers have the ability to adjust the proportion, size, and type of wood fibers and the amount of bonding material to suit particular job needs.

GYPSUM BOARD AND GYPSUM SHEATHING

Both types of materials are listed in the building code as shear wind-resisting materials, but their use is discouraged in earthquake regions of the country. Gypsum board and similar products lack the flexibility of other products. Yes, shear wind forces are resisted, but the result of repetitive cycles of alternate direction loading on gypsum board results in larger and larger nail holes.

STRAIGHT OR LAPPED SIDING

Provided each board and stud intersection is nailed with two nails, this system can resist lateral loads. Of all of the systems listed, it is the least efficient at its job because of the spacing of the fasteners.

FOAM CORE PANELS

A manufactured product in which solid structural foam takes the place of wood or metal studs between interior and exterior sheathing. In almost every way, a foam core panel may be treated as you would a wood shear wall as far as shear wind resistance is concerned.

BRICK, CLAY MASONRY, CONCRETE MASONRY, AND CONCRETE

All these materials can be used to create shear walls if assembled in the proper way. They are generally used where forces exceed those permitted for wood walls, where the construction type does not permit combustible materials, and/or where the height of the structure exceeds the limit set for wood, which are three (3) stories.

STEEL

Where force levels exceed those permitted for all other materials or where dimensional constraints limit the width of shear walls, steel plate shear walls are used.

SHEAR WALL PLUS FRAME

In areas susceptible to earthquakes and high winds, codes for shear wall design now require builders to use let-in bracing or costly plywood site-built assemblies. Two manufacturers are now helping to streamline construction of shear walls by providing premanufactured modular products that are cost-effective and easy to design, specify, install, and inspect.

Resource B: Sample Planning Document

Florida State University School Knowledge Center

Facilities Program

Prepared by:

FSUS Knowledge Center Building Committee

Physical Plant Department Facilities Planning Section

TABLE OF CONTENTS

IV. Building Committee Members

The persons listed below were appointed by the chairman of the Campus Development and Space Committee; to serve as the Building Committee for this project. This facilities program document represents the product of a comprehensive planning effort undertaken by this Committee, each member of which contributed the essential information required by the design professionals to conceptualize and develop the project. Every attempt has been made to include all of the information necessary to complete this project. In the event that questions develop during the design process concerning these requirements, the Building Committee shall advise on these matters.

It is expected that this Committee, working in conjunction with the University's assigned construction project administrator, shall monitor the development of the design and assist the design professional by explaining program requirements, refining design concepts, providing technical review of submittals, and assisting in furniture and equipment selection and procurement. The coordination and scheduling of all design activities relating to this project shall be the responsibility of the construction project manager assigned to this project working in conjunction with the Building Committee. All questions relating to Committee contact, design presentations and submittals, submittal dates, and similar events shall be coordinated with the construction project manager through these offices.

Ms. Donna Shrum
Library Media Specialist Building Committee Chair

Dr. Thomas Hart
Professor of Information Studies

Ms. Connie Lane
FSUS Technology Coordinator

Ms. Delores McCoy
FSUS Library Media Specialist

Ms. Adele Smith
FSUS Assistant Professor

Dr. Karen Singh
FSUS Professor

Mr. Homer Tedder
Parent

Dr. Walt Wager
Educational Research Professor

Ms. Robin Leach
Disabled Student Services

Mr. Vie Paramore
ACNS Engineer

Mr. Mark Bertolami
Physical Plant Department

V. Introduction

Description of Project History:

Florida State University School Library (FSUS) was built in 1954 and was constructed to support school program needs of that time. This facility no longer meets many of the educational needs of today's students. As cited in recent Southern Association of College and School's (SACS) Recommendations, the visiting committee stated that the school should "expand and remodel the media center and acquire current technology consistent with the mission of a laboratory school."

FSUS is a department of the Florida State University College of Education (COE) but is funded independently. Through reports of the COE Information Technology and Library Resources Committee (ITLRC), Faculty Council, and Teacher Education Advisory Council (TEAC), indications reflect that the COE as well as FSUS needs to reevaluate the use of its media and technology facilities and to establish long term goals.

In collaboration with the College of Education and the School of Information Studies, the Florida State University School developed a concept paper (see Exhibit 3 in the Appendix of this document) which describes the ideas behind the proposed new facility. The collection will include information for education as well as about education. Kindergarten through twelfth grade students will use the Knowledge Center as it supports their information needs; undergraduate and graduate college students will use the Center to observe, to work with younger students, to locate information for their own needs, and to plan with each other and with professionals in the Knowledge Center.

Upon the completion of this and future phases of construction, the Knowledge Center will combine the materials and staffs currently located in the Curriculum Resource and Learning Resource Centers of the College of Education, as well as some materials from the School of Library and Information studies. The Center will house advanced learning and information technologies that will not only offer high-tech methods to accomplish conventional goals, but will revolutionize teaching. Education professionals will be able to access vast libraries of data in a variety of formats to create truly individualized learning experiences for each student. It is expected that, when completed, this facility will serve as a local, state, and regional demonstration hub where advanced teaching and learning strategies can be observed and cutting-edge learning materials can be evaluated.

General Project Description:

It is planned that this facility will be built adjacent to the Florida State University School. The design professional shall assist the University and the Building Committee in determining the exact location for the building based upon a site analysis study that shall be conducted as part of this project. The Center will be designed to accommodate both present and future programs that will provide innovative learning opportunities and access to a multitude of information types for students ranging from kindergarten through postgraduate school. Within the program framework, learners will have the opportunity to research, observe, and participate actively in their own education. The Center will become a place where educational theory is developed, applied, examined, and reflected upon by research teams of professors, practicing educators, librarians, and college students.

Support for this program and the proposed facility shall be a collaborative effort, which will include the following:

a. staffing and supervision for facility use,
b. materials and technology needs assessment,
c. program development and implementation,
d. funding resources via partnerships, grants, etc., and
e. liaisons to promote interest in the facility throughout the community, the Florida DOE, the state of Florida, and beyond.

The mission of the College of Education is to prepare future teachers and to explore, through research, issues which impact education. The mission of FSUS is based on the philosophy that quality education thrives in an environment where the involvement of all members of the school family are valued and encouraged. Embodied in this philosophy is the recognition of the school's two-fold purpose: (1) to provide a quality education for K-12 students and (2) to serve as a model laboratory in developing and testing educational innovations which benefit public schools throughout the state. The core of the mission is to empower students to use their skills and knowledge to learn independently; to address academic, personal, career, and community problems (individually or in groups); and to make thoughtful decisions. This project shall provide a unique opportunity for the University, the University School and the College of Education to make a symbolic statement as to its heritage and ambitions.

Outline of Project Goals and Objectives:

The establishment of this state-of-the-art facility shall promote the implementation of the following goals and objectives:

Goals:

1. Establish a clearly defined relationship with the University and encourage more active involvement with various colleges, schools and departments.
2. Improve articulation both internally (K-12 faculty and staff) and externally (FSU, DOE, other public schools) in the areas of curriculum development, teaching strategies and practices, and research investigations and dissemination.

Objectives:

a. To serve as a teacher education center where in-service and pre-service teachers may observe exemplary instructional practices.
b. To serve as a model site for exploring and refining innovative teaching techniques.
c. To provide a setting where faculty and graduate students can design, demonstrate, and analyze the effectiveness of new instructional materials and innovative educational technology.
d. To provide an environment for the systematic evaluation of materials and techniques which are adaptable to other public schools in Florida.
e. To serve as a vehicle for the dissemination of research findings which have proved effective.

Outline of Desired Design Objectives:

The design objectives outlined below will provide adequate spaces within the facility to meet the specified project goals and objectives:
a. To provide information resources for students, ranging from kindergarten through post-graduate, as well as faculty.

   b. To provide adequate space for literature review, research, teacher education training, ITV and multimedia productions, distance learning, graphic productions, conferencing, professional development, and technical processing.

   c. To provide delivery systems which will facilitate access to information from a wide variety of sources and from varying mediums, e.g., video, global electronic communications via the Internet systems, satellite transmissions, and the like.

   d. To provide access from classrooms at FSUS and the College of Education to the networked resources in the Center.

   e. To provide a secure environment for the Center's collection, the users of the facility, and the facility itself.

   f. To accommodate the potential for future expansion of the facility.

Design Professional's Scope of Work:

The design professional shall be responsible for providing all architectural and engineering services required for this project. All additional consulting services shall also be provided by the design professional on an as-needed basis. The following is a brief description of the anticipated scope of services. More information regarding these services can be found in the Program Area section of this document.

1. *Program Review:*

The design professional shall be responsible for reviewing this facilities program document and becoming thoroughly familiar with the program requirements. Following the review of this program, the design professional shall meet with the Physical Plant Department's construction project manager and the Building Committee to discuss any questions concerning the scope of work.

2. *Architectural Design:*

The design professional shall be responsible for the preparation of all phases of architectural design, commencing with site analysis/selection and schematic design and continuing through the development and submittal of completed construction bid documents. More information regarding the site selection phase is provided in the Program Area section of this document. At the time of this programming effort, it does not appear that any extraordinary architectural consulting services are required in order to complete this project; however, the design professional shall be responsible for providing any such architectural services should they become necessary. It is expected that the design professional shall have demonstrated adequate experience in the design and construction of this type of facility.

3. *Engineering Design:*

The design professional shall be responsible for the preparation of all phases of engineering design, commencing with schematic design and continuing through the development and submittal of completed construction bid documents. In general, engineering design shall include all civil, structural, mechanical, electrical, telecommunications, and plumbing disciplines necessary to complete the project.

4. *Bidding and Construction Administration:*

The design professional shall be responsible for assisting the University with the advertisement and opening of all bid documents. The design professional shall provide all required construction administration and inspection services in accordance with State

University System (SUS) and FSU requirements. The following list provides more detail on these administrative services:

   a. Assist in the opening and evaluation of bids and provide recommendations of award to the BOR/University.

   b. Provide contract administrative services.

   c. Provide inspection of work in progress to the extent that the design professional can certify to the BOR/University that the work is being accomplished in strict compliance with the contract documents.

   d. Provide for the inspection of completed work and certify without qualification to the University that the work has been completed in accordance with the contract documents.

   e. Recommend an acceptable construction schedule based upon the milestones outlined in this program; scheduling of work so as to minimize the impact of related construction noises, disruptions, and inconveniences to the students, faculty and staff of the Florida State University School. Work schedules shall be closely developed and coordinated with the Building Committee and the Physical Plant Department.

5. *Cost Control:*

During the design of this project, it is essential that the Building Committee and the Board of Regents Office of Capital Programs (BOR OCP) be kept informed as to estimates of probable construction costs. Accordingly, the design professional shall provide at each submittal an estimate of construction costs.

If, during any phase of this project, it becomes evident that the construction cost exceeds available budget, then the design professional shall work with the Building Committee and BOR/University staff to resolve all cost over-runs. The design professional is encouraged to provide recommendations for reasonable cost savings whenever possible.

The ultimate programmatic requirements for this project more than likely exceed the available project budget. As will be demonstrated in the Program Area section of this document, the Building Committee has attempted to outline a probable phasing schedule for this project. Accordingly, the design professional shall examine this schedule and investigate the possibility of developing a series of add alternates which may be appropriate to maximize the effectiveness of the available funding. Therefore, it is expected that the design professional shall consider the development of add alternates during early stages of the design phase. All add alternates must be approved by both the Building Committee and the BOR/University prior to the advertisement of bids.

6. *Governmental Interaction:*

As required, the design professional shall be responsible for assisting the University in meeting the requirements of all applicable state statutes and local ordinances which deal with construction activity and/or property development. This legislation includes, but is not limited to, the BOR (FSU) / City of Tallahassee Development Agreement, state and local growth management statutes, City of Tallahassee and Leon County environmental, site plan, concurrency/consistency, and zoning reviews, possible environmental review by the Florida Departmental of Environmental Protection (FDEP), and possible environmental review by local water management districts.

Prior to the commencement of the design phase, the design professional shall consult with the Physical Plant Department to discuss this item in greater detail. Regardless of governing jurisdiction, it is expected that the design professional shall be capable of providing the necessary assistance to meet all legislative requirements.

VI. Academic Plan

1. *Give the date and program numbers of all relevant academic program reviews. Explain how the proposed facilities program meets the recommendations of the last academic program review.*

The most recent academic program review was conducted by the SACS Committee for FSUS (excerpts from the SACS report are presented in Exhibit 5 in the Appendix of this document). The review team cited several weaknesses in the present school library media center facilities and program. Specifically these deficiencies are identified in Item 1 of Section V "Space Needs Assessment" of this document. As such, it shall be the charge of the design professional to provide a design solution to solve the problems and deficiencies stated therein.

2. *List the recommendations of the review consultant.*

The following is a list of the recommendations contained in the SACS report:
   1. Space allocated to the Library Media Center should be increased either through a new facility or through remodeling of the existing facility.
   2. Increase funding for ongoing collection development and acquisition, replacement of audiovisual equipment, and the purchase of periodicals and non-print media is needed.
   3. Additional non-professional clerical and technical help should be employed.

3. *Explain how the proposed facility meets the recommendations or justify any variation.*

It is expected that the construction of a new facility will assist the Florida State University School in addressing the majority of the issues outlined in the SACS report. This new facility will represent a significant improvement in the size and quality of the learning environment assigned to this School's library. Issues such as spatial flexibility, lack of materials storage space, unsuitable furnishings and equipment, and appropriate types of space/functions will be addressed in this project.

As a multi-phased project, the construction of a new Knowledge Center represents a long term commitment on the part of the Florida State University School to address not only the School's spatial needs but also its academic programs.

4. *If the proposed facility is not part of an approved academic plan, provide information to explain the need and justify the establishment of new academic programs.*

The Florida State University School is part of an approved academic plan for the University's College of Education, in addition, this project is closely aligned with the recommendations of the most recent DOE Educational Plant Survey and the SACS report. Therefore, this item is not considered relevant.

VII. Space Needs Assessment

1. *Describe the facilities problem in terms of current and future facility deficiencies: describe the proposed solution and what alternative solutions were considered.*

The relevant academic program review was conducted by the SACS Committee for FSUS. The review team cited the following weaknesses in the school library media center facilities and programs:

1. The existing facility is poorly designed and lacks flexibility.
2. The existing facility does not provide adequate space for students or for the utilization of equipment by individuals and groups.
3. There is a lack of production facilities as well as storage and shelf space for materials.
4. There is no suitable shelving and furniture for elementary students.
5. There is an insufficient number of non-professional staff to perform clerical and technical tasks.
6. The inadequate facility severely limits the library media center program.
7. The total collection lacks the breadth, depth, timeliness, and range of formats to meet the needs of the school's program.
8. Funding for rebuilding and maintaining the collection is inadequate.

Construction of the new Knowledge Center will rectify most of the problems outlined above. This new facility will result in a significant improvement in the size and quality of the learning environment assigned to this School's library. Additional issues such as spatial flexibility, lack of materials storage space, unsuitable furnishings and equipment, and appropriate types of space/functions will be addressed in this project.

In addition to the SACS report, the Department of Education Educational Plant Survey recommended the construction of new media center facilities. An excerpt of the plant survey presented as Exhibit 4 in the Appendix of this document.

As a multi-phased project the Knowledge center shall be planned such that the infrastructure can support approximately 10,000 nsf of future growth. This future growth component represents the relocation of the Curriculum Resource Center and the Learning Resource Center presently located at the College of Education to the Knowledge Center. The construction of a new Knowledge Center represents a long term commitment on the part of the Florida State University School to address not only the School's spatial needs but also its academic programs.

2. *If a new facility is proposed, provide reasons why other alternatives were not chosen and why a new facility is the best solution.*

A number of other avenues have been explored to ease both the physical and programmatic burdens present in the existing Media Center, including the following:

- *Increasing facility operating hours for student accessibility.*
  The current center already operates at maximum accessible hours for students, faculty/ and COE users. Existing resources do not allow for extending these hours any further.
- *Renovation or reclamation of existing space.*
  All existing space in the School is adequately utilized for other diverse educational activities and needs. Simply stated, there is no other space available within the facility to convert into a Knowledge Center.
- Consideration was also given to locating the Knowledge Center within the existing Center as a "second floor" addition. This alternative was deemed to be an inordinately expensive solution which would not render adequate usable space. A second floor solution would also require extended disruption of services during most of the construction time.

3. *Provide quantitative analysis indicating how the proposed amounts and types of space were arrived at using requirements of programs to be housed.*

The general facility requirements for this project are based primarily on the recommendations developed as a result of the Department of Education Educational Plant

Survey. The Space Summary provided in the Program Area section of this document documents both the Plant survey results and the programmatic requirements as determined by the Building Committee. Variations from the Plant Survey are due the unique programmatic and technological requirements and the diversity of the user group present in a laboratory school. The specific space sizes programmed for the proposed facility were determined by overlaying the requirements of Chapter 6A-2, F.A.C.

The space requirements outlined in this program are based upon reasonable architectural assumptions. It shall be the responsibility of the design professional to review and become thoroughly familiar with the space needs listed in this document during the preliminary design phase of this project and validate that these space provisions satisfy the school's needs.

VIII. Analysis of Impact on Master Plan

Upon its completion the Florida State University Campus Master Plan did not envision a specific project dedicated to the construction of a Knowledge Center at the Florida State University School. Since that time, however, the needs of both the University and the Florida State University School have evolved to the point where the need for this facility is strongly evident.

Though the project is not contained in the existing Campus Master Plan, it is contemplated in the current project to update the master plan. Specifically, the University's master planning consultants have been apprised of this project's current programming and planning activities and have been instructed to include it in the update.

It is expected that prior to the submittal of the campus master plan update, the design professional shall have completed the site analysis phase for the Knowledge Center. This information will be transmitted to the master planning consultants for inclusion in the campus master plan update. Additionally, it is not envisioned that the construction of the Knowledge Center will create any significant master planning issues. Although the available area is limited, it has been determined that there is sufficient open space for the construction of this facility on the School's campus. It is also expected that adequate utility capacity is available for this project.

IX. Site Analysis

The Florida State University School is located in the northwest corner of the main campus of Florida State University. Its campus lies on approximately 20 acres of land at the southeast corner of the intersection of Call Street and Stadium Drive. The School is comprised of a complex of educational, administrative, and recreational facilities.

As described earlier, this project anticipates the design professional's participation in the final determination of a project site. The Program Area section describes the location of two potential sites. Therefore, in the absence of a final site, the Site Analysis information outlined below depicts general conditions of the entire FSUS campus and is not site specific. The design professional shall have access to all existing documentation concerning the physical characteristics of this portion of the campus for reference.

A. Site Topography and Soil Conditions

In general, the topography of the University School site slopes from an elevation of approximately 85 feet above mean sea level (AMSL) at Call Street to approximately 65 feet AMSL at the open conveyance ditch along the southern boundary of the site.

According to the *Florida State University State Lands Management Plan* and the *U.S. Department of Agriculture Soil Survey Adas of Leon County*, the project site contains only one prominent soil type, "36—Orangeburg Urban Land 2–5% slope." The *Atlas* describes this soil series as consisting of well drained, moderately permeable soils, formed in loamy and clayey deposits, located primarily on rolling uplands with a water table below 72'.

At the time of this programming effort there has been no sub-surface soil testing performed in conjunction with this project. The design professional shall be responsible for the required testing of soil conditions and verification of site topography.

B. *Site Water Table, Flood Hazard and Storm Water Drainage Requirements*

According to the Federal Emergency Management Agency (FEMA) Flood Zone/Maps, the site is not designated as an area of significant flooding. It is expected that this project shall provide all required stormwater improvements since it involves the creation of additional impermeable surface area. These improvements may include the relocation of components of the existing stormwater system, the creation of a stormwater detention area, and/or connection to the Center's existing stormwater system. It is expected that the design professional shall make recommendations for any necessary stormwater system improvements which may be necessary as a result of this project.

C. *Vehicular and Pedestrian Circulation*

As mentioned previously, the Florida State University School is located at the intersection of Call Street and Stadium Drive, a busy, poorly designed "T" intersection. Murphree Street and Bryan Street, located immediately north of the School also serve as local streets and means of access to both the School and the rest of the University.

Vehicular access to the School is provided at three access points; two of which are small parking areas and access drives off Stadium Drive, the third an entrance drive at the front (north side) of the School.

Call Street and to a lesser extent Stadium Drive serve as major pedestrian and bicycle paths for University students to access the main campus. The Call Street corridor as it runs through the main campus is the primary pedestrian/bicycle route from the west and there is every expectation that, as the University grows, this corridor will be even more heavily used.

Expectations are high that the Knowledge Center will be heavily utilized not only by the students and faculty of the Florida State University School but also by those in the College of Education as well as other off-campus user groups. It should also be noted that the hours of operation of this facility will differ from that of the normal operation of the balance of the school facility, thus presenting unique design requirements to insure the ultimate safety of the users and the facility itself.

It is of paramount importance that the users and staff of the Center be provided a means of access to the facility that is safe and secure at all times. Critical to this issue is the need to keep students, especially those of grade-school age, from having to cross vehicular paths or other potentially hazardous obstacles to reach the Center. However, safe and secure access for both vehicular and bicycle parking is required during all hours of operation. Of course, all access must also accommodate mobility-impaired persons.

The design professional shall be responsible for assisting the University in maintaining the integrity of all pedestrian and vehicular circulation routes around the project site during the construction process.

Finally, the design professional shall be aware that the City of Tallahassee is in the process of designing a series of improvements which will correct existing problems at the Call Street/Stadium Drive intersection. These improvements will include a realignment of Stadium Drive with Bryan Street. During the site selection phase of this project, the design professional shall investigate the progress of these road improvements to determine potential impacts on the siting of the Knowledge Center. Additionally, the design professional shall consult with the Facilities Planning Section of the Physical Plant Department to determine the long range transportation strategies that are being incorporated into the University's Campus Master Plan Update.

D. *Site Vegetation*

To assist in the design of this project, the design professional shall be provided with information contained in the University's tree survey, which documents tree location, size and species. This survey will be made available to the design professional for consideration during the design process.

The design professional shall consult with the Grounds Department in the Physical Plant Department on all matters relating to landscaping and existing vegetation.

It is imperative that, during the construction phase, construction activity shall have no negative impacts on existing vegetation. Accordingly, the design professional shall recommend sites for construction staging areas as well as incorporate landscaping protection features in the construction documents where necessary.

E. *Archaeological History*

The *Florida State University State Lands Management Plan* indicates that there are no archaeological sites in the vicinity of the project site.

Per the BOR's "Professional Services Guide," the design professional shall be responsible for petitioning, on behalf of the University, the Florida Department of State, Division of Historical Resources for an assessment of the proposed site to verify this determination of historical or cultural resources.

F. *Location of Existing Utilities and Proximity of Utilities to the Project Site*

The most recent utility survey plans for the main campus shall be made available to the design professional and his consultants. The design professional shall be responsible for examining the condition and capacity of the various utility systems, which will be required of this project as well as for making recommendations for all necessary improvements. The University does not maintain an inventory of City-maintained utilities, which serve the campus. The design professional shall be responsible for acquiring all such information.

Additionally, the design professional shall consult BR-276, "Design for Utility Improvements, the Florida State University" to insure that all utility improvements, especially those which might impact central utility systems, are consistent with the requirements of this project.

The following is an overview of existing utility service provided to the project site:

Chilled Water:

It is expected that the proposed facility's chilled water needs shall be served by the soon to be completed Satellite Utilities Plant located immediately east of the Florida State University School. The School is presently served by two 6" lines located along the eastern-most boundary of the school site. The design professional shall be expected to examine the condition and capacity of the existing chilled water distribution system and make recommendations as to the optimum means of serving the new facility as well as any other production/distribution improvements that may be necessary.

Steam:

The School is presently served by a 4" supply and a 2" return steam line running in a route from the west side of Salley Hall (Building 46) to the eastern end of the northernmost classroom wing (Building 123).

The design professional shall be expected to examine the condition and capacity of the existing steam distribution system and make recommendations as to the optimum means of serving the proposed Knowledge Center as well as any other production / distribution improvements that may be necessary.

Electric:

Primary electric service is provided to the site via an underground route from Manhole W40 located in front of Salley Hall from which a 2W4F line runs southwest to Manhole W62 located at the east end of the middle classroom wing (Building 125).

The design professional shall be expected to examine the condition and capacity of the existing electric distribution system and make recommendations as to the optimum means of serving the new facility as well as any other production / distribution improvements that may be necessary.

Sanitary Sewer:

Existing sanitary sewer service is provided for the School via a 6" force main connecting a lift station located at the east end of the courtyard between the center and southernmost classroom wings (Buildings 125 and 127) to the 12" main line located beneath Call Street.

The design professional shall be expected to examine the condition and capacity of the existing sanitary sewer system and make recommendations as to the optimum means of serving the new facility as well as any other production / distribution improvements that may be necessary.

Storm Sewer:

In general the topography of the University School site slopes from an elevation of approximately 85 feet above mean sea level (AMSL) at Call Street to approximately 65 feet AMSL at the open conveyance ditch along the southern boundary of the site. The on-site structured conveyance system collects and transfers the majority of stormwater to the eastern boundary of the site, then turns in a southerly direction until it reaches the conveyance ditch. The conveyance of stormwater for the western edge of the School site, including the retention area located at the northwest corner of the School's campus, is to the southwest, passing under Stadium Drive and into the open conveyance ditch that parallels Stadium Drive. This conveyance ditch then turns to the east, crosses underneath Stadium Drive, and runs parallel to the School's southern boundary.

The design professional shall be expected to examine the condition and capacity of the existing stormwater distribution system and make recommendations as to the optimum means of serving the new facility as well as any other production / distribution improvements that may be necessary. The design professional shall also take into account the previously mentioned Call Street/Stadium Drive intersection improvements currently under design by the City of Tallahassee to determine any potential impacts on stormwater conveyance in this area of the main campus and, more importantly, on the proposed Knowledge Center.

Telecommunications:

The nature of a facility like the proposed Knowledge Center generates an extensive programmatic need for a variety of telecommunications systems, including especially voice and data transmission. The design professional shall be responsible for identifying and providing for all the required systems described in the Program Area section of this document and connecting these components to the existing distribution systems that serve the School. The design professional shall consult with the University's Office of Telecommunications and Academic Computing Network Services for a determination of existing systems type, location, and capacity and coordination during the design and construction phases. The design professional shall also become familiar with the University's long-range telecommunication plans.

Well Water:

A water well supplying the Satellite Utilities Plant is located at the eastern edge of the School. Work on the establishment of this well should be completed prior to the commencement of the construction of the Knowledge Center.

Natural Gas:

The City of Tallahassee maintains the gas distribution system throughout the main campus. At this time, it is not expected that gas service shall be a requirement of this project. However, the design professional shall be responsible for verifying this assumption during the design phase. If gas service is determined to be a programmatic need, then all work relating to the gas distribution system on campus must be coordinated with the appropriate City of Tallahassee utility departments.

Irrigation:

There is no irrigation water service in or around either of the sites proposed for the construction of the Knowledge Center.

G. Architectural significance of any structure on site and the proximity and significance of structures on adjacent sites which will have an impact on the project:

It is expected that the design of this project shall be sensitive and complimentary to the existing architectural features and qualities of the facilities which surround it.

The design professional shall become familiar with the activities to be conducted within the proposed facility and their relationships with the College of Education. The design professional shall recommend to the University any additional improvements which may be necessary to achieve a greater degree of compatibility between the proposed facility and its neighbors.

H. Any unusual site condition which may impact the cost or design of the project.

Two issues of critical concern in the development of this project are the existing site topography and the resulting stormwater conditions and the possible intermingling of pedestrian and vehicular circulation.

I. Direction of prevailing winds:

In the summer, the prevailing winds are from the south/southeast. In the winter, the prevailing winds are from the north and south. It is not expected that prevailing winds shall have a significant impact on the design of this facility. The design professional shall, however, be sensitive to downstream effects of any mechanical exhaust which may be vented from this facility.

X. Program Area

The information contained in this section of the document relates to the specific spatial and site requirements for the construction of the proposed Knowledge Center. This information conveys the Building Committee's attempt to describe the function, size and spatial relationship of the spaces programmed for construction as well as siting of the facility within the school boundaries. The resulting Space Summary and Bubble diagram are included at the end of this section. Additionally Exhibit 6 located in the appendix of this document contains additional programmatic data relating to size, utility, environmental, and furnishing and equipment requirements.

It is expected that the design professional shall become thoroughly familiar with these spatial requirements and descriptions and that, prior to the commencement of the design phase, the design professional shall have the opportunity to discuss these requirements with the Building Committee to insure a mutual understanding. All questions relating to the spaces programmed for this project shall be addressed to the Building Committee.

As mentioned in the Scope of Work description in the Introduction of this document, the design professional shall be expected to assist the Building Committee and the University in determining a final site for this project. The following section explains further the requirements of this phase after which the spatial requirements of this project are outlined.

Site Selection Phase:

At this point in the project's development, a final site for the construction of the Knowledge Center has not been determined. In recommending approval of the concept of this project, the University's Campus Development and Space Committee requested that the design professional assist the Florida State University School and the University in making this determination. This recommendation was later approved by then President Lick and serves as the basis for this portion of the design professional's scope of work. It is expected that the final site recommendation shall be reviewed by the Campus Development and Space Committee for approval prior to initiation of the design phase.

It is expected therefore that prior to the commencement of the design phase, a site selection phase shall be conducted. In conducting this phase, the design professional shall be expected to become thoroughly familiar with the campus of the Florida State University School and its immediate surroundings including all facilities and their functions, natural features, utility systems, pedestrian/vehicular circulation patterns, parking, future development plans, etc. The design professional shall analyze the two areas proposed for construction described below as well as other possible areas on the FSUS campus that the design professional feels are worthy of consideration. The design professional shall discuss the site selection criteria described above with the Building Committee as well as recommending other considerations if known.

It is also expected that this phase of the work shall be completed within 30 days of the notice to proceed and that multiple copies of a final site selection report shall be provided to the Building Committee and the Physical Plant Department which include both graphic and narrative analyses. A final site shall be agreed upon by the design professional and the Building Committee prior to submission to the Campus Development and Space Committee for consideration. The design professional shall be expected to assist in the presentation of the final site analyses to this Committee if required.

The campus of the Florida State University School is severely constrained not only by its own facilities but also by its surroundings. On its southern and eastern perimeters, existing recreational and athletic facilities provide no opportunity for the School to expand. To the north and west, Call Street and Stadium Drive serve to lock in the School's boundaries as well. Therefore, possible sites are limited to the existing campus of the School.

There are two general areas on this campus which offer possible sites. The first is the area west of the School's existing Auditorium (Building 124) and east of Stadium Drive. This is an existing open space and offers the convenience of adjacent parking and service drives. In addition, the site is close enough to the School so that some facilities, such as restrooms, could possibly be shared. Covered pedestrian access would also be facilitated utilizing this site.

The second general area is the open space between the front classroom wing (building 123) and the Stone Building (Building 50) to the north. The Stone Building houses the majority of the University's College of Education under whose auspices the School is administered. This site offers several unique advantages including the potential of a symbolic bridge or connection between the School and the College of Education. Though equally undeveloped as the first site described, unfortunately this site is severely sloped and would most likely require a modification to the access drive which serves the front of the School to protect the students.

The description of these two sites does not suggest that others may not be equally suitable as well. Therefore, the design professional is encouraged to survey the entire campus of the Florida State University School and discuss other general areas with the Building Committee.

These simple observations by no means provide the necessary information to select an adequate site for this project. It is expected that the design professional shall be responsible for this site selection analysis and that, working with the Building Committee, a final site shall be recommended to the Campus Development and Space Committee for final consideration.

To assist in this analysis, the design professional shall have access to all existing information about the Florida State University School campus including utility plans, tree surveys, and the like. In addition, the Building Committee has proposed the following site selection criteria for the design professional to consider.

1. *Safety:*

It is expected that the Knowledge Center shall be heavily utilized not only by the students and faculty of the Florida State University School, but also by those of the College of Education as well as other on-campus and off-campus user groups . It is however of paramount importance that students be provided a safe facility which is also safely accessed. Therefore, consideration should be given to siting this facility in such a manner that students, especially those of grade-school age, do not have to cross vehicular paths or other obstacles. Of course, all access must also accommodate mobility impaired-persons.

Since this facility could also have an evening-user component, the site must provide safe and secure access during hours of darkness. Exterior lighting, convenient parking, and well designed landscaping are also critical components.

2. *Expansion:*

It is envisioned that this project represents only the first phase of a construction program that will eventually provide all of the appropriate types and quantities of spaces that are necessary in a successful facility of this kind. The Building Committee has attempted to outline all of the spaces which will be provided in this phase as well as in subsequent phases. Accordingly, the final site must provide opportunities for future expansion that are reasonable and convenient and can accommodate future expansions. The space summary located elsewhere in this section of the program provides a breakdown of phasing by space type and square footages. This summary suggests that upon completion of this first phase the Knowledge Center will provide 8,678 net assignable square feet of space.

In considering expansion, the design professional should consider both horizontal and vertical expansion possibilities. Ideally, all infrastructure components will be sized to accommodate the ultimate build-out, though this depends largely upon available budget.

3. *Symbolism:*

This project provides a unique opportunity for the University, the Florida State University School and the College of Education to make a symbolic statement as to its heritage and ambitions. It has been suggested previously that this facility could serve as a symbolic link between the School and the College. In addition, considering the School's prominent location on the western edge of the Main Campus, this project should also serve as an important entry image for the entire University to those travelling onto campus from Call Street, Stadium Drive and Murphree Street. The design professional shall have access to information contained in the University's Campus Master Plan Update which further defines these campus-wide goals.

4. *Infrastructure:*

Also critical to the siting of this facility is the need to provide the necessary infrastructure systems to accommodate the Center's programs. In considering a site, the design professional must provide for the necessary utility components, including chilled water, steam, electrical, telecommunications (including fiber optic), solid waste disposal, exterior lighting, and stormwater. The Physical Plant Department shall provide the design professional with all existing information on these systems to assist in the determination of a site. It is important to note that this project shall be responsible for funding connections to all of these utility systems.

Program Area Activities

A successful school media program is one that accommodates a diverse and varied number of activities occurring in the same facility, often simultaneously. The spatial allocations and relationships within the facility should provide for efficient flow of traffic and flexible adaptation of spaces. Both a space summary and relationship diagram are located at the end of this section.

At any given time, students may be found reading, using reference materials for research, receiving instruction, listening and viewing multimedia materials, accessing electronic information resources, developing video projects, or producing a television program. Staff size will be limited in terms of the operation and supervision of these activities; therefore, the design of the Knowledge Center must consider the need for supervision of all areas from various points throughout the facility. Interior walls should incorporate vision panels so as not to obstruct vision into these areas.

The Building Committee has also completed forms that describe the size, utility, environmental and furnishings/equipment requirements of each of these spaces. Copies of these forms are contained in Exhibit 6 of the Appendix. Because of rapidly evolving technology utilized in the areas of Distance learning and Interactive Video the equipment list provided with these spaces are preliminary. A final equipment list will be submitted , reviewed and approved by all appropriate University and BOR departments prior to acquisition. Thus, the design professional shall work closely with the building committee, the FSU Office of Telecommunications and the FSU IRM office in the accommodations for the final equipment applications.

The following is a brief description of the spaces that are programmed for inclusion in the Knowledge Center

1. Entrance

This area shall be a functional transition space between the building's exterior and interior. This area should have opportunities for displays, both floor and wall type, traffic control by staff, and be located in proximity of the circulation area within the Reading Room.

2. Reading/Stacks/Copy Room (3388 nsf)

The Reading Room is the main area of the Knowledge Center where many diverse activities will occur that require a variety of environmental controls. This space should provide a comfortable environment planned to stimulate student interest and encourage use of the facility. The Reading Room provides for the following activities: circulation and control of materials; reference and research; browsing; displays; individual, small, and large group study or instruction; use of traditional audio visual equipment and various multimedia technologies; access to information-delivery systems of electronic resources outside the school. Key environmental concerns for this area include humidity, temperature, lighting, and acoustics.

Space allocations for the following activities are to be incorporated as part of the Reading Room: reading areas for both elementary and secondary students which will provide for simultaneous use by individual, small, and large groups of differing ages and grade levels; stacks; periodicals; computer workstations; circulation.

Reading areas—At least 25% of the area should be available for student seating. Mixed seating should include tables and chairs appropriate for elementary-aged children as well as secondary students (adults). Computer terminals/workstations should also accommodate both young children and adults for the purposes of individual listening and viewing. Consideration should be given to a flexible system for concealed utility floor boxes with pop top covers for electrical cable, coaxial cable, voice and data lines.

Circulation Desk—This area should be highly visible to allow visual supervision of as much of the Reading Room as possible and should also be accessible to the main entrance/exit, technical processing, and periodical storage areas.

On-line public access catalog (OPAC)—Multiple terminals providing access to the library catalog and other information resources should be located in several areas throughout the reading room.

Vertical files—Space should be provided to accommodate file cabinets for vertical files.

Periodicals—Sloped display shelving is required to display current issues of magazines, newspapers, and journals.

3. Periodical Storage (141 nsf)

This area is dedicated to the storage of back issues of periodicals that are available for reference and research and therefore should contain the maximum amount of shelving storage possible. This area should be in the proximity of the Circulation Desk for supervision and control purposes.

4. Technical Processing (401 nsf)

This is the area in which all materials and equipment for the Knowledge Center are received, cataloged, processed, and distributed. Clerical duties related to the management of the media program also take place in this area. The space should be designed to accommodate the logical sequence of events related to receiving, processing, and repairing materials, i.e., built-in work stations, counters, multiple electrical outlets, a wet sink, wall shelving, shelf list cabinet, and wall cabinets for storage. A special delivery door and access to a vehicular service drive should be considered in the design of this area. A restroom for staff use should also be located in the area. This space should provide access to the Reading Room in the proximity of the Circulation Desk.

5. Graphics Production Lab (351 nsf)

This area should be designed for the production of instructional media, i.e., slides, transparencies, posters, charts, dry mounting and laminating, binding, and other graphic and photographic functions. This space should be divided into two separate functional areas, one for media production and one for graphics production. The media production area will be used for activities using traditional photography, still video, copy stands, and multimedia computer workstations. The graphics production area will house equipment for the balance of the functions listed above as well as 3 built-in workstations for computer and typing uses, wall shelving, and storage cabinets for supplies. Student safety ia a key concern in this area since this space will house heat-producing and cutting equipment accessible for student use.

In addition, a special area of this room shall be designated for the school publishing center. This area will require a computer work station, a work area for assembling and binding books, and storage for supplies. This area should be located adjacent to the Technical Processing area and in the proximity of the Professional Library.

6. Professional Library (611 nsf)

In addition to meeting the needs of student users, the Center's collection includes professional materials and information services. This space should provide a comfortable, inviting environment in which faculty and staff may review materials to help teachers keep up-to-date with trends, developments, techniques, and research in general and specialized educational fields.

The space should be equipped with telephone, computer/ typewriter, listening and viewing equipment, professional journals and other resources. It should be located adjacent to the Graphics Production area and in the proximity of the Reading Room.

7. Conference Rooms (3 @ 120 nsf)

These spaces should be located in a quiet and easily supervised area. These areas should be acoustically treated and equipped for multipurpose use (lecture, video, slide presentations, etc.) and should have movable walls/partitions to allow for the combination of two or all three areas into a single larger space. One permanent projection screen and podium should be provided and be installed so that they can serve the larger combined space.

8. Staff Offices (3 @ 140 nsf)

All administrative/management functions, i.e., planning, and selection of materials for the media program will take place in these spaces. In addition to a desk, these areas should include wall shelving for professional materials and files, a computer workstation and a telephone for use by the librarian.

9. AV/CC Storage (650 nsf)

This space should contain various storage facilities for small and large instructional equipment (AV and closed circuit equipment, portable projection screens, maps, globes, etc.), rolling projection carts, parts for repairs, supplies, etc. Lockable cabinets need to be provided for storage of some equipment and supplies. Contained within this space should be an area designated for equipment repair with multiple electrical outlets. This space should be located near the graphics production area and the television control room.

10. Closed Circuit T.V. (450 nsf)

This space should provide for the specific equipment and space to accommodate video production activities. Special lighting is required for the portion of this area to be used as a student production studio. The area should be partially partitioned for a small control room to house special equipment and to direct the production of video programming. Vision panels should be incorporated into the walls between the studio and reading room and the studio and control room. Counters, shelving, and cabinets to accommodate video recorders, television receivers and special audio equipment are required for this area. This area should be acoustically designed and treated to restrict sound reverberation.

11. Group Projects and Instruction (766 nsf)

A large classroom-sized area with acoustical treatment and provisions for visual control by staff should be provided for the following types of activities:

Group viewing/instruction—Furnishings should include tables and chairs for approximately 30 students and equipment for presentations using all forms of media.

Distance learning—This classroom space should accommodate up to 30 students in an interactive instructional setting. The design of this space, especially the interactive telecommunications system, shall be closely coordinated with the FSU Office of Telecommunications as well as the FSU IRM Office. As previously mentioned due to the rapidly evolving technology utilized in this type of facility, it is not possible to determine exact specifications for equipment which may be installed so far in the future. The Building Committee will provide a final list of equipment during the design phase. This list shall first be reviewed and approved by all appropriate University and BOR departments prior to the acquisition.

The equipment necessary to operate such a space will be provided for, where possible, from the furnishings/equipment line of the construction budget. If, during the design process, it becomes evident that this is not possible, then the design professional shall design this classroom in such a manner that a future installation of the necessary equipment can be accomplished with minimal difficulty. These design criteria in fact apply to all telecommunication, lighting, mechanical and other related systems.

This interactive classroom control room located in the TV distribution room shall also be considered as an on-site distribution point as well. The capability to extend programs to the balance of the school shall also be provided. As a general principle, all environmental controls should be accessible not only to the instructor, but to the TV distribution/control room as well.

It is known that these types of classrooms have very specific acoustic, electrical, mechanical, and related requirements. It is expected that the design professional shall work with the Building Committee and staff from other University departments to develop the technical information and design of this space.

12. Video Editing (2 @ 70 nsf)

This area shall provide an area for students and staff to perform editing of video and audio productions. Design should address acoustic concerns and should be adjacent to the television studio.

13. TV Distribution (234 nsf)

The television distribution system originates in this area and extends to all classrooms and instructional areas inclusive of the Group Projects area. This space also acts as a control room to store and operate the associated audio, visual, and telecommunications equipment for the operation of the distance-learning classroom. It is a multi-channel system capable of local origination or playback of programming on videotape decks or live broadcasts. . All "head-end" equipment is mounted in a television equipment rack in the distribution area.

14. LAN Control

This space provides for the location of the data distribution equipment, fiber optic cable termination, level 5 cable termination, and electronic equipment for data routing and distribution for the entire school facility.

The design professional shall review the program document prepared for a recent technologies project entitled "Retrofit For Technology" prior to the design of this space. As this space will be the hub of the communications network the design professional shall work closely with the FSU Office of Academic Computing and Network Services in the design and coordination of this space with the balance of this facility, the school and the University.

15. Secondary Skills Lab (766 nsf)

A large classroom-sized area with acoustical treatment and provisions for visual control by staff should be provided for the following types of activities:

Group viewing/instruction—Furnishings should include tables and chairs for approximately 30 students and equipment for presentations using all forms of media.

Distance learning—This classroom space should accommodate up to 30 students in an interactive instructional setting. The design of this space, especially the interactive telecommunications system, shall be closely coordinated with the FSU Office of Telecommunications as well as the FSU IRM Office. Again, due to the rapidly evolving technology utilized in this type of facility, it is not possible to determine exact specifications for equipment which may be installed so far in the future. However, the Building Committee shall provide a final list of equipment during the design phase. This list shall first be reviewed and approved by all appropriate University and BOR departments prior to the acquisition.

The equipment necessary to operate such a space will be provided for, where possible, from the furnishings/equipment line of the construction budget. If, during the design process, it becomes evident that this is not possible, then the design professional shall design this classroom in such a manner that a future installation of the necessary equipment can be accomplished with minimal difficulty. These design criteria in fact apply to all telecommunication, lighting, mechanical and other related systems.

This interactive classroom control room located in the TV distribution room shall also be considered as an on-site distribution point as well. The capability to extend programs to the balance of the school shall also be provided. As a general principle, all environmental controls should be accessible not only to the instructor, but to the TV distribution/control room as well.

It is known that these types of classrooms have very specific acoustic, electrical, mechanical, and related requirements. It is expected that the design professional shall work with the Building Committee and staff from other University departments to develop the technical information and design of this space.

Square Footage Variances from Approved Facilities List

Upon analysis of the spatial and functional requirements of the activities to be conducted within the Knowledge Center the Building Committee has determined that in the best in of the FSUS Media Program the following variances from the Department of Education Plant Survey recommendations should be requested.

Reading /Stacks /Copy (3388 nsf)—The Building Committee recommends that the area allocated to the Media Reading, Stacks, and Copying Rooms be combined to create a single more flexible space.

Technical Processing (401 nsf)—The Building committee is recommending to increase the area allocated to this space (329 nsf) by reassigning space from Graphics production area (72 nsf).

Graphics Production (351 nsf)—The Building Committee recommends that the programmed square footage for this area be reduced from the recommended (423 nsf). The excess space will be reassigned to the Technical Processing space (72 nsf).

Professional Library / Textbook Storage (611 nsf—The Building Committee is recommending that due to the related functions of these two spaces, they be combined into one common space. (328 + 282 nsf)

Conference Rooms (3 @ 120 nsf)—The Building Committee is recommending that rather than provide a single conference room of the recommended 275 NSP the facility would be better served by providing a larger space that has the capabilities of being sub-divided into three smaller rooms. The additional space required for this variance would be achieved by reducing the A/V, Closed Circuit Storage space (85 nsf) and the Secondary Skills Development Lab (40 nsf).

Staff Offices (3 @ 140 nsf)—The Building Committee is recommending that due to the present staffing levels and the future levels required by the additional functions of the facility That 3 staff offices be provided. The space required for one of the additional programmed offices, is provided for in the Secondary skills development lab (110 nsf). The space required for the third staff office will be acquired by reducing the A/V, Closed Circuit Storage space allocation (135 nsf).

A/V, Closed Circuit Storage (650 nsf)—The Building Committee is recommending that the due to the related functions of these areas they be combined. However the combined square footage (941 nsf) exceeds the programmed area by 291 nsf.

The excess area will be applied to the Conference area (85 nsf), the Staff offices (135 nsf), and the Group Projects and Instruction area (71 nsf).

Closed Circuit T.V. (450 nsf)—The Building Committee is recommending that the programmed square footage for this area be reduced from the recommended 659 nsf. The excess space will be divided among the T.V. Distribution Room (140 nsf) and the Video Editing Rooms (69 nsf).

Group Projects and Instruction (746 nsf)—The Building committee is recommending to increase the allocated (471 nsf) by redistributing some space from A/V, Closed Circuit Storage (71 nsf) and the Secondary Skills lab (224 nsf) o this space.

Video Editing (2 @ 70 nsf)—The Building Committee is recommending that the space allocated for a Dark Room be reassigned to this type space. The additional area required to meet the programmatic objectives will be obtained by reducing the Closed Circuit T.V. area (69 nsf).

T. V. Distribution (234 nsf)—The Building committee is recommending to increase the allocated (94 nsf) by redistributing some space from Closed Circuit T.V. area (140 nsf).

Secondary Skills Development Lab (746 nsf)—The programmed square footage for this area will be reduced from the recommended 1140 nsf. The excess space will be divided among the Staff Offices (110 nsf), the Conference Rooms (40 nsf), and the Group Projects and Instruction area (204 nsf).

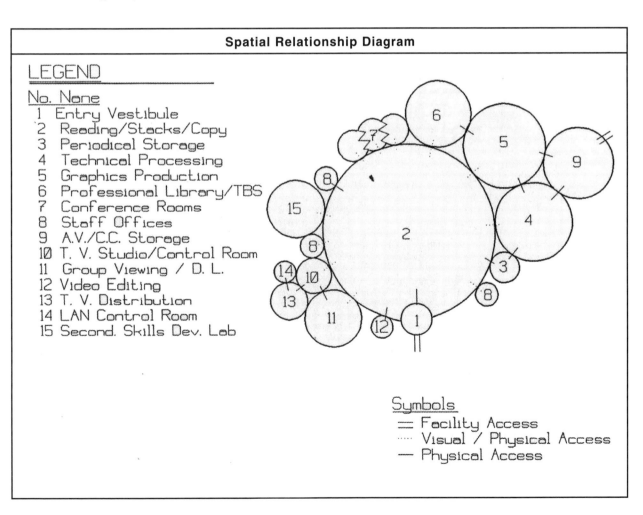

Spatial Relationship Diagram

LEGEND

No. None
1 Entry Vestibule
2 Reading/Stacks/Copy
3 Periodical Storage
4 Technical Processing
5 Graphics Production
6 Professional Library/TBS
7 Conference Rooms
8 Staff Offices
9 A.V./C.C. Storage
10 T. V. Studio/Control Room
11 Group Viewing / D. L.
12 Video Editing
13 T. V. Distribution
14 LAN Control Room
15 Second. Skills Dev. Lab

Symbols
= Facility Access
..... Visual / Physical Access
— Physical Access

Florida State University School Knowledge Center Space Summary (Programmed)

SPACE NO.	SPACE NAME	ACCESS	DOE SURVEY	NO. OF SPACES	AREA (NSF)	TOTAL AREA
1	Entry Vestibule	P		1	N/G	0
2	Reading/Stacks/Copy	P	3388	1	3388	3388
3	Periodical Storage	R	141	1	141	141
4	Technical Processing	R	329	1	401	401
5	Graphics Production	R	423	1	351	351
6	Professional Library/TBS	R	329	1	611	611
7	Conference Rooms	P	235	3	120	360
8	Staff Offices	R	175	3	140	420
9	A / V, C.C. Storage	S	941	1	650	650
10	Closed Circuit T.V.	P	659	1	450	450
11	Group Projects and Instructi	P	471	1	766	766
12	Video Editing	R	71	2	70	140
13	T.V. Distribution	S	94	1	234	234
14	LAN Control room	S		1	N/G	0
15	* Secondary Skills Dev. Lab	P	1140	1	766	766
16	* Textbook Stor.	R	282	1	0	0
	SUB-TOTAL (NSF)		8678			8678
	Net : Gross Factor (32%)		2777			2777
	TOTAL (GSF)		**11455**			**11455**

* Space Identified in the   Plant Survey but not within the Media Center

XV. Project Schedule

The proposed schedule for the design, bidding, and construction of this project is listed below in both tabular and graphic form. It is expected that the design professional shall review this schedule prior to the commencement of design and make any recommendations for adjustment. Refinements to this schedule must be made in consultation with the design professional, the Building Committee, the Physical Plant Department, and the Board of Regents Office of Capital Programs (BOR OCP).

First Year

Mar 15   Facilities program expected to be transmitted to the BOR OCP for review and approval.

Apr 01   Facilities program expected to be approved. A/E selection process is expected to begin.

Aug 01   A/E selection process expected to be completed, contract negotiations completed, Notice to Proceed issued to design professional to commence design phase.

Second Year

Jul 01   Design phase expected to be completed, 100 % Construction Documents submitted, including review by the Office of the State Fire Marshal. Project advertised for bids.

Aug 01   Bids opened.

Sep 15   Contract awarded, and Notice to Proceed issued to contractor to commence construction phase.

Third Year

Aug 01   Substantial completion expected.

Sep 01   Final completion expected.

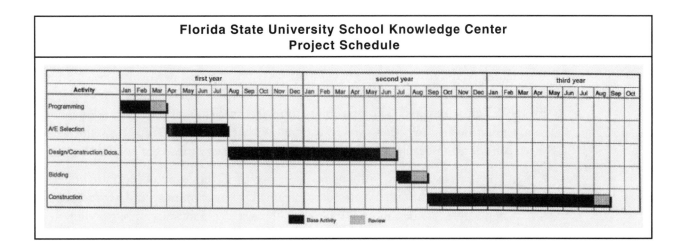

XVI. Program Funds

Funding for this project will be derived from a series of PECO appropriations allocated to the Florida State University School for the specific purpose of addressing DOE survey-approved projects. As explained earlier, the construction of a media center, or Knowledge Center, was approved during the School's most recent DOE survey.

The following is a summary of the various allocations which will be utilized to complete this project.

Source	First Yr	Second Yr	Third Yr	Fourth Yr	Total
PECO for Lab (Survey Recommended Projects)	$ 475,415	$ 337,135	$ 342,625	$ 360,082	$1,515,257 Schools

It should be noted that, although not all of the funding is currently in place, it is expected that the anticipated funding will be in place in sufficient time for the commencement of the design and construction phases. There is sufficient funding presently in hand to commence with the selection of the design professional and enter into a contract for the completion of the design phase. By the time this phase is completed, it is expected that there will be sufficient funding to bid the project and enter into a construction contract.

FUNDS REQUIRED
Planning $ 113,850   Construction $ 1,248,361   Equipment $ 153,046
Total $ 1,515,257

Operating expenses for this facility will be provided in a manner similar to the existing funding formula for laboratory schools.

XVII. Project Budget Summary

This project's estimated Project Budget Summary can be found on the following page. This summary includes a breakdown of all project costs including site development, construction, and construction related costs such as design fees and furnishings/equipment. . The design professional shall be responsible for verifying these estimated costs prior to the commencement of this project and during its duration. The design professional is encouraged to make recommendations for adjustments where necessary.

All costs outlined in the Project Budget Summary are based primarily upon current dollar values. No inflationary factors have been utilized in developing either construction or administrative costs unless otherwise noted.

Figures relating to some site-development costs are based primarily upon assumed allowances and do not reflect "take-off" calculations. During the design process, it shall be the design professional's responsibility to review these and other costs and make recommendations for any necessary adjustment. Other factors or influences which have been considered in developing the Project Budget Summary are listed below:

1. The costs associated with impact fees assessed as the result of local growth management legislation have not been included in this summary. If determined to be applicable, the design professional shall assist the University in responding to or developing information pertinent to the estimating of these fees.

2. Costs associated with concurrency or consistency have likewise not been included. The design professional shall similarly assist the University in responding to this item.

3. Site-utility estimates do not include the costs of any applicable tap fees. It is assumed that the cost of construction is capable of fulfilling these costs.

4. It is assumed that artwork will be required for this project.

5. Because this project will be funded from a series of PECO allocations, it is assumed that the necessary funding for the contracting of the design and construction phases will be available for obligation. There exists presently sufficient funds to commence the A/E selection phase and the design phase. Funding for the construction phase will be based in part on future (Third Year and Fourth Year) allocations.

6. The conversion factor of 1.32 utilized on the following page to convert NASF to GSF is based upon examples of related types of facilities constructed throughout the state. It should be noted that this conversion factor represents a target figure and that actual net-to-gross ratios shall be determined by two factors: the design of the facility and the available budget.

7. Similarly, the Construction Cost per GSF is based in part upon BOR construction cost data for library space as well as local school district historical data for the construction of similar types of facilities.

8. The Building Committee has attempted to determine a budget figure for the acquisition of furnishings and equipment for this project. Since DRS allocations are not use specific (that is, allocated for planning, design and construction), a portion of the FY 1995-96 allocation has been set aside for furnishings/equipment acquisitions. During the design phase, it may be necessary to adjust this furnishings/equipment line to accommodate construction cost which is the Building Committee's highest priority for the use of these allocations. However, the design professional shall not assume that a possible reassignment of funds shall accommodate an inefficient or wasteful design. The maintenance of this project's Capital Outlay Implementation Plan (COIP) shall be monitored by the Physical Plant Department, the BOR Budget Office and the BOR Office of Capital Programs.

PROJECT BUDGET SUMMARY
Florida State University
Florida State University School Knowledge Center

BUILDING EXPANSION COSTS:

NASF/GSF CONSTRUCTION TOTAL

Space Type	NASF	Factor	GSF	Cost per GSF	Cost
Library	8,678	1.32	11,455	$ 84.50/GSF	$ 967.944

Subtotal Building Construction Cost: **$ 967,944**

SITE DEVELOPMENT COSTS:

Site Improvements (grading, lighting, paving, landscaping)	$ 50,000
Site Utilities	$ 30,000
Stormwater Mitigation	$ 30,000
Fiber Optic Link	$ 10.000
Subtotal Site Development Costs:	$ 120,000

Subtotal Building Construction and Site Development Costs: **$ 1,087,944**

CONSTRUCTION RELATED COSTS:

Professional Fees		$ 93,850
Architectural Fees	$ 83,850	
Site Selection Analysis	$ 5,000	
Planning Contingency	$ 5,000	
Inspection Services		$ 50,000
Surveys and Tests		$ 20,000
Furnishings/Equipment		$ 153,046
Artwork (@ 1/2 of 1% of Construction/Site Development Costs)		$ 5,417
Telecommunications		$ 25,000
Contingency (@ 7.4% of Construction/Site Development Costs)		$ 80,000

Subtotal Construction Related Costs: **$ 427,313**

TOTAL BUDGET COST ESTIMATE: **$ 1,515,257**

XVIII. Appendix

The following exhibits represent additional information relating to the programming and design of this project. They are included for information purposes only; questions relating to their content should be addressed to the Building Committee. The following is a brief description of each Exhibit.

Exhibit 1: Project Location Map

The Project Location Map contained in this Exhibit illustrates the location of the Florida State University School on the Main Campus.

Exhibit 2: Site Location Plan

The Site Location Plan identifies the two preliminary sites that have been proposed for consideration by the Building Committee.

Exhibit 3: FSUS / COE Concept Paper

This Exhibit contains a copy of a Concept Paper prepared by the FSUS, FSU/COE, and the FSU/SLIS that defines the vision, goals, and mission of the Knowledge

Exhibit I
Florida State University School Knowledge Center—Project Location Map

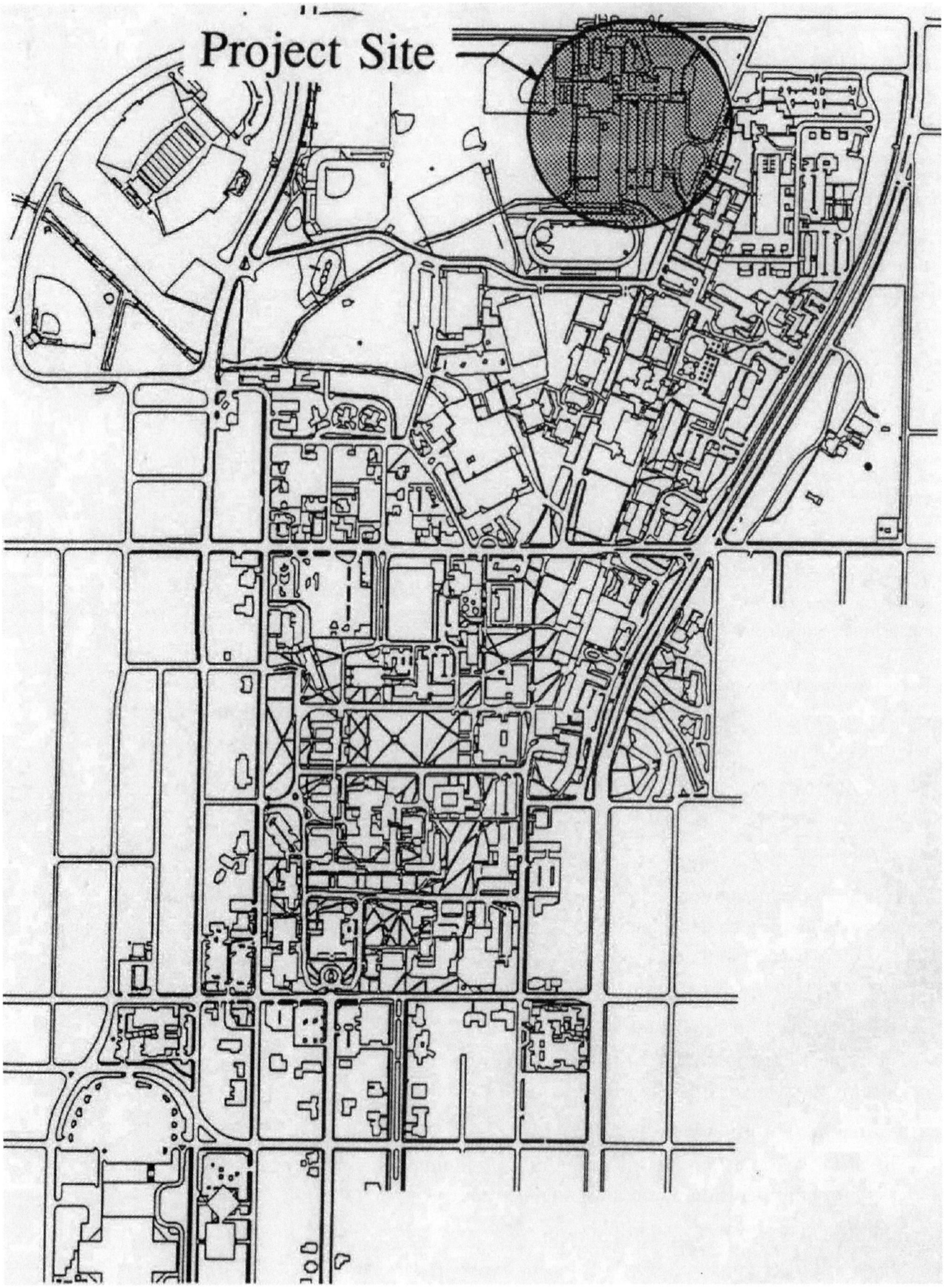

Project Site

Exhibit 2
Florida State University School Knowledge Center—Site Location Plan

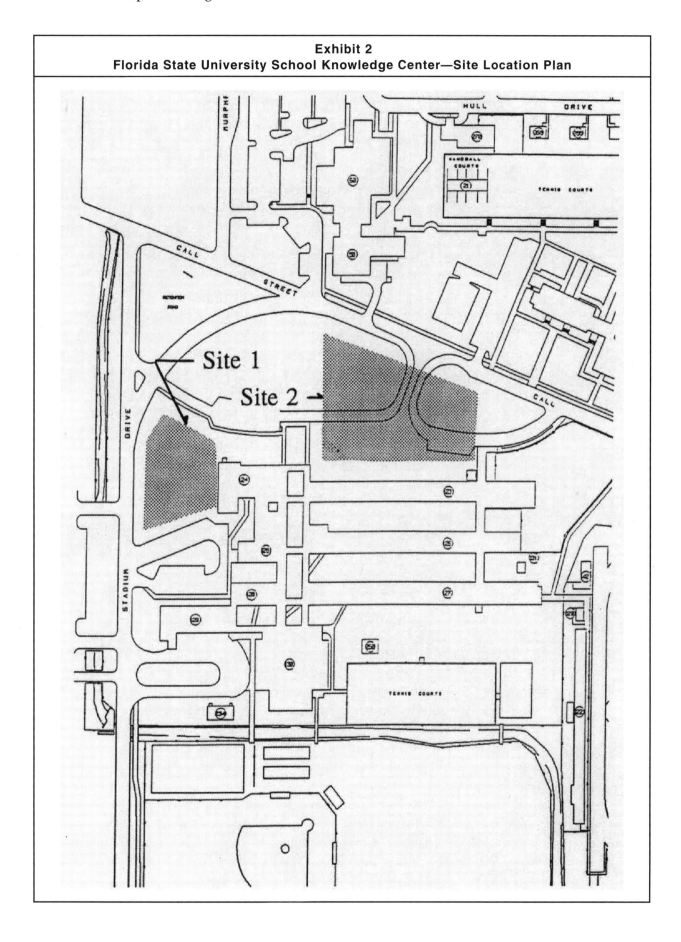

Center. This information is contained in this program document for the design professional's reference.

Exhibit 4: DOE. Educational Plant Survey

This Exhibit contains an excerpt from the most recent Department of Education Educational Plant Survey that attests to the need for the spaces programmed for the proposed Knowledge Center.

Exhibit 5: SACS Report

This Exhibit contains an excerpt from the most recent SACS accreditation report which delineates the deficiencies in the FSUS' existing media programs.

Exhibit 6: Data Collection Forms

The Data Forms contained in this Exhibit outline the specific programmatic requirements of the spaces anticipated for construction in the Knowledge Center.

Exhibit 7: FSU Standard Telecommunications Specification

The FSU Office of Telecommunications has produced the attached "FSU Standard Telecommunications Specification" to assist the design professional in the design, layout, and specification of telecommunications systems and equipment The design professional shall verify that this version of the Specification is the most current. Additionally, the design professional shall consult with the FSU Office of Telecommunications on all matters related to the design of these systems.

Exhibit 3 - FSUS / COE Concept Paper

The Florida State University Knowledge Center

A Proposal for Leading Florida's Learners into the 21st Century

ABSTRACT

The attached paper describes an innovative and exciting project proposed by Florida State University's Developmental Research School, College of Education, and School of Library and Information Studies. The project - currently called the Knowledge Center - revolves around the construction of a new library media faculty for the Florida State University School (FSUS). This structure will be the focal point of a unique cooperative effort in which students from kindergarten through graduate school will develop the knowledge and skills necessary to function in an information-rich and technologically sophisticated environment The program will also prepare future teachers and school library media specialists for educational leadership roles by providing opportunities for them to practice innovative educational approaches and work with high-tech learning tools. Interwoven with these learning and preparation aspects of the program will be a variety of research activities, for the Center will serve as a setting where professors and graduate students can observe real learning in action and develop, apply, and evaluate educational theory. Finally, the program will have an outreach component It will serve as a local, state, and regional demonstration hub where advanced teaching and learning strategies as well as cutting-edge learning materials can be observed and evaluated.

This project proposal, which was initiated by the FSUS professional staff to further the school's mission, received quick and enthusiastic support from the College of Education and the School of Library and Information Studies. Implementation of the program will reflect a collaborative vision and cooperative effort

The next page of this paper provides a quick overview of the proposal. The rest of the document supplies background and supporting information.

PROPOSAL OVERVIEW

What is the Knowledge Center?

The Knowledge Center is both a cooperative *program* and a joint-use *facility*.

The *program* will provide innovative learning opportunities and access to all types of information for students ranging from kindergarten through graduate school. Within the program framework, learners will experience, research, observe, and participate actively in their own education.

The *facility* will be built on the campus of the Florida State University School. It will house traditional and cutting-edge information materials and learning technologies.

What FSU units will cooperate to create the Knowledge Center? The Knowledge Center would be a joint project of The College of Education The School of Information Studies The Florida State University School Other FSU Colleges and Schools

Who else might be involved with the Knowledge Center?

Other entities that might be involved at the planning or implementation stages are

The Leon County Library System and the Leon County School District which might cooperate on program and collection development

The State Department of Education which might use the Knowledge Center as a demonstration site for innovative teaching approaches technologies, and materials.

Corporate sponsors who might donate newly developed materials and technologies to the Center for early testing, use, and demonstration.

The FSU Center for Professional Development which might cooperate on distance learning opportunities and in-service training.

What commitment will be required of the University?

Support from the University must include

Moving the expansion plans for the Stone Building up on the priority list

Moving plans for constructing the FSUS Knowledge Center building through the FSU system as a high priority.

Approving the blending of the Stone Building expansion funds (which will come from the Public Education Capital Outlay and Debt Service Trust Fund [PECO]) with FSU School funds set aside for expansion of the media center. Overseeing the joint development of short-range and long-range plans by the three cooperating Florida State units. Supporting the solicitation of corporate donations for the Center.

For more explanation, please read on. The attached paper provides background and supporting information.

The Florida State University Knowledge Center:
A Proposal for Leading Florida's Learners
into the 21st Century

Some might call the Knowledge Center a twenty-first-century library, but we prefer to *think* of it as an evolving, kaleidoscopic, nonstop learning event Its program will lure youngsters with the joy of a story well told and engage their minds with the excitement of information. It will move them from depending on others to fill their information needs to functioning independently in a knowledge-rich world. Yet, it will also foster a vital interdependence as children work together locally and globally. The Knowledge Center's impact on learning will be sweeping in scope and interdisciplinary in nature.

High-tech learning tools will support all of the Knowledge Center's learning activities. Children who use the Knowledge Center may

- consult a touch-screen terminal to choose resources from a vast array available in the Knowledge Center or from distant locations via futuristic interlibrary loan.
- use their own palm-sized computers to download stories or information they want to take home to share with family members.
- create video and computerized electronic stories or term papers.
- send their newly created projects to friends in learning groups across the world.
- participate in lifelike teleconferences with their peers in dozens of countries.
- cooperate via satellite and computer networks with far-flung learning pals to address global problems. The technology and instant communication will be an essential and enriching element of their daily learning.

While the program will certainly engage youngsters who attend the Florida State University School (FSUS), it will also provide an unmatched real-world setting where graduate and undergraduate students can experience a new teaching and learning paradigm. As they practice their new educational approaches, aspiring teachers and school library media specialists and their professors will have unprecedented opportunities to observe, research, and work directly with young learners.

The Knowledge Center program will be headquartered in a new joint-use facility constructed on the FSUS campus to serve as the school's library media center. The facility will house informational materials (both print and electronic) and learning technologies appropriate for students of all ages, but the walls of this building will not imprison the information or learning devices. Instead, fiber optic pathways that extend across and off the campus will allow learners twenty-four-hour access to much of the information.

As impressive as this facility will be, the technologically supported program is the heart of this proposal. In order to delineate the concepts underlying this program, this proposal is structured into the following four sections:

1. Envisioning **Our Mission**. Describes foundational educational concepts thatunderlie the Knowledge Center (p. 2).
2. **Achieving the Vision**. Explains how the educational ideas can come to life in the Knowledge Center (p. 4).
3. Reaping the **Benefits**. Focuses on benefits that will accrue to students associated with FSU (p. 7).
4. Sharing the **Vision**. Discusses ways in which other local, state, regional, and national groups will also benefit from the Knowledge Center (p. 9).

A conclusion (p. 11) will summarize and reiterate necessary support from the University.

ENVISIONING OUR MISSION

Most children enter school at the age of four or five and exit some twelve years later. Many eventually rejoin the schooling stream, some leaving and returning several times over the next decades. Just what is the goal of all this schooling? How should a school shape its students? What final forms do we aim to create?

Current leaders in school restructuring, reform, and renewal efforts describe desirable outcomes in terms similar to those agreed upon by the Knowledge Center planning team. Those ideas are illustrated in Figure 1 on the next page and are presented in three layers:

- Overriding Goals
- Supporting Skills and Knowledge
- Core of the Mission

Overriding Goal. Our broadest outcome is effective and productive citizens who both enrich and respect their country and their world. Socially, they must function capably in multicultural settings; economically, they must be keen global competitors.

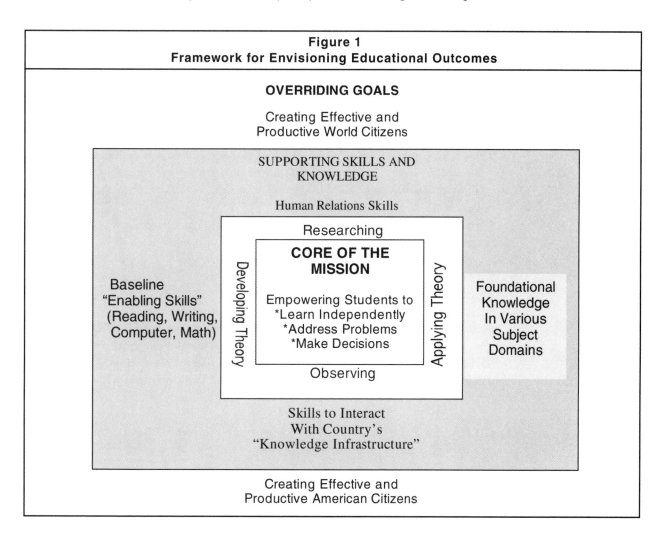

Figure 1
Framework for Envisioning Educational Outcomes

OVERRIDING GOALS

Creating Effective and
Productive World Citizens

SUPPORTING SKILLS AND
KNOWLEDGE

Human Relations Skills

Researching

CORE OF THE MISSION

Empowering Students to
*Learn Independently
*Address Problems
*Make Decisions

Developing Theory

Applying Theory

Observing

Baseline
"Enabling Skills"
(Reading, Writing,
Computer, Math)

Foundational
Knowledge
In Various
Subject
Domains

Skills to Interact
With Country's
"Knowledge Infrastructure"

Creating Effective and
Productive American Citizens

Supporting Skills and Knowledge. Effective and productive world citizens have gained supporting skills and knowledge in school. They can cooperate and work on teams when necessary. They have baseline "enabling skills" (abilities in reading, writing, computer operation, and mathematics) that support additional learning in science, history, and other concept-rich subjects. Finally, because the world of information is expanding exponentially, world citizens know how to interact with the country's knowledge infrastructure to locate, use, and create information as needed.

The four types of supporting skills and knowledge depicted on Figure 1-human relations abilities, enabling skills, foundational knowledge, and information skills-can be discussed separately but cannot be isolated in the learning process. Instead, learning in all four areas is intertwined. Enabling skills are practiced and improved in a social context, and foundational knowledge can be constructed successfully when students must identify and locate information for themselves.

Core of Our Mission. In the past, many considered the development of supporting skills and foundational knowledge to be the primary goals of education. However, we agree with our contemporaries who insist that schooling has more important aims. We believe that the core of our mission is to empower students to use their supporting skills and knowledge to learn independently; to address academic, personal, career, and community problems (individually or in a group); and to make thoughtful decisions.

Bordering *this* mission core are additional activities unique to university faculty and students. They will use the Center as a research setting where they can observe real learning in action and develop and apply educational theory.

This framework of ideas supports the Knowledge Center program. Our next step is to enliven the framework by showing how the vision can be achieved.

ACHIEVING THE VISION

Three fourth-graders dash through the Knowledge Center doors and hurry over to their friend, Mr. Simmons, a school library media intern. Their questions overlap: "Is it time for aw conference yet? Can you help us get started? Will you look at the questions we've written?'

Mr. Simmons smiles at their energy and leads them to a nearby table where the books, videotapes, artifacts, and computer printouts full of information about folktales are arranged. Together, they examine and polish the children's questions. Finally, Mr. Simmons announces, "OK, I think we're ready." They all move to the conference comer of the Knowledge Center.

The children, barely able to sit still, perch on the edges of three small chairs while Mr. Simmons adjusts the complex equipment in the comer. Suddenly, directly in front of them three more images appear, projected into the air, and the children begin a long-distance conference with three youngsters at an experimental United Nations school in Somalia. Together, the six trade folktales from their divergent cultures and explore the messages those tales convey. Mr. Simmons directs the exchange when necessary, and when the 30-minute conference is over, sends the children back to their classroom to report their findings and share the videotaped conversation with their classmates. There, students will include the information in a chapter of the class book they are writing about folktales from around the world.

This scene hints at myriad educational activities that build the supporting skills and knowledge specified in Figure 1. The children involved had worked cooperatively to accomplish a complex task. They had identified their information need, located materials, used them to develop questions for their conference, participated in the long-distance discussion, and presented their findings to classmates. The other children in the class will take the newly created information, write about it, draw appropriate illustrations, edit it, and add it to a long-term class project

The students will have used reading, writing, presentation, computer, information, and human relations skills and will have added to their foundational knowledge in social studies (especially multicultural concepts), literature, and science (because many of the folktales describe scientific phenomenon that can be investigated). An undercurrent of the lesson is the collaborative planning and unit development by the library media intern and the classroom teacher.

Can this scene ever be a reality? Advancing technologies are leading us in this direction, but the mere existence of technologies does not guarantee an impact on the learning of children. After all, the technologies may exist but not be widely available in schools, or the adults who work with children may not be trained to use the high-tech equipment to support compelling learning activities. The Knowledge Center program will provide both necessary access to and appropriate experience with using technology to foster learning scenes such as the one above.

The planning for this Center begins at the FSU program level. The combined creative energies, talents, and funds from three dynamic units (the College of Education, the School of Library and Information Studies, and the FSUS) will provide the impetus and the ongoing inspiration for the program. The Center's program will focus on three main tasks:

- Fostering, originating, and developing learning opportunities.
- Preparing educators for present and future roles.
- Providing essential resources and technologies.

Fostering, Originating, and Developing Learning Opportunities. The learning opportunities that originate in the Center will be supported by current research in cognitive science. These investigations into how people learn tell us that every student must construct his or her own understandings of the world based on experiences. As educators, we now realize that we cannot give students knowledge; but we can give them learning experiences in places like the Knowledge Center to that they can create their own understandings.

Preparing Educators for Present and Future Roles. The Center's learning opportunities will also demonstrate the power of a new way of thinking about teaching. Aspiring classroom teachers and school library media specialists will move away from the image of themselves and their textbooks as the sole dispensers of knowledge. Instead, they (and the professors and teachers with whom they work) will use the Knowledge Center's resource-rich environment to help students discover their own paths to learning.

Educational planning teams will be the norm for the Knowledge Center. Professors, classroom teachers, school library media specialists, instructional designers, and technicians will pool their ideas, special skills, and talents to create integrated learning experiences that break down the walls of subject domains and allow children to interact with a world of ideas.

These beginning educators will leave their Knowledge Center experience with a vision of educational practice at its **best** and with the skills to implement that vision in other locations around the state and country.

Providing Essential Resources and Technologies. A range of materials and technologies must be available to support the learning experiences of individual students so that each can learn in the way that suits him or her best Some of the materials and technologies will be traditional. For example, print resources will probably always have a place in education. Other parts of the collection (such as a wide-ranging set of multicultural realia that will allow a hands-on approach for children studying world cultures) may be less traditional but still not high-tech.

More futuristic resources will also be available. The Center will house networked CD-ROM learning stations, laser disk information access, and satellite downlink and uplink capabilities. We cannot predict the entire range of technologies that might be appropriate within the next fifty years. For that reason, the Knowledge Center facility must be large and flexible enough to accommodate rapid technological advancement.

The materials and equipment housed in the Knowledge Center will range not only from traditional to futuristic but also from beginning to advanced. For the FSUS students, resources appropriate for kindergarten through twelfth grade will be available. Additional information, designed for undergraduate and graduate students, will also be in the facility. Most of the materials (and also the management staffs) currently located at the Stone Building's Learning Resources/Curriculum Center and at the Harold Goldstein Library Science Library will be moved to the Knowledge Center. The collection will truly be a rich and deep database that includes information for education as well as about education.

All of these resources will, of course, be expensive, but the Knowledge Center planning team is convinced that the Center will attract corporate sponsors interested in placing their newly-developed materials and technologies in a demonstration site. Corporate donations such as these often include the use of a technician who spends time working with and training the local staff.

Access to these exciting learning resources and technologies will have to be as open as possible. Kindergarten through twelfth grade students will use the Center at all times of the day to work on class and individual projects and participate in distance learning. Undergraduate and graduate learners will be in the Center during days and evenings to observe, work with students, locate information for their own tasks, plan with each other and with professionals in the Knowledge Center, and take part in distance education. Throughout the day and evening hours, the Center will serve as a research site where educational theory is developed, applied, examined, and reflected upon by research teams of professors, educators, and students.

Because of these multi-type activities, we recommend that Knowledge Center implementation plans include extended physical access to the facility and that twenty-four hour electronic access be available to as many resources as possible.

The plan is ambitious, but the benefits to students from kindergarten through graduate school make the Knowledge Center program essential. Those benefits are the subject of our next section.

REAPING THE BENEFITS

After the last bell of the school day, a diverse group of professionals hurries into the Knowledge Center. Brad Simmons, a school library media intern, starts the meeting. "We're here to begin planning the electronic term paper project for the eleventh grade U.S. history students. Let's start by reviewing what experiences the students in those classes have had with locating and using information and with the production equipment." The two history teachers and their teaching intern describe the students' background.

Brad hesitates when they finish, unsure of what to ask next. The school library media specialist with whom he is working steps into the discussion. "Let's shift our thinking a little now and try to delineate the essential questions we want the students to address, the content and processes they will use, and the product we want them to create." As a pan of this exchange, the technician in ifie group describes possible production activities. Students will be able to use the Center's camcorder to videotape footage of interviews or local historical scenes, integrate those scenes with segments pulled from the U.S. history laser disk set, add their own narration, and create a computerized path through the information. This year, they win also be able ask learning partners at schools around the world to videotape a specific scene and send it to them via the satellite network.

Gradually the structure of the unit takes form. By the end of an hour, the group has a plan that divides teaching and preparation responsibilities among all the members and sets a tentative schedule.

The Knowledge Center will provide a learning platform for hundreds of students a year. Those who will most directly benefit from the program include

- Students attending FSUS (about 900 a year).
- Students from the College of Education (as many as 1500 a year).
- Students from the School of Library and Information Studies (as many as 140 a year).

Kindergarten through Twelfth Grade Students

Students attending the FSU School will benefit most directly from the Knowledge Center because of the wealth of new learning opportunities (like me one being planned above) that include

- **Expanded access to information.**
- **A new focus on the processes of using and creating information.**
- **Access to guidance from well-trained teaching teams.**

Expanded Access to Information. Foundational information related to every subject domain and appropriate for every student at the school will be available in or through the Knowledge Center. Students will use telecommunications systems to locate information across the world. Human experts will be a part of this information network and will communicate with students as time and technology permit All of these activities involve students in interacting with the world's "knowledge infrastructure" (see Figure 1), an essential supporting skill.

New Focus on the Processes of Using and Creating Information. Once students have found the information for a challenging assignment in perhaps social studies or science, they must read, interpret, analyze, evaluate, and synthesize it. Most of these activities involve refining their "enabling skills" (see Figure 1), a process that will be made more effective by the available technologies. Appropriate computer software will allow for mathematical analysis and display, word processing, desktop publishing, and graphic design. Students will also use Web design tools (or similar programs) to create individual and group projects like that planned by Brad Simmons and the planning team at the first of this section.

Access to Guidance from Well-Trained Teaching Teams. The information inundation could be overwhelming, but at each step of the process, students will be supported by planning team members. Each professional on the team will be a specialist but will also be able to act as a generalist. The teacher will be the subject-matter expert; the school library media specialist will be the information-access-and-use (or process) specialist; the technologist and technicians will support equipment use.

Graduate and Undergraduate Students

Skills attained by graduate and undergraduate students like Brad and the teaching interns at the first of this section will include

- **Functioning as a part of an educational planning team.**
- **Using technology to support the creation of learning environments.**
- **Dealing positively with change.**

Functioning as a Part of an Educational Planning Team. At the Knowledge Center, graduate and undergraduate students will work in planning teams on the complex tasks of conceptualizing, designing, implementing, and managing learning situations. They will also cooperate with each other and with their professors to research various aspects of the new teaching and learning paradigms. All this practice is important because beginning educators sometimes envision their role as one of isolation from other professionals. Yet active interdependency and collaboration are essential in today's complex education and information environments.

Changing deeply entrenched understandings of educators' roles is incredibly difficult because they rest on subconscious cultural "scripts" that dictate our behavior. The Knowledge Center program will provide a stage upon which new scripts can be visualized and practiced. Professors, teachers, school library media specialists, instructional designers, instructional technologists, and administrators will all have a chance to try new teaching and instructional roles.

Using Technology to Support the Creation of Learning Environments. In addition to rehearsing collaboration, graduate and undergraduate students will also practice using the Knowledge Center's advanced learning and information technologies. Equipment and systems already available allow rapid information processing and transfer, communication with libraries at distant sites, interactive viewing of learning materials, and live two-way television broadcasts. Technologies now in development will permit instant retrieval of print, visual, or audio materials from distant libraries; transmission of photographic quality video; live television broadcast directly to classrooms from remote scientific or historical locations; and tours of ancient, dangerous, or unreachable sites via virtual reality (artificial environments experienced by users who are wearing special goggles containing video screens and motion-sensitive gloves that control the video databases of the site).

These advanced learning and information technologies will not merely offer high-tech ways to accomplish conventional goals but will revolutionize teaching. Education professionals will soon be able to access vast libraries of data in a variety of formats to create truly individualized learning experiences for each child.

Dealing Positively With Change. Perhaps as important as the collaborative planning skills and the technological abilities will be the attitude toward change fostered by the Knowledge Center program and facility. Educators who experience the program will feel the reality of new working environments. They will learn to accept (yet evaluate rigorously) new teaching approaches. These undergraduate and graduate students will be equipped to lead schools into the twenty-first century.

Students associated with FSU will benefit directly from the Knowledge Center, but the positive impact will also flow beyond the campus boundaries. The local, state, and national benefits and recognition that the Knowledge Center will generate are described in our next section.

SHARING THE VISION

A dozen young teenagers enter the Knowledge Center singly and in small groups and hurry to the adjacent distance learning room. The last trio arrives just as their teacher's image appears on a large video monitor in the front of the room and greets them in Japanese, the language and culture the class is studying. Because the students are clearly visible on the teacher's monitor at her broadcast site in a distant state, she is able to speak individually to each, asking for an update of their current project on Asian art.

One 13-year-old girl speaks eagerly, directing her comments toward the monitor where unobtrusive television cameras photograph her and send the image to her teacher's location. "I got the most <u>incredible</u> video from a library in Michigan about the art of paper making. I finally understand why it's an art form in the Orient"

"Great!" the teacher responds. "Mr. Simmons, can you and Andrea share part of that video with us during our next class?"

Brad, the school library media intern, sits slightly behind the students but still within range of the cameras. As site facilitator, he provides logistical and informational support under the supervision of the Center's professional staff. "We can do better than that! Andrea has made arrangements with her art teacher to do a paper-making demonstration for the class. She'll use the video to give background information. Then, the next week if there is time, Andrea hopes to have a speaker from the University who win discuss the effect that the invention of paper had on China and later on Japan."

As this interchange takes place, several visitors at the side of the room watch and take notes. Two are from a rural, southern school district and have been asked by their superintendent to make a recommendation concerning two-way, televised distance education for their district. Another is from the Florida Department of Education and is evaluating the computer-controlled communication system recently donated by an educational corporation. A fourth visitor is gathering information for a research study on the social aspects of learning in distance education.

Distance education experiences are occurring more and more frequently across the country, but classes like the one above that is fully supported with advanced technology and information access are still relatively rare. Educators understand that in theory the classes can take place, but believing in the reality is difficult until the experience is made concrete.

The Knowledge Center will make change concrete and will function as a hub where educators can experience it. Agencies and educators that will benefit include

- Local education and information agencies.
- State and regional educational entities.
- National educational leaders and practitioners.

Local Education and Information Agencies. Nearby school and library Systems will be able to cooperate with and benefit from the Knowledge Center. Both collections and programs can be shared. Distance education opportunities for school-age students can be extended to any appropriately equipped location, and adult distance classes offered through the Knowledge Center will demonstrate a commitment to lifelong learning. For all levels, the rich resources (both human and informational) available at the University can enhance the educational experiences at a relatively low cost to the participating districts and students.

State and Regional Educational Entities. The Knowledge Center will become both a demonstration site for advanced teaching and learning strategies and a collection site of educational materials. As a demonstration site, the Center will provide concrete, observable examples of the most current teaching and learning innovations. Resource-based learning, cooperative learning, technologically supported teaching, team planning/teaching, and many other theory-based techniques will be parts of the Knowledge Center program that visitors will observe.

Working with the Florida Department of Education, the Center can also provide access to a complete collection of textbooks and related media (including the equipment required for each). Educators throughout the state and region will examine and evaluate these materials at the Center.

National Educational Leaders and Practitioners. The innovative teaching and learning examples will also be made available nationally. The concrete experiences can be shared via interactive teleconferences that enable educators from around the nation to observe events and discuss outcomes with participants. Videotapes and laser disks that contain the same information in noninteractive form can also be distributed.

The planning team for this project firmly believes that the cutting-edge, practice-based research about learning produced in the Knowledge Center will be applied to educational settings all over the country. The research findings will be distributed nationally in respected educational journals as well-as over electronic research dissemination networks.

CONCLUSION

We acknowledge the ambitiousness of the Knowledge Center, but when we re-envision the evolving, kaleidoscopic, nonstop learning events that will take place there and the outcomes depicted in Figure 1, we wonder: Can the University decline the opportunity to develop this unprecedented joint-use facility and cooperative program? The clear answer is that the Knowledge Center must become a reality.

Some start-up steps have already been taken. For example, FSUS has received $500,000 in PECO funds that will be directed to the project, and a proposal has been submitted to the FSU Physical Plan Section through its advisory board to initiate the process of planning for construction. Other activities that should be accomplished soon include:

- Dissemination of information throughout the University to identify other units that might wish to be involved.
- Establishment of an advisory council to assist in the development process.
- Development of a plan to seek additional funding and partners.

But if all aspects of the Knowledge Center are to emerge as depicted in this paper, the University must nurture and shape the project over the next several years by

- Moving the expansion plans for the Stone Building up on the priority list.
- Moving plans for constructing the FSUS Knowledge Center building through the FSU system as a high priority.
- Approving the blending of the Stone Building expansion funds (which will come from the Public Education Capital Outlay and Debt Service Trust Fund [PECO]) with FSU School funds set aside for expansion of the media center.

- Overseeing the joint development of short-range and long-range plans by the three cooperating Florida State units.
- Supporting the solicitation of corporate and other donations for the Center.
- Assisting in providing personnel on a start-up basis.

By serving students at all levels and by functioning as a research site, the Knowledge Center will promote the missions of the cooperating FSU units and of the University at large as well as serve the broader educational community. It will serve as a model for others and will place FSU at the forefront of educational and technological change. In addition, it will set an example of the wise use of facilities, personnel, and informational resources in a collaborative partnership.

As it is now conceived, the Knowledge Center will play a central part in leading Florida's learners into the 21st century. We urge Florida State University to accept the challenge of presiding over this innovative program that will influence education throughout the state, region, and nation.

This paper has been prepared by Judy M. Pitts in cooperation with Dr. Thomas Hart, Dr. Fran Kochan, Dr. Robert Lathrop, Dr. F. William Summers, Dr. Landra Rezabek, Ms. Constance Lane, Ms. Donna Shrum, and Ms. Dolores McCcy. Special acknowledgements go to Dr. Shirley Aaron for allowing use of her term 'Knowledge Center' and to Dr. Dianne Obergfor her description of the 'scripts' that guide role perceptions.

Exhibit 6—Knowledge Center Data Collection Forms

Space 1—Entrance: Physical Data

SPACE: 1 - Entrance	QUANTITY: 1

PHYSICAL DATA	
AREA area: N/G suggested dimension:	**COMMUNICATION** phone: public computer: 3 P.A.: 1 CCTV: 1
ACOUSTICS internal source: people external isolation: none	**ILLUMINATION** natural: preferred ambient: indirect none glare task: yes controls: dimmer
MICRO-CLIMATE temperature: 70-77 degrees humidity: 60%	**SERVICES** electric: 110, floor water: none
FINISHES walls: paint, glass floors: quarry tile ceiling: acoustical tile	**ACCESS** public
RELATION adjacency: main reading room/ circulation area, proximity: entrance to FSUS, parking	**OCCUPANCY** present: 15 future: 15
ACTIVITY DESCRIPTION 1. traffic control 2. visible control by staff 3. display area	

NOTE: Covered access to school. Access to pay phone, blue light emergency phone, and school-wide public address system

Space 1—Entrance: Furniture/Equipment

SPACE: 1 - Entrance   QUANTITY: 1

FURNITURE/EQUIPMENT

DESCRIPTION	no.	size	util*	N/E
bulletin board	2			new
recessed wall hung display case	2		e,c	new
recessed traffic grates	1			new
recessed interior fiber traffic mats	1			new
automatic door for handicap access	1		e	new
Floor Model Display Case	1		e,c,d	new

* e=electric, v=voice, d=data, c=cable TV

Space 2—Reading Room/Stacks/Copy: Physical Data

SPACE: 2 - Reading Room/Stacks/Copy   QUANTITY: 1

PHYSICAL DATA

AREA
area: 3,388   sq. ft.
suggested dimension: 50 x 68

COMMUNICATION *
phone: 4
computer: 24
P.A.:   1
CCTV: 4

ACOUSTICS
internal source: people, machines
external isolation: none

ILLUMINATION
natural: minimal (controlled)
ambient: fluorescent/incandescent
task: yes
controls: dimmer, multi-zoned, black out
            capabilities

MICRO-CLIMATE
temperature: 70-77 degrees
humidity: 60%

SERVICES*
electric: 110
water: none

FINISHES
walls: paint, glass
floors: carpet
ceiling: acoustical tile

ACCESS
public
restricted (circulation area)

RELATION
adjacency: all areas of the center
proximity:

OCCUPANCY
present: 93 (+4staff) =97
future: 93 (+4staff) =97

ACTIVITY DESCRIPTION
1. elementary and secondary student reading areas
2. visible control by staff
3. workstations for media specialists
4. flexible areas to accommodate large groups for teleconferences, programs, etc.
5. shelving to house collection of approx. 15,000 items
6. computer workstations to access online catalog and other information resources
7. circulation area allowing visual control over reading room and entrance
8. programs for large groups

* Underfloor Grid application

Space 2—Reading Room/Stacks/Copy: Furniture/Equipment

SPACE: 2 Reading/Circulation   QUANTITY: 1

FURNITURE/EQUIPMENT				
DESCRIPTION	no.	size	utilty	N/E
intermediate children's chairs	28			new
intermediate children's tables	7			new
adult chairs	52			new
adult tables	13			new
seated computer workstations	8			new
stand-up computer workstations	6			new
staff desk	2			new
secretarial chair	3			new
circulation desk with 2 computer workstations (variable height to accomodate children & adults)	1			new
chair, high swivel	2			new
network printer	1			new
modem	1			new
telephone	4			new
step stools	4			new
book truck	4			new
wood shelving stacks for 15,000 items (1,500 linear ft.)				new
slanted shelving for periodicals				new
vertical files cabinets (28 drawers)				new
microfiche cabinet	1			new
microfiche reader/printer (coin op)	1			new
newspaper rack	1			new
atlas stand	1			new
dictionary stand, table top	1			new
ceiling mounted TV (27 in)	1			new
portable sound system	1			new
podium	1			new
copy machine - leased	1			ex
wall clock	1			new
bulletin boards (number & size to be determined by available wall space)				new
book display stand	1			new
portable white marker board	1			new
pass daters, electric	1			new
pass desk and chair	1			new
electric wall/ceiling mounted projection screen	1		e	new
carpeted story steps	1			new
theft detection device	1			ex

Space 3—Periodical Storage: Physical Data

SPACE: 3 - Periodical Storage   QUANTITY: 1

PHYSICAL DATA	
AREA area: 141 sq. ft. suggested dimension: 10 x 15	**COMMUNICATION** phone: 1 computer: 1 P.A.: 1 CCTV: 1
ACOUSTICS internal source: people external isolation: none	**ILLUMINATION** natural: minimal ambient: fluorescent/incandescent task: no controls: dimmer
MICRO-CLIMATE temperature: 70-77 degrees humidity: 60%	**SERVICES** electric: 110 water: none
FINISHES walls: paint / glass floors: carpet ceiling: acoustical tile	**ACCESS** restricted
RELATION adjacency: reading room/ circulation area, proximity: technical processing	**OCCUPANCY** present: 4 future: 4

ACTIVITY DESCRIPTION
1. storage area for 3-5 years of back issues of magazines
2. accessible to circulation area and copy machine

Space 3—Periodical Storage: Furniture/Equipment

SPACE: 3 - Periodical Storage   QUANTITY: 1

FURNITURE/EQUIPMENT				
DESCRIPTION	no.	size	util*	N/E
built-in shelving (wall, island)		max		new
book truck	1			ex
step stool on rollers	1			new

* e=electric, v=voice, d=data, c=cable TV

Space 4—Technical Processing: Physical Data

SPACE: 4 - Technical Processing   QUANTITY: 1

PHYSICAL DATA

AREA
area: 401 sq. ft.
suggested dimension: 20 x 20

COMMUNICATION
phone: 2
computer: 3
P.A.: 1
CCTV: 1

ACOUSTICS
internal source: machines, people
external isolation: none

ILLUMINATION
natural: minimal
ambient: fluorescent
task: yes
controls: standard

MICRO-CLIMATE
temperature: 70-77 degrees
humidity: 60%
air changes: normal

SERVICES
electric: 110, floor, wall plug mould
water: yes

FINISHES
walls: paint
floors: carpet, vinyl
ceiling: acoustical tile

ACCESS
from circulation area

RELATION
adjacency: reading room/ circulation area, graphic productions
proximity: librarian's office, equipment storage area

OCCUPANCY
present: 4
future: 4

ACTIVITY DESCRIPTION
1. provides workspace for cataloging & processing of new materials, storage of unprocessed items and supplies, repair of books, non print items, and other materials,
2. accessible to circulation area

Space 4—Technical Processing: Furniture/Equipment

SPACE: 4 - Technical Processing   QUANTITY: 1

FURNITURE/EQUIPMENT				
DESCRIPTION	no.	size	util*	N/E
built in shelving		max		new
counters w/computer work stations	2		e,v,d	new
secretarial chair	3			
desk for library assistant	1			
built in cabinets		max		new
book trucks	3			new
bulletin board	1			new
large sink	1		w	new
work table 36" x 72"	1			new
18" stool	2			
28" stool	2			
telephone	1			new
typewriter	1			ex
locking key cabinet	1			new
engraver	1			
legal files, 4 drawer	4			
shelf list catalog	1			
wall clock				
staff restroom	1			new

* e=electric, v=voice, d=data, c=cable TV, w=water

Space 5—Graphics Production: Physical Data

SPACE: 5 - Graphics Production   QUANTITY: 1

PHYSICAL DATA

AREA	COMMUNICATION
area: 351 sq. ft. suggested dimension: 15 x 23	phone: 1 computer: 3 P.A.: 1 CCTV: 1

ACOUSTICS	ILLUMINATION
internal source: machines, people external isolation: none	natural: minimal ambient: fluorescent task: yes controls: zone

MICRO-CLIMATE	SERVICES
temperature: 70-77 degrees humidity: 60%	electric: 110 water: yes

FINISHES	ACCESS
walls: paint floors: carpet, vinyl ceiling: acoustical tile	restricted

RELATION	OCCUPANCY
adjacency: technical processing proximity: professional library	present: 6 future: 6

ACTIVITY DESCRIPTION
1. provides work space for production of instructional materials and visuals, multi-media workstations, word processing, laminating, etc.
2. provides area for school publishing center
3. accessible to technical processing area and professional library

Space 5—Graphics Production/Pub. Ctr.: Furniture/Equipment

SPACE: 5 - Graphics Production/Pub. Ctr   QUANTITY: 1

FURNITURE/EQUIPMENT

DESCRIPTION	no.	size	util*	N/E
built in shelving (max)				new
bulletin board	1			new
built in cabinets w/w (max)				new
counters w/computer workstations	2		e,d	new
secretarial chair	3			new
work table	1			new
18" stool	2			new
28" stool	2			new
light table	1		e	new
large sink	1		w	new
roll laminator	1		e	ex

Space 5—Graphics Production/Pub. Ctr.: Furniture/Equipment *(Cont'd.)*

SPACE: 5 - Graphics Production/Pub. Ctr   QUANTITY: 1

FURNITURE/EQUIPMENT				
DESCRIPTION	no.	size	util*	N/E
laminator stand	1			new
poster maker	1		e	ex
lettering machine (Ellison type)	1			new
typewriter	1		e	new
typing table	1			new
computer workstation for publishing center with storage for art supplies	1		e,d,v	new
laser disc player	1		e	ex
still video camera	1			ex
laser printer	1		e	ex
35 mm camera	1			
tripod	1			
copy stand	1			ex

Space 5—Graphics Production: Furniture/Equipment

SPACE: 5 - Graphics Production   QUANTITY: 1

FURNITURE/EQUIPMENT				
DESCRIPTION	no.	size	utilty	N/E
Kodak photo CD player	1			new
dual audio cassette recorder	1			new
pull out storage unit for charts, maps, and posters	1			new
ELMO visual marker	1		e	new
tracing board	1			new
wall colck	1		e	new
paper cutter	1			ex

Space 6—Professional Library/TBS: Physical Data

SPACE: 6 - Professional Library/TBS   QUANTITY: 1

PHYSICAL DATA	
AREA area: 611 sq. ft. suggested dimension: 20 x 30	**COMMUNICATION** phone: 1 computer: 4 P.A.: 1 CCTV: 2
ACOUSTICS internal source: machines, people external isolation: none	**ILLUMINATION** natural: minimal ambient: fluorescent task: yes controls: dimmer
MICRO-CLIMATE temperature: 70-77 degrees humidity: 60%	**SERVICES** electric: 110, floor water: no
FINISHES walls: paint floors: carpet ceiling: acoustical tile	**ACCESS** restricted
RELATION adjacency: reading room/ graphics production	**OCCUPANCY** present: 10 future: 10

ACTIVITY DESCRIPTION
1. provide for reading, listening, viewing, evaluation, and selection of professional and instructional
   materials by faculty
2. accessible to reading room and graphics production

Space 6—Professional Library/TBS: Furniture/Equipment

SPACE: 6 - Professional Library   QUANTITY: 1

FURNITURE/EQUIPMENT				
DESCRIPTION	no.	size	util*	N/E
built in shelving				new
wall cabinet	1			new
rectangular tables	2			new
chairs	8			new
cluster of lounge furniture	1		v	new
occasional tables	2			new
computer workstations (carrels)	3		e,d,	new
secretarial chairs	3			new
laser printer	1		e	new
telephone	1		v	new
typewriter	1		e	new
typing table	1			new
calculator	1			new
file cabinet, legal	2			new
wall clock	1		e	new

* e=electric, v=voice, d=data, c=cable TV

Space 7—Conference Room: Furniture/Equipment

SPACE: 7 - Conference Room   **QUANTITY:** 3

FURNITURE/EQUIPMENT				
DESCRIPTION	no.	size	util*	N/E
built in shelving				new
file cabinet	1			new
rectangular table	1			new
chairs	4			new
mini blinds for privacy	1			new
utilities for multipurpose use			e,d,c	
white marker board	1			new
in one conference room only:				
podium	1			new
ceiling mounted projection screen	1			new

* e=electric, v=voice, d=data, c=cable TV

Space 7—Conference Room: Furniture/Equipment

SPACE: 7 - Conference Room   **QUANTITY:** 3

FURNITURE/EQUIPMENT				
DESCRIPTION	no.	size	util*	N/E
built in shelving				new
file cabinet	1			new
rectangular table	1			new
chairs	4			new
mini blinds for privacy	1			new
utilities for multipurpose use			e,d,c	
white marker board	1			new
in one conference room only:				
podium	1			new
ceiling mounted projection screen	1			new

* e=electric, v=voice, d=data, c=cable TV

Space 8—Staff Offices: Physical Data

SPACE: 8 - Staff Offices   QUANTITY: 3

PHYSICAL DATA

AREA area: 140 sq. ft. critical dimension: 10 x 12	**COMMUNICATION** phone: 1 computer: 1 P.A.: 1 CCTV: 1
ACOUSTICS internal source: machines, people external isolation: none Extend walls to underside of roof deck	**ILLUMINATION** natural: minimal ambient: fluorescent task: incandecsent controls: standard, dimmer
MICRO-CLIMATE temperature: 70-77 degrees humidity: 60%	**SERVICES** electric: 110
FINISHES walls: paint, glass floors: carpet ceiling: acoustical tile	**ACCESS** restricted
RELATION adjacency: reading room proximity:	**OCCUPANCY** present: 2 future: 2

ACTIVITY DESCRIPTION
1. provides quiet workspace for administrative functions for library media specialist
2. will accommodate interviews and planning with teachers
3. accessible to circulation area

Space 8—Staff Offices: Physical Data

SPACE: 8 - Staff Offices   QUANTITY: 3

FURNITURE/EQUIPMENT

DESCRIPTION	no.	size	util*	N/E
desk	1		e,v	new
swivel chair	1			new
legal file cabinet	1			new
tall book case	1			new
computer workstation	1		e,d	new
telephone	1		v	new
modem	1		d	new
arm chair	1			new

* e=electric, v=voice, d=data, c=cable TV

Space 9—AV/CC Storage: Physical Data

SPACE: 9 - AV/CC Storage   QUANTITY: 1

PHYSICAL DATA

AREA	COMMUNICATION
area: 650 sq. ft. suggested dimension: 35 x 20	phone: 1 computer: 3 P.A.: 1 CCTV: 2

ACOUSTICS	ILLUMINATION
internal source: machines, people external isolation: none	natural: none ambient: fluorescent task: yes controls: standard

MICRO-CLIMATE	SERVICES
temperature: 70-77 degrees humidity: 60%	electric: 110, Multiple Quad outlets

FINISHES	ACCESS
walls: paint floors: carpet ceiling: acoustical tile	secure

RELATION	OCCUPANCY
adjacency: graphics production proximity: technical processing	present: 4 future: 4

ACTIVITY DESCRIPTION
1. provides storage for small and large audio visual equipment on shelves, in cabinets, or on large rolling carts
2. provides storage for supplies and other types of multimedia such as large multi-cultural kits
3. accessible to reading area

Space 9—AV/CC Storage: Furniture/Equipment

SPACE: 9 - AV Storage   QUANTITY: 1

FURNITURE/EQUIPMENT

DESCRIPTION	no.	size	util*	N/E
various AV, multimedia equipment either existing, or to be purchased later				
built in shelving, 12-15 inches deep for storage of various projectors, tape decks, kits, etc.				
built in locking storage cabinets				
storage cabinets with drawers				
storage for portable projection screens and wall maps				
double duplex plug molding			e	
work area for equipment maintenance			e,d,c	
work area for processing kits				
legal file cabinet	1			new
step ladder	1			new
wall clock	1			new

* e=electric, v=voice, d=data, c=cable TV

Space 10—Closed Circuit T.V.: Physical Data

SPACE: 10 - Closed Circuit T.V.   QUANTITY: 1

PHYSICAL DATA	
AREA area: 350 sq. ft. suggested dimension: 15 x 24	**COMMUNICATION*** phone: 1 computer: 1 P.A.: 1 (switched) CCTV: 1
ACOUSTICS internal source: machines, people external isolation: adjacent spaces Extend walls to underside of roof deck.	**ILLUMINATION** natural: none ambient: fluorescent, color corrected task: yes controls: dimmer
MICRO-CLIMATE temperature: 70-77 degrees humidity: 60%	**SERVICES** electric: Multiple, floor grid
FINISHES walls: acoustically treated, glass floors: carpet ceiling: acoustical tile	**ACCESS** Restricted
RELATION adjacency: group viewing T. V. Distribution Video Editing proximity: Reading room	**OCCUPANCY** present: 8 future: 8
ACTIVITY DESCRIPTION 1. Preparation of live video productions	

*This area should be coordinated with the T.V. Distribution Space requirements

Space 10—Closed Circuit T.V.: Furniture/Equipment

SPACE: 10 - Closed Circuit TV   QUANTITY: 1

FURNITURE/EQUIPMENT				
DESCRIPTION	no.	size	util*	N/E
built in shelving				new
bulletin board	1			new
external communications channel ducting to permit distance learning connections			e,d,c	new
built in cabinets				new
computer workstation			e,d	new
telephone	1		v	new
special effects computer	1		e,d	new
special effects generator	1		e,d	new
microphone mixer	1		e	new

Space 10—Closed Circuit T.V.: Furniture/Equipment *(Cont'd.)*

SPACE: 10 - Closed Circuit TV   QUANTITY: 1

FURNITURE/EQUIPMENT				
DESCRIPTION	no.	size	util*	N/E
audio amplifier	1		e	new
hand microphones w/ stands	4			new
pressure zone microphones	1			new
lavaliere microphones	6			new
audio compressor/limiter	1		e	new
black and white monitors	3		e	new
color preview monitors	4		e	new
easel	1			new
turntable	1		e	new
VHS cassette recorder for production	2		e	new
VHS editing cassette recorder	1		e	new
VHS editing controller with cables	1		e	new
headphones for camera operators, etc.	7			new
dual cassette recorder/CD player	1		e	new
video distribution amplifier	1		e	new
audio distribution amplifier	1		e	new
waveform monitor	1		e	new
cyclorama (black, blue, and white)	1			new
modular production console w/ shelves	1		e,d	new
mobile edititng console	1			new
wall clock	1		e	new
studio lights on tripods w/ filters	3		e	new
surge protected multiple outlet strip	4			new
anchor desk	1			new
2 place love seat	1			new
upholstered, armed side chairs	4			new
28 " high stools	2			new
low table	1			new
secretary chairs for production/editing	4			new
vectorscope	1		e	new
studio monitor speakers	1			new
character generator	1		e,d	new
racks and rack mounts as needed				
cameras	3			new
tripods	3			new
dolleys	3			new

e=electric, v=voice, d=data, c=cable TV

Space 11—Group Projects and Instruction: Physical Data

SPACE: 11 - Group Projects and Instruction   QUANTITY: 1

PHYSICAL DATA	
AREA area: 766 sq. ft. suggested dimension: 25' x 30'	**COMMUNICATION*** phone: 1 omputer: 24 P.A.: 1 (switched) CCTV: multiple
ACOUSTICS internal source: machines, people external isolation: none (Extend walls to underside of roof deck.)	**ILLUMINATION*** natural: None ambient: fluorescent-video compatible controls: dimmable
MICRO-CLIMATE temperature: 70-77 degrees humidity: 60%	**SERVICES*** electric: 110 water:
FINISHES walls: paint / acoustic panel floors: carpet ceiling: acoustical tile	**ACCESS** restricted
RELATION adjacency: Closed Circuit T.V. proximity: T.V. Distribution	**OCCUPANCY** present: 30 future: 30

ACTIVITY DESCRIPTION
1. Classroom type space accommodating up to 30 students in an interactive instructional setting.
2. Space should be flexable to allow for setup for a variety of interactive activities including computers, video, audoe and connection to remote sites for distance learning applications.
3. Accessible to closed circuit T.V. studio.

* Equipment requirements should be coordinated with the closed circuit T.V., T.V. Distribution room and Group Projects and Instruction for interactive and distance learning.

Space 11—Group Projects and Instruction: Furniture/Equipment

SPACE: 11 - Group Projects and Instruction   QUANTITY: 1

FURNITURE/EQUIPMENT				
DESCRIPTION	no.	size	util*	N/E
teacher multi-media work station	1		e,v,d	new
white marker board (classroom)	1			new
student desks or tables (special voice activated audio system)	30		e,v,d	new
large video monitor	2		e,c	new
horizontal camera station	1			
2 section wall wireway duct with 22 outlet boxes, 4 jacks each				new
floor outlet boxes	1		e,d	new
portable multi-media workstations	6			new
chairs	32			new
wall clock	1			new
cameras (2 floor, 1 ceiling)	3			new
ceiling mounting bracket for camera	1			new

* e=electric, v=voice, d=data, c=cable TV, w=water

Note: This room will contain unique communication services and equipment requirements to be coordinated with the Closed Circuit T.V.. and T.V. distribution rooms.

Space 12—Video Editing: Physical Data

SPACE: 12 - Video Editing   **QUANTITY: 2**

PHYSICAL DATA

AREA area: 70 sq. ft. suggested dimension: 7 x 10	**COMMUNICATION** phone: computer: 1 P.A.: 1 (switched) CCTV:
ACOUSTICS internal source: machines, people external isolation: none	**ILLUMINATION** natural: none ambient: fluorescent task: yes controls: dimmable
MICRO-CLIMATE temperature: 70-77 degrees humidity: 60%	**SERVICES** electric: 110 Multiple outlets water: None
FINISHES walls: paint, Acoustic Panel floors: carpet ceiling: acoustical tile	**ACCESS** restricted
RELATION adjacency: reading room (visual) proximity:	**OCCUPANCY** present: 2 future: 2

ACTIVITY DESCRIPTION
1. Provides workspace for students (2) to do mechanical editing of audio video productions.

Space 12—Video Editing: Furniture/Equipment

SPACE: 12 - Video Editing   **QUANTITY: 2**

FURNITURE/EQUIPMENT

DESCRIPTION	no.	size	util*	N/E
work table	1		e,d	new
chairs	2			new
secure cabinet for equipment storage	1			new
VHS editing cassette recorder	2		e	new
audio cassette deck	1		e	new
bulletin board	1			new
microphone for audio dubbing	1			new

* e=electric, v=voice, d=data, c=cable TV, w=water

Space 13—T.V. Distribution: Physical Data

SPACE: 13 - T.V. Distribution   **QUANTITY:** 1

PHYSICAL DATA

AREA area: 234 sq. ft. critical dimension: 15' x 15'	**COMMUNICATION** phone: 1 computer: multiple P.A.: 1 (switched) CCTV: multiple
ACOUSTICS internal source: machines, people external isolation: none	**ILLUMINATION** natural: none ambient: fluorescent-video compatible task: yes controls: standard
MICRO-CLIMATE temperature: 70-77 degrees humidity: 60%	**SERVICES** electric: 110
FINISHES walls: paint / acoustic panel floors: carpet (non-static) ceiling: acoustical tile	**ACCESS** restricted
RELATION adjacency: group projects and instruction, sec. skills dev. lab proximity: closed circuit T.V.	**OCCUPANCY** present: 4 future: 4

ACTIVITY DESCRIPTION
1. control center for school wide integrated information delivery, retrieval and management system, including closed circuit cable TV, video, satellite reception
2. accessible to closed circuit TV Studio

NOTES: Integrated information delivery system will allow remote scheduling and control from individual classrooms of audio visual equipment such as video tape machines, laser disc players, interactive compact discs (CDI), etc. using any of the following distribution methods: broadband, baseband, fiber optic, satellite, microwave, or codec paths.
This system will also permit access to remote sites for distance learning and teaching applications.

Resource C: Sample Contract and Request for Bids

Sample Contract for Architects

Owner Name (owner would be the school system)

<u>(Specific state laws or arbitration the apply)</u>

THIS CONTRACT made as of *[DATE]* by and between the [SCHOOL SYSTEM] acting by and through its [AGENT], hereinafter called the Owner, and *[ARCHITECT]*, hereinafter called the Architect, for the following project: *[PROJECT]*.

A. Basic Contract
   1. The Architect shall provide Basic & Additional professional services for the Project in accordance with the Project Program and with the Terms and Conditions of this Contract.
   2. The Owner shall compensate the Architect, in accordance with the Terms and Conditions of this Contract, as follows:
   [TOTAL COMPENSATION]
   3. This Contract is a [Lump-Sum, Fixed-Fee—this statement may vary for situations] amount for all Services and Responsibilities required to complete the Project. If there are professional services required beyond the scope of this Contract, those services will be negotiated. Services beyond the scope of the Contract must be authorized in writing by the Owner before the work is performed.
   4. By signature on this Contract, the declaration is made that the Architect is professionally qualified, registered, and licensed to practice in the State of XXXX.

B. The Architect's Basic Services
   1. The Architect's Basic Services consist of the five phases described below which are to be inclusive of the necessary structural, civil, mechanical and electrical engineering services and other services as outlined in the Project Program.
   2. The Architect's Additional Services shall consist of site survey, geotechnical investigation, warranty inspection and record mylar drawings. The Architect shall furnish, as part of the geotechnical investigation, the services of a soils engineer to determine soil bearing values and other necessary subsoil conditions.
   3. The Architect shall schedule design review conferences, which shall include the Owner and other interested parties, to discuss review comments. The Architect

shall take minutes of all meetings and distribute typewritten copies to all parties attending the meeting within ten (10) calendar days.

4. The Architect shall review the Project Program and project budget furnished by the Owner and make recommendations for the requirements of the project. The Architect shall establish the requirements and all design parameters in agreement with the Owner that shall then be incorporated into the Project Program.

5. The Architect shall be responsible for providing the local building code official with a set of plans and specifications at each review phase. If there is not a local jurisdiction for building code review, the Owner will coordinate the review with the XXXX State Building Code Division.

6. The Architect shall be responsible for the professional quality, technical accuracy, and the coordination of all designs, drawings, specifications and other services furnished under this Contract. The Architect shall, without additional compensation, correct or revise and errors, deficiencies or omissions in the designs, drawings, specifications, estimates and other services.

7. Neither the Owner's review, approval or acceptance of, nor payment for, the services required under this Contract shall be construed to operate as a waiver of any rights under this Contract or of any cause of action arising out of the performance of this Contract. The Architect shall remain liable to the Owner for any and all damages caused by the Architect's negligent performance of any of the services furnished under this Contract.

8. The rights and remedies of the Owner provided for under this Contract are in addition to any other rights and remedies provided by law.

9. When commissioning services are required and/or requested by the Owner, the Architect shall cooperate with the Owner in selecting a Commissioning Agent. The Architect shall participate in commissioning of the project and all project systems at no additional cost to the Owner. The Commissioning Agent shall be under separate contract to the Owner.

C. Schedule

The Architect shall submit a Schedule for the Owner's review and approval outlining all time frames, projections and milestones for all reviews, meetings, investigations, design phase efforts and other portions of the overall project including, but not limited to, a projected bid opening date and construction time frame. Changes and/or alterations to the Schedule shall not be permitted without the approval of both the Architect and Owner.

D. Schematic Design Phase

1. The Schematic Design Phase shall commence with the signing of this Contract and shall be complete with the Owner's approval of the Schematic Design Documents.

2. The Architect shall prepare, for approval by the Owner, Schematic Design Documents, consisting of drawings, outline specifications and similar documents illustrating the scale and relationship of project components.

3. The Architect shall provide *[NUMBER ( )]* set(s) of Schematic Design Documents including Estimate of Construction to *[AGENCY POINT OF CONTACT]*, and *two (2)* set(s) of the same to the Owner for review.

E. Design Development Phase

1. The Design Development Phase shall commence with the Owner's approval of the Schematic Design Documents and shall be complete with the Owner's approval of the Design Development Documents.

2. The Architect shall provide a certified Site Survey describing all physical characteristics, legal limitations, grades and lines of streets, alleys, pavements and adjoining property; rights of way, restrictions, easements, covenants, encroachments, zoning, deed restrictions, boundaries and contours of the site; locations, dimensions and complete data pertaining to existing buildings, other improvements and trees; and full information concerning available service and utility lines both public and private.

3. The Architect shall provide a Geotechnical Investigation which shall include, but not be limited to, test borings, test pits, determinations of soil bearing values, percolation tests, and evaluations of hazardous materials with a written report and recommendations.

4. The Architect shall prepare, for approval by the Owner, Design Development Documents consisting of drawings, sketches, specifications, Estimate of Construction Cost, and similar documents necessary to fix and describe the size and character of the entire Project as to the architectural, structural, mechanical, electrical systems and other elements as defined in the Project Scope.

5. The Architect shall provide *[NUMBER ( )]* set(s) of Design Development Documents, including the Estimate of Construction Cost, to *[AGENCY POINT OF CONTACT]* and *two (2)* set(s) of the same to the Owner for review.

F. Construction Documents Phase

1. The Construction Documents Phase shall commence with the Owner's approval of the Preliminary Design Documents and shall be complete with Owner's approval of the final Plans and Specifications and the final Estimate of Construction Cost.

2. Based on the approved Preliminary Design Documents and any adjustments required in the Project Program and/or fixed limit of Construction Cost, the Architect shall prepare, for approval by the Owner, Construction Documents. These documents, which shall consist of Plans and Specifications and a final Estimate of Construction Cost, shall set forth in detail, the requirements for the construction of the entire Project.

3. During the preparation of the Plans and Specifications, the Architect shall advise the Owner of any adjustments to previous estimates of Construction Cost indicated by changes in Owner requirements or general conditions and revise said estimate accordingly.

4. The Construction Documents Phase shall constitute 100% of the design effort inclusive of any responses and alterations due to comments received upon review from the Owner, building codes officials, user groups or other interested third parties.

5. The Architect shall assist the Owner in filing the required documents for the approval of governmental authorities having interest in the Project.

6. The Architect shall provide *[NUMBER ( )]* set(s) of Plans and Specifications along with the final estimate of Construction Cost to *[AGENCY POINT OF CONTACT]*, and *two (2)* set(s) of the same to the Owner for final review. This final review shall constitute a submission of the Plans and Specifications at 95% completion of the design effort where the remaining 5% shall consist of incorporating final review comments and inclusion of the "Boiler Plate."

7. The Architect shall request the "Boiler Plate" and essential bidding information from the Owner upon submission of the Plans and Specifications for final review.

8. The Architect shall incorporate review comments and make all corrections, additions, or deletions to the Plans and Specifications prior to distribution for bidding purposes, without the use of addenda, unless approved by the Owner.
9. The Architect shall furnish and distribute *[NUMBER ( )]* set(s) of Plans and Specifications for bidding purposes, and one set to the Owner as a record office set.

G. Bidding Phase
1. The Bidding Phase shall commence with the incorporation of final review comments and the Owner's approval of the Plans and Specifications and the final Estimate of Construction cost and shall be complete with the issuance of the Notice To Proceed of the Construction Contract.
2. The Architect, following the Owner's approval of the Plans and Specifications and the final Estimate of Construction Cost, shall assist the Owner in obtaining bids and in awarding the Construction Contract(s). Any interpretation of the Plans and Specifications, by the Architect, will be issued to all plan holders by addenda. The Architect will not issue any addenda within seven (7) days of the bid opening without the permission of the Owner.
3. The Architect shall arrange, attend and conduct a pre-bid walk-through for the project unless the Owner specifically requests no walk-through.

H. Construction Cost of the Project
1. Construction Cost does not include the fees of the Architect, the cost of the land, rights-of-way, or other costs that are the responsibility of the Owner but shall be the total estimated cost to the Owner of all elements of the Project designed and/or specified by Architect.
2. Estimates of Construction Cost prepared by the Architect must represent his best judgment based upon the latest published cost data and general conditions of the construction industry in the area where the project is to be constructed and does not constitute a guarantee to the Owner that bids or negotiated prices will not vary.
3. When the fixed limit of Construction Cost is established in conjunction with the Project Program, the Architect shall determine, with the interaction of the Owner, what materials, equipment, components, systems, and types of construction are to be included in the Plans and Specifications, and to make reasonable adjustments in the Project Program to bring it within the fixed limit. The Architect may also include up to four (4) Additive Alternates, with the interaction of the Owner, to the Base Bid to ensure the bids will be within the fixed limit of Construction Cost.
4. If the final Estimate of Construction Cost exceeds the fixed limit of Construction Cost (including any Alternates and bidding contingencies), the Owner may:
   a. Give written approval of an increase in the fixed limit of Construction Cost; or
   b. Confer with the Architect in revising the Project to reduce the final Estimate of Construction Cost. Such revisions shall be at the expense of the Architect.
5. If the lowest responsible bid exceeds the fixed limit of Construction Cost (including any Alternates and bidding contingencies), the Owner may:
   a. Give written approval of an increase in the fixed limit of Construction Cost; or
   b. Negotiate deductive changes, not to exceed [7%—this percent may vary] of the total cost of the project with the lowest responsible bidder; or

    c. Confer with the Architect in revising the Project to reduce the final Estimate of Construction Cost and rebid the Project. Such revisions shall be at the expense of the Architect and shall constitute his sole responsibility to the Owner in this regard.

I. Construction Phase—Administration of Construction Project

  1. The Construction Phase shall commence with the issuance of the Notice To Proceed of the Construction Contract and shall be complete when the Contractor has completed the corrections from the warranty inspection.

  2. The Architect shall provide administration of the Construction Contract as set forth in Paragraphs 1 through 13 of this Article inclusive of the General Conditions of the Contract for Construction, AIA Document A201, XXXX Edition.

  3. The Architect shall be the representative of the Owner throughout the duration of this Contract and as such shall advise and consult with the Owner. The Architect shall have authority to act on behalf of the Owner to the extent provided in the General Conditions of the Construction Contract unless otherwise modified in writing.

  4. The Architect shall arrange and conduct a pre-construction meeting, in cooperation with the Owner, after the Owner has given Notice to Proceed to the Construction Contractor. The Architect shall take minutes of the meeting and distribute typewritten copies to all parties attending the meeting within five (5) calendar days.

  5. The Architect shall visit the project site a minimum of *[NUMBER ( )]* times to familiarize himself with the progress and quality of the work and to determine if the Project is proceeding in accordance with the Plans and Specifications. The Architect shall conduct monthly job meetings with the Contractor's and Owner's representatives. The Architect shall take minutes of the meeting and distribute typewritten copies to all parties attending the meeting within five (5) calendar days. The Architect shall furnish the Owner with written field reports on a form approved by the Owner within five (5) calendar days of a project site visit. Any representative of the Architect shall be subject to the Owner's approval.

  6. Based on observations at the site and the Contractor's Form XXX, Periodic Estimate for Partial Payment request, the Architect shall determine the amount owing to the Contractor and shall act upon the Contractor's Periodic Estimate for Partial Payment within seven (7) days of receipt. Certification of the Contractor's Form XXX shall constitute a representation by the Architect to the Owner that the work has progressed to the point indicated; that to the best of the Architect's knowledge, information and belief, the quality of the work is in accordance with the Plans and Specifications; and that the Contractor is entitled to payment in the amount certified. If, in the Architect's opinion, the Contractor is not entitled to the amount indicated on Form XXX, he shall evaluate what percentage is due, inform the Owner, and then return the Periodic Estimate for Partial Payment to the Contractor for revision.

  7. The Architect shall be the interpreter of the requirements of the Plans and Specifications. All interpretations, responses to requests for information, and decisions concerning the Plans and Specifications shall be in writing and issued to the Contractor and Owner by the Architect.

8. The Architect shall have authority to reject work that does not conform to the Plans and Specifications. The Architect shall advise the Owner of any and all rejected work and, if in his reasonable opinion, it may be necessary to stop work. The Owner will issue any Stop Work Orders to the Contractor.

9. The Architect shall review, approve, or take other appropriate action on shop drawings, samples, and other submissions by the Contractor to ensure compliance with the Plans and Specifications.

10. The Architect shall, in consultation with the Owner, prepare Change Orders and ascertain that Change Order amounts are fair and reasonable. The Owner is the approving authority and the Architect shall not order any work done without prior approval by the Owner.

11. The Architect shall conduct inspections as part of his contracted site visits to determine the Dates of Substantial Completion and Final Completion. The Architect shall not authorize Substantial Completion nor Final Completion without the approval of the Owner.

12. The Architect shall receive, review and approve or reject written warranties, operation and maintenance manuals and related materials required of the Contractor in accordance with the Plans and Specifications.

13. The Architect shall furnish the Owner a set of [specify type of] drawings and incorporate changes made during the construction process which reflect the as-built conditions. The [specify type of] drawings shall be provided to the Owner not less than thirty (30) calendar days after the date of Substantial Completion. The Architect shall also furnish the Owner with a full set of Record Drawings in AutoCad electronic media format.

J. Warranty Period and Inspection

1. The warranty period shall be as defined in the Specifications as beginning upon Substantial Completion and continuing for one (1) calendar year from the date of Final Acceptance of the Project by the Owner. The warranty period for some items may extend beyond the one (1) calendar year from Final Acceptance but for which the Architect shall not be required to visit the site or perform warranty inspections.

2. The Architect shall provide his services as defined in this Contract for the full term of the warranty period.

3. The Architect shall conduct a warranty inspection within thirty (30) calendar days prior to the expiration of the warranty period to determine if any defects in the work exist. The Architect shall notify the Owner, both verbally and in writing of defects, and whether or not the defective work is covered by the warranty. All warranty work or repairs shall be under the direction of the Architect. The Architect shall notify the Owner of defective work and shall then, in conjunction with the Owner, notify the Contractor in accordance with the General Conditions of the Construction Contract.

K. Payments to the Architect

1. Payments for the Architect's Basic Services shall be made as follows:

$_____upon completion of the Schematic Design Phase.

$_____upon completion of the Design Development Phase.

$_____upon completion of the Construction Documents Phase.

$_____upon completion of the Bidding Phase.

$_____upon completion of the Construction Phase.

2. Payments for the Architect's Additional Services shall be made as follows:

   $_____upon completion and acceptance of the Site Survey.

   $_____upon completion and acceptance of the Geotechnical Investigation.

   $_____upon receipt of the Record [type of] Drawings.

   $_____upon completion of Warranty.

3. Payments for the Architect's Supplemental Services shall be made as follows:

   $_____unit cost per additional trip to Construction Site if requested by the Owner.

4. Until the work is Substantially Complete, the Owner will pay ninety (90%) percent of the amount due the Architect on account of progress payments. The remaining amount due, other than that specified for Warranty Inspection or Record [specify type of] Drawings, will be paid to the Architect upon completion and Final Acceptance of the Project.

5. If the Owner determines that any representations on the pay request submitted by the Architect are wholly or partially inaccurate, the Owner may withhold payment of sums otherwise due the Architect until the inaccuracy and its cause have been corrected to the Owner's satisfaction.

6. Each request for payment submitted by the Architect shall be on Form XXX provided by the Owner. The Architect, shall provide certification, with his request for final payment after Final Acceptance of the Project, that all bills for materials, supplies, utilities and for all other items or services furnished or caused to be furnished and used in the execution of this Contract have been fully paid to date and that there are no unpaid claims or demands of State or Federal Agencies, sub-contractors, consultants, employees, or any others resulting from or arising out of any work done under this Contract.

7. Payments for Reimbursable Expenses, as defined in this Contract, shall be made upon presentation, review and approval of the Architect's statement of actual expenses.

8. A fee will be negotiated for work done on Change Orders only if the Change Order is Owner initiated. Change Orders, as a result of errors, lack of foresight, lack of coordination between disciplines, omissions or negligence by the Architect shall be performed at his expense and shall include all associated construction costs related to that portion which is over and above what the Owner would have paid if the Change had been incorporated in the Plans and Specifications.

9. The Architect shall not be reimbursed nor receive additional fees for time extensions of the Construction Contract for: lack of or poor responsiveness to shop drawings; requests for information; pay requests; all Change Orders other than Owner-initiated Change Orders. Should the Construction Contract be delayed for an extended period, regardless of fault or cause, any additional fees for the Architect shall be determined after Substantial Completion or after all claims and/or disputes have been resolved. Fees shall be limited to additional site visits, processing of pay requests, and participation in disputes/claims between Owner and Contractor as defined herein.

L. Reimbursable Expenses

1. Reimbursable Expenses are in addition to the fees for Basic and Additional Services and are actual expenses incurred by the Architect, his employees, or his consultants in the interest of the Project as specified in the following paragraphs.

2. Expense of transportation, lodging and per diem when traveling in connection with the Project, for other than the site visits specified above, if authorized in writing in advance by Owner.

3. Actual expenses under this Article shall be reimbursed per the unit costs listed on Form XXX as negotiated with the Owner. Costs incurred by the Architect without the prior written consent of the Owner shall be at the Architect's expense.

M. Owner's Responsibilities

1. The Owner shall provide information regarding his requirements for the Project Program.

2. The Owner or his representative shall examine documents submitted by the Architect and shall render decisions pertaining thereto.

3. The Owner shall furnish and pay for the structural, mechanical, chemical and other laboratory tests, inspections and reports as required.

4. The Owner shall furnish and pay for accounting and insurance services as may be necessary for the Project, and such auditing services as he may require to ascertain how or for what purposes the Architect or Contractor has used the moneys paid under this Contract and/or the Construction Contract.

5. If the Owner observes or otherwise becomes aware of any fault or defect in the Project or non-conformance with the Plans and Specifications, he shall give prompt notice thereof to the Architect.

6. The Owner shall prepare for the Architect, upon the Architect's request, the necessary bidding information, wage rates, and the General and Supplementary General Conditions of the Construction Contract, commonly called the "Boiler Plate," for inclusion into the Specifications.

N. Relationship

The relationship of Architect to Owner under this Contract is that of an Independent Contractor. The Architect is not an employee of XXXX, is not carrying out the regular business of XXXX and is not subject to the supervision and control of XXXX. Each of the parties will be solely and entirely responsible for their own acts and the acts of their employees. No benefits are provided by XXXX to the Architect or the Architect's employees.

O. Successors and Assigns

The Owner and the Architect, each binds himself, his partners, successors, legal representatives, and assigns to the other party to this Contract, and to the partners, successors, legal representatives and assigns of such other party in respect to all covenants of this Contract. Neither the Owner nor the Architect shall assign or transfer his interest in the Contract without written consent of the other.

P. Termination of Contract

1. The Architect or Owner may terminate this Contract upon giving written notice to the other that such party has failed to fulfill its obligations under this Contract. In the event of such default, the Architect or Owner shall notify the other and allow ten (10) calendar days upon receipt for correction action. Should no satisfactory corrective action be taken by the defaulting party, the other shall have right to terminate the Contract.

2. The Owner may terminate this Contract without cause at any time upon giving written notice to the Architect. If the Contract is terminated for the convenience

of the Owner, the Architect shall be paid for all services rendered prior to receiving the written notice.

   3. If the Architect fails to fulfill his obligations and the Contract is terminated, the Owner may prosecute the Project to completion by contract or other means available. The Owner may hold the Architect liable for any and all additional costs incurred due to the Architect's failure to perform. The rights and remedies available to the Owner provided herein are in addition to any and all other rights and remedies provided by law or equity.

Q. Ownership of Documents

   1. All documents developed under this Contract are and shall become the property of the Owner whether the Project for which they are made is or is not executed.

   2. The signing of this Contract shall constitute a complete transfer of ownership, intellectual property and copyright of all documents from the Architect to the Owner upon Substantial Completion of the Project. Such transfer shall not be construed by the Architect as a grant for usage nor can it be revoked by the Architect.

   3. The Owner agrees to indemnify and hold harmless the Architect from any and all claims, demands and causes of action of any kind or character arising as a result of reuse of the documents developed under this Contract.

R. Architect's Records

The [owner] shall have access to all records, correspondence, and files of the Architect, its employees, engineers, or consultants pertaining to the contract administration undertaken on behalf of the [owner]. This access shall be continuing and survive the termination of the Contract for either cause or convenience. Such records shall be kept in a generally recognized format and shall be available to the Owner, Auditor, the Fiscal Analyst or his authorized representative at mutually convenient time for a period of three (3) years after completion and acceptance of the Project by the Owner.

S. Contingent Fees

The Architect warrants that he has not employed or retained any person, partnership, or corporation, other than a bona fide employee or agent working for the Architect to solicit or secure this Contract, and that he has not paid or agreed to pay any person, partnership, or corporation, other than a bona fide employee or agent, any fee, or any other consideration, contingent upon the making of this Contract.

T. Late Addenda

The Architect agrees not to issue any addenda within seven (7) calendar days prior to the date of the bid opening for the project without first securing permission from the Owner.

U. Extent of Contract

This Contract represents the entire and integrated agreement between the Owner and the Architect and supersedes all prior negotiations, representations or agreements, whether written or oral. This Contract may be amended only by written instrument signed by both Owner and Architect.

V. Venue

In the event of mediation, arbitration, or litigation concerning the Contract, venue shall be the [court with jurisdiction], and the Contract shall be interpreted according to the Laws of [state].

W. Indemnity and Hold Harmless

The Architect shall indemnify and hold harmless the State of XXXX from and against all damages, claims and liability arising out of the negligent acts, errors or omissions of the Architect, its officers, agents, consultants, and employees, including all judgments, awards, losses, expenses, costs and attorneys' fees.

X. Insurance

1. The Architect shall procure and maintain liability insurance sufficient for protection from claims, actions, damages and liability due to or arising out of bodily injury, automobile accidents, personal injury, sickness, disease, death or other incidents for himself and all his employees and from claims, actions, damages and liability to or destruction of property including losses resulting therefrom.

2. The Architect shall procure and maintain per claim professional liability insurance at limits of: *[AMOUNT]* for protection from and against all claims, actions, damages and liability caused or arising out of negligent acts, errors or omissions of the Architect, its officers, agents, consultants, and employees.

Y. Dispute Resolution Between Owner and Contractor

1. In the event a dispute arises between the Owner and Contractor, or any other party, whether during construction or thereafter, the Architect shall advise and consult with the Owner in attempting to resolve the dispute, whether informally or by mediation, arbitration, or litigation. The Architect will make himself and/or his agents and employees available and shall permit inspection of his records. In the event that it is ultimately determined that the Architect did not cause or contribute to the damages or expenses alleged, the Architect shall be reimbursed by the Owner for all costs reasonably incurred upon resolution of the dispute. If there is no formal finding of fault, the Architect and Owner shall negotiate terms for payment. The Owner will not be required to reimburse the Architect at any time prior to the final determination and resolution for the responsibility of any claim or dispute.

2. In the event the Architect caused, in whole or in part, the dispute or controversy, the Architect shall bear his costs for participating in the resolution.

Z. Dispute Resolution Between Owner and Architect

1. Any and all controversies, disputes, claims or other matters between the parties arising out of or related to this Contract, or breach thereof, shall be decided and settled by arbitration in accordance with the [arbitration rules of the state of XXXX].

2. Each party shall be responsible for and bear its own costs of any arbitration, except those awarded by arbitration.

3. Good faith effort and attempt shall be made by both parties to decide and settle any and all controversies, disputes, claims or other matters prior to initiating arbitration proceedings either through negotiation or mediation. Mediation shall be conducted by a neutral third party in accordance with rules agreed to in writing by the parties.

4. The complaining party shall, at a minimum, provide notice of any claim, dispute or potential for legal proceedings pursuant to the applicable statute(s) of limitations as provided in [XXXX] state law. However, a complaining party may demand initiation of a resolution through arbitration upon 15 calendar days written notice to the other party of the conditions that give rise to the complaint or dispute.

5. [County and State] shall be the venue for all arbitration proceedings. [state] law shall govern any arbitration. All arbiters shall be certified by the American Arbitration Association.

6. When written demand for arbitration has been made, the manner of arbitration with regard to the selection and number of arbiters shall be mutually agreed upon in writing by both parties. If the parties cannot agree, petition shall be made to the [appropriate court].

7. During arbitration and resolution of any dispute, complaint or claim, the Architect shall continue with scheduled performance of work in accordance with this Contract. The Owner shall continue to make payment in accordance with the provisions of this Contract except in those areas involving the complaint, dispute or claim.

AA. Employment

1. The Architect shall be familiar with and be responsible for and adhere to all Federal and State requirements regarding employment practices.

2. All hiring and other employment practices of the Architect shall be in accordance with Federal Equal Employment Opportunity Commission regulations and shall be nondiscriminatory, based on merit and qualifications without regard to race, color, religion, creed, political ideas, sex, age, marital status, physical or mental handicap, or national origin.

This Contract entered into as of the day and year first written above.

ARCHITECT

(Signature)

(Title)

Taxpayer's I.D. No.
Is this firm incorporated?   no   yes
OWNER

(Owner Representative)
Date

Sample Request for Bids to Select Contractors

NOTICE TO CONSTRUCTION MANAGERS
XXXXXXXX announces that Construction Management Services will be required for the project listed below:

Project and Location:
Project No.: XXXXX
Project: XXXXXXXXXXXX
Location: XXXXXXXXX

This project consists of a new XXXXXX facility located XXXXXXXX to serve XXXXX, XXXXX and XXXXX. The building site is located on XXXX Street between XXXXX and the XXXXXXX, across from the XXXXXXX. The facility is expected to be approximately XXXXX gross square feet. The project will include relocating a parking lot along with the construction of other related site improvements. The construction budget is approximately $XXXXXXX with a total anticipated project budget of $XXXXXXX.

The contract for construction management will consist of two phases. Phase one is pre-construction services, for which the construction manager will be paid a fixed fee. Phase one services include value engineering, constructability analyses, development of a cost model, estimating, and the development of one or more Guaranteed Maximum Prices (GMP's) at the 50% or the 100% Construction Document phase. If the GMP is accepted, phase two, the construction phase, will be implemented. In phase two of the contract, the construction manager becomes the single point of responsibility for performance of the construction of the project and shall publicly bid trade contracts, encouraging the inclusion of [any special groups to be included]. Failure to negotiate an acceptable fixed fee for phase one of the contract, or to arrive at an acceptable GMP within the time provided in the agreement, may result in the termination of the construction manager's contract.

Selection of the finalists for interviews will be made on the basis of construction manager qualifications, including experience and ability; past experience; bonding capacity; record-keeping/administrative ability; critical path scheduling expertise; cost estimating; cost control ability; quality control ability; qualifications of the firm's personnel, staff and consultants. Finalists will be provided with a copy of the latest documentation prepared by the project architect/engineer, a description of the final interview requirements and a copy of the XXXXX's standard construction management agreement.

The Selection Committee may reject all proposals and stop the selection process at any time. The construction manager shall have no ownership, entrepreneurial or financial affiliation with the selected architect/engineer involved with this project.

Instructions:

Firms desiring to provide construction management services for the project shall submit a letter of application and a completed XXX "Construction Manager Qualifications Supplement." Proposals must not exceed XX pages, including the Construction Manager Qualifications Supplement and letter of application. Pages must be numbered consecutively. Submittals, which do not comply with these requirements or do not include the requested data will not be considered. No submittal material will be returned.

All applicants must be licensed to practice as general contractors in the State of XXXX at the time of application. Corporations must be registered to operate in the State of XXXX by the Department of XXXX, Division of Corporations at the time of application. As required by Section XXXXX, XXXXX Statues, a construction management firm may not submit a proposal for this project if it is on the convicted vendor list for a public entity crime committed within the past 36 months. The selected construction management firm must warrant that it will neither utilize the services of, nor contract with, any supplier, subcontractor, or consultant in excess of $XXXX in connection with this project for a period of 36 months from the date of placement on the convicted vendor list.

The XXX Construction Manager Qualifications Supplement forms and the Project Fact Sheet may be obtained on line at *www.XXXXX* or by contacting: XXXXXXX, Facilities Planning and Construction,
XXXXXXXXX Address
XXXXXXX telephone, XXXXXX facsimile.

For further information or questions, please contact XXXXXX, XXXXX Director, XXXXX telephone, at the address listed above.

Submit six (6) bound copies of the required proposal data. Submittals must be received in the XXXXX Facilities Planning & Construction Office by XXXXX local time, XXXX Day, XXXXXX date. Facsimile (FAX) submittals are not acceptable and will not be considered.

Index

About the Author

Dr. Thomas Hart is Professor Emeritus in the College of Information at Florida State University where he led the school library media program for 34 years. He is the author of seven major books on school library media center issues. He recently served as visiting professor at Nanyang Technological University in Singapore where he developed a significant policy statement for knowledge management in Singapore's schools. An active member of various professional organizations, Dr. Hart has served in various leadership roles. His most recent book is *The Knowledge and Information Society* (2000).

The DVD features video tours, commentaries by both this book's author and the school library media specialist of each facility, and before-and-after comparisons of remodeled library facilities. The DVD can be viewed on either a DVD player or a computer with a DVD-compatible drive. The above disk also features an additional planning document as well as PowerPoint presentations showcasing technological developments, library decor, and more. These are accessible on Windows PCs by opening up 'My Computer,' right clicking on the DVD icon, and left clicking 'Open.'

116 x 166